T0418239

The Non-Cycle Mystery Plays

Between the beginning of the tenth and the end of the sixteenth centuries, in all parts of Great Britain from Aberdeen to Cornwall, performances of liturgical and mystery plays are on record. This book, first published in 1909, is a collection of early-English religious plays with a detailed introduction written by the editor Osborn Waterhouse. *The Non-Cycle Mystery Plays* will be of interest to students of drama, performance and theatre studies.

The Non-Cycle Mystery Plays

Together with
'The Croxton Play of the Sacrament'
and
'The Pride of Life'

Edited by
Osborn Waterhouse

Routledge
Taylor & Francis Group

First published in 1909
by Kegan Paul, Trench, Trübner & Co.

This edition first published in 2015 by Routledge
2 Park Square, Milton Park, Abingdon, Oxon, OX14 4RN

and by Routledge
711 Third Avenue, New York, NY 10017

Routledge is an imprint of the Taylor & Francis Group, an informa business

© 1909 Osborn Waterhouse

All rights reserved. No part of this book may be reprinted or reproduced or utilised in any form or by any electronic, mechanical, or other means, now known or hereafter invented, including photocopying and recording, or in any information storage or retrieval system, without permission in writing from the publishers.

Publisher's Note
The publisher has gone to great lengths to ensure the quality of this reprint but points out that some imperfections in the original copies may be apparent.

Disclaimer
The publisher has made every effort to trace copyright holders and welcomes correspondence from those they have been unable to contact.

A Library of Congress record exists under LC control number: 09019859

ISBN 13: 978-1-138-92015-6 (hbk)
ISBN 13: 978-1-315-68730-8 (ebk)

The Non-Cycle Mystery Plays,

TOGETHER WITH

THE CROXTON PLAY OF THE SACRAMENT

AND

THE PRIDE OF LIFE.

RE-EDITED FROM THE MANUSCRIPTS

BY

OSBORN WATERHOUSE, M.A.,

WITH INTRODUCTION AND
GLOSSARY.

LONDON:

PUBLISHED FOR THE EARLY ENGLISH TEXT SOCIETY

BY KEGAN PAUL, TRENCH, TRÜBNER & CO., LTD.,

DRYDEN HOUSE, 43 GERRARD STREET, SOHO, W.

AND BY HENRY FROWDE, OXFORD UNIVERSITY PRESS,

AMEN CORNER, E.C.

1909.

To my Friend and former Teacher,

Professor Moorman,

GRATEFULLY DEDICATED.

PREFACE.

EVEN in the preparation of so small a volume as this, one lays oneself open to many obligations. My heartiest thanks I owe to Miss L. Toulmin-Smith for permission to print from her editions of the *Brome Play;* to Mr. Walter Rye for rediscovering an eighteenth-century transcript of the *Norwich Play;* and to Mr. E. E. Kitchener and E. F. M. for valuable help in reading proof. Dr. Furnivall's unfailing kindliness to, and encouragement of, his editors are too well known to call for mention.

Topsham, Devon, Feb. 2, 1909.

CONTENTS.

INTRODUCTION.

I.

GENERAL.

THE miscellaneous character of the contents of the present volume rendered it somewhat difficult to select a title which would adequately and fittingly describe such a collection of plays. Apart from the "morality," *The Pride of Life*, which has been included on account of its early date, and the *Play of the Sacrament*, a miracle play, the collection comprises those remains of our early-English, religious drama, not contained in the four great cycles of mystery-plays. The term "non-cycle mysteries" is, however, not intended to suggest that they have never formed part of some mystery-cycle, which question is rather reserved for discussion in dealing with each piece individually.

Although three of the plays are fragmentary, and all the Biblical ones handle subjects treated in the cycles, their interest is not thereby diminished; and their importance, in so far as they supply much additional information with reference to the history and development of our early drama, is by no means insignificant. The manuscript containing the three "offices," known as the *Shrewsbury Fragments*, is the only English example of plays representing the drama in transition from the liturgical play to the mystery proper; the Newcastle and Norwich plays supply us with interesting details, the one of the methods of composition, the other of the mode of performance and staging of the respective plays; the two Abraham plays, in comparison with the four plays in the cycles upon the same subject, show us something of the variety with which this popular story was treated; the Croxton *Play of the Sacrament* is the only preserved text of a miracle play, the existence of which type in England, as well as on the Continent is amply proved by various official records; and *The Pride of Life* serves as a link between the morality plays of the later form and construction and the dance-of-death plays.

The preservation of the four great cycles of plays has naturally led to the emphasizing of the cyclical form and cyclical method of performance as the typical one in England, and has also resulted in the ignoring to a large extent of the plays and recorded performances which do not come into this category. The number of documents which have been lost and the number of performances the record of which also has not been preserved, are immense, but still sufficient evidence is to hand to indicate how widespread and popular the performances were, that the greatest possible variety of treatment did exist, and that the cycle and the cyclical mode of performance were by no means universal.

Between the beginning of the tenth and the end of the sixteenth centuries, in all parts of Great Britain from Aberdeen to Cornwall, performances of liturgical and mystery plays are on record; Dublin has them too, and John Bale's religious plays, *God's Promises* and *John the Baptist*, were performed as far west as Kilkenny. Local circumstances, such as the amount of ecclesiastical influence and the number and wealth of the trade-guilds, were often the factors determining the magnificence, or insignificance, and the mode of performance of the plays. Thus cycles of all sizes appear to have existed: York has preserved forty-eight plays, Coventry forty-two, Wakefield thirty, and Chester twenty-five; while we learn from various municipal records that Beverley had thirty-six, Norwich thirteen, Newcastle twelve, Worcester five, Bungay in Suffolk at least five but very probably more, Lincoln probably four, and that Chelmsford, Ipswich and other places also possessed cycles. The length of the cycle depended largely upon the number and prosperity of the guilds: the formation of new guilds necessitated the inclusion of a new play or the division of existing plays: a lack of funds in particular guilds, on the other hand, led to the dropping or amalgamation of certain plays. Thus for example, the Norwich play of *The Creation* was sometimes preceded by the *Fall of the Angels*, while at other times it was the first play of the series; again, a list of the York plays drawn up in 1415 gives the number as fifty-one, a second, undated list as fifty-seven, and the manuscript preserves forty-eight; and the thirty-eight Beverley plays of 1390 were thirty-six in 1520: further we learn from the accounts of the latter that in 1411 a play was added, and that in 1495 another play was divided.

Another custom seems to have existed at Aberdeen which

possessed two series of plays ; the Passion and Nativity cycles were not amalgamated, but the former was performed at Corpus Christi and the latter at Candlemas.

The occasions on which such plays were performed were equally various and numerous as the plays themselves. The most popular of all days appears to have been Corpus Christi, which comes at a time of the year when the weather is suitable for such performances, and which received additional ecclesiastical importance in 1311 at the Council of Vienne, when Clement V confirmed a bull enacted by Urban IV. In England the plays were very intimately connected with the Corpus Christi procession, although instances of their dissociation are not unknown ; at Newcastle, for example, the procession took place in the morning and the plays were performed in the afternoon. Other days too were popular. A cyclical play at Chelmsford appears to have been given on Midsummer Day, or a day soon following, while Chester, Norwich, New Romney, and probably Leicester, performed their respective plays at Whitsuntide. This, also, was exceptionally the case with the plays at York in the year 1569, Whit Tuesday being the day selected. On an earlier occasion (1426), in the same town, the plays were given on Corpus Christi Day, and the procession postponed until the day following. At Lincoln the performance took place on St. Anne's Day, and at Beverley on St. Mark's Day. The Edinburgh Candlemas and Corpus-Christi performances have already been referred to. On at least one occasion, a cycle of plays is recorded to have been performed at a royal entry, viz., at Aberdeen in May 1511, for the entertainment of Queen Margaret, the wife of James IV, as Dunbar tells :

> " The streittis war all hung with tapestrie,
> Great was the press of peopill dwelt about,
> And pleasant padgeanes playit prattelie." [1]

The number of pageants used and the number of " stations " at which performances were given, are by no means coincident with the number of plays : custom varied considerably. The thirty-six plays of the Beverley cycle were given at six consecutive "stations " in the course of one day ; the forty-two Coventry plays were allotted to ten or twelve pageants each of which covered several incidents, and were only performed at three " stations," the whole

---

[1] Dunbar: *The Quenis' Reception at Aberdein* (ed. J. Small, Scott. Text Soc., ii. 251).

being also performed within the day; while at Chester, where the
plays were given at Whitsuntide, nine were performed on the
Monday, nine on Tuesday and seven on Wednesday, all at numerous stations; and at York, in 1399, the number of "stations" was
limited by statute to twelve, but afterwards varied between twelve
and sixteen. A cyclical play at Chelmsford, given on the Monday
after Midsummer Day in 1562, is further peculiar in that it was
played "in a 'pightell' or enclosure, upon a scaffold with a stage
for the spectators," and appears to have been taken on circuit to
other towns, since on the following day it was performed at
Braintree and later at Malden. At Coventry the plays were only
given at three, or at most, four "stations," while the customs at
Leicester, Lincoln, Norwich and Worcester have not been definitely
recorded. On two occasions, 1409 and 1411, performances are
recorded at Skynners' Well,[1] London, which, according to the
description of them preserved, must have been of the nature of
mystery plays and were evidently given on a very extensive scale;
the play of 1409, " whiche endured Wednesday, Thorsday, Friday
and on Soneday was ended," showed "how God created Heaven and
Earth, out of nothing, and how he created Adam and so on to the
Day of Judgment"; and in 1411, "begaune a gret play from the
begynnyng of the worlde, at the skynners' welle, that lastyd vij
dayes contynually; and there ware the moste parte of the lordes
and gentylles of Ynglond."

The performance of these mystery-cycles, with few exceptions,
took place annually: occasionally, however, other cyclical plays
were substituted for the mystery-cycle. Thus, for example, at
York, in 1535, for the latter was substituted *The Creed* play,
which was performed every tenth year, generally, however, in
addition to the craft-plays, and in 1488 and 1558 by *The Paternoster* play: in 1550 and 1552 the performances were omitted
because of plague, and in 1564, 1565 and 1566, because of war
and sickness. At Lincoln, too, the *Ludus Corporis Christi* was apparently at various times replaced by *Ludus de Pater Noster, Ludus
Sancti Laurentii, Ludus Sanctae Susannae, Ludus de Kyng Robert
of Cesill* or *Ludus de Sancta Clara*, according as the authorities
determined.

The records of performances of single plays of both types, mystery and miracle, are numerous and widespread. A single play, for

---

[1] Also referred to as Clerkenwell.

example, was frequently selected from a cycle for separate performance, as was often the case at Chester. Thus, in 1488, *The
Assumption* was performed before Lord Strange at the High Cross;
in 1515, the same play, in conjunction with *The Shepherds* play, in
St. John's Churchyard; in 1576, *The Purification*, by the Smiths
at Alderman Mountford's on Midsummer Eve, and finally, in 1578,
The Shepherds play with others, at the " High Cross on the Roodee "
before the Earl of Derby and Lord Strange.[1] Thus, to cite further
examples, Aberdeen had a *Resurrection* play ; the Digby *Burial and
Resurrection* was played, one part on Good Friday and the other
part on Easter day ; in 1584 at Coventry a *Destruction of Jerusalem* play was performed ; at Hull a *Noah* play ; at Leconsfield a
Christmas *Nativity* play and an Easter *Resurrection* play ; at
Leicester a *Herod* and a *Shepherds* play ; at Winchester in 1486 a
Christi discensus ad Inferos ; and at Canterbury the *Three Kings
of Coleyn.*   Plays of a nature very much akin to these few representative ones already mentioned, based upon apocryphal sources
and other early Church writings, are equally numerous ; in 1528,
at Dublin, was performed the *Deaths of the Apostles*, and at Shrewsbury in 1565, *Julian the Apostate*. Most numerous of all, however,
are the records of plays upon incidents drawn from the life of some
saint ; and this is not to be wondered at, since not only had each
church its patron saint, but also each craft-guild, the honouring of
whom was certainly one of the first duties of the members of the
guild. St. George and St. Thomas of Canterbury naturally occupy
the foremost places, but are by no means alone ; thus, London,
Coventry and Dunstable have records of plays of St. Catherine ;
Braintree of St. Swithin, St. Andrew and St. Eustace ; and Lincoln of Saints Laurence, Susanna, Jacob and Clara ; to mention
but a few of the multitude of references available.

Unlike the cycles, these single plays were intended as occasional
rather than annual events. Local conditions determined their time
and manner of performance. In a still larger degree than cyclical
plays they served to adorn court festivities (as for example at
Windsor in 1416, when Henry V invested the Emperor Sigis-
mund with the Order of the Garter), banquets, royal entries, and
to celebrate particular saints' days. Still performances on the
usual festivals are very numerous, although somewhat irregular ;

[1] E. K. Chambers, *Mediæval Stage*, ii, 355, quoted from Morris and
Furnivall.

thus, for example, Dublin and Lichfield had performances at Christmas, Leicester on New Year's Eve, Lichfield and other towns at Easter, Hull on Plough Monday, Reading at Bartlemastide, etc.

Moreover, long after Biblical plays ceased to be liturgical in character, the church continued to serve the people as theatre, and the surplices of the clergy as part of the necessary costumes of the actors. As late as the sixteenth century the performance of plays in the church, indeed, was a very common occurrence, as is proved by the church records at Halstead, Heybridge and Braintree, to quote three out of many examples ; and from the same accounts we learn, too, that money was collected by some method or other from the spectators, on behalf of the ecclesiastical funds. Thus, in 1523, to quote an example from Braintree, a *St. Swithin* play, acted in the church on a Wednesday, realized £6 14s. 11½d., the expenses of which were £3 1s. 4d., leaving a net gain of £3 13s. 7½d. due to the church. Similar records are numerous. The churchyard, also, continued to be a popular place for performances, as was the case at Bungay in 1566 ; while at Dublin, Hoggin Green (now College Green), at Chelmsford a " pightell," at Canterbury the Guildhall, and at Reading the market-place, were distinguished as places chosen for plays. This small list, however, illustrates rather than exhausts, the variety of places which were used for the purpose.

An interchange of plays, players, and stage-effects, between towns having performances, was also a frequent occurrence. Thus, a play which had proved popular at one place was often taken to a neighbouring town or village. So we learn that between 1429 and 1490, players from New Romney often, and players from Ruckinge (1431), Wytesham (1441), Ham (1454), Hythe (1467), Folkestone (1479), Rye (1480), and Stone (1490), acted at Lydd ; while in 1490, the chaplain of the Guild of St. George at New Romney, went to see a play at Lydd, with a view to its reproduction in his own town. New Romney itself, although, as is evident, well provided with its own players, was often visited by those from other towns : in 1399 from Hythe, 1422 Lydd, 1426 Wittersham, 1429 Herne, 1430 Ruckinge, 1474 Folkestone, 1488 Appledore, 1489 Chart and Rye, 1491 Wye, 1494 Brookland, 1499 Halden, and 1508 Bethersden. The two which we have quoted are, moreover, by no means isolated examples. Records of the borrowing and lending of wardrobes are also very numerous : the Chelmsford wardrobe was apparently very valuable, was at various times noted down in inventories, and the lending of it became a regular and valuable source of income to the churchwardens. To multiply further examples would be valueless and tedious : but sufficient has been said in these few opening lines to indicate, inadequately perhaps, the variety of, and extent to which single plays flourished, how widespread they were, and how important a part in the national life they played ; and that a considerable amount of dramatic activity, which has too often been overlooked, did exist outside the limits of the great cycles and the few others which were believed to have existed. With these few introductory, general remarks we turn to an individual consideration of the separate plays.

II.

FRAGMENTS OF LITURGICAL PLAYS, DISCOVERED AT SHREWSBURY.

On January 4th, 1890, in a letter to *The Academy*, the Rev. Prof. Skeat first called public attention to the discovery of these plays, and a week later, in the same journal, published the text of the manuscript : upon these two articles the following account of the manuscript and its contents is based.[1]

The manuscript in question (Mus. iii. 42) was discovered at Shrewsbury, in the library of the school, by Dr. Calvert : of this document Dr. Calvert made a transcript and sent it to Dr. Clark, who in turn handed it to Prof. Skeat. Certain problems which this transcript suggested to the latter scholar, led him to seek their solution in the original. The manuscript, Prof. Skeat tells us, originally consisted of forty-three leaves ; five quires of eight leaves, and one quire of three leaves : the ninth leaf had been cut out. The first leaf is a palimpsest, and originally contained what is written on the back of the second leaf. The first thirty-six leaves, written with care, and rubricated, contain the following Latin anthems, carefully set to music :—

[1] In the summer of 1905 I visited Shrewsbury School for the purpose of collating the MS., but could find no responsible person who could give me permission to see it ; and at the end of the summer holidays in the same year I wrote to the headmaster of the school for permission to consult it, but have not yet received a reply to my letter : I have, therefore, been compelled to base my text and much of the material in this introduction upon the articles of Prof. Skeat ; fortunately a scholar of such eminence that one can rest assured the version of the text and facts respecting the manuscript are to be implicitly relied upon.

In this connection Professor Skeat also points out that Langland, in *Piers Plowman,* clearly followed the text of anthems three and four. The portion of the manuscript, however, which is of most immediate interest to us, begins upon leaf thirty-eight, where the rubric, *Luke ii.* 8, is followed by some English verses written in the same hand, but somewhat smaller, accompanied by marginal notes, which Prof. Skeat, upon examination of the original, discovered to be the cues for the actor whose part the manuscript contains. The same authority assigns the manuscript to the beginning of the fifteenth century. The text of the *Shrewsbury Fragments* is also given in Prof. Manly's *Specimens of the Pre-Shaksperean Drama,* Vol. I.: the present text is based upon a collation of those of Professors Skeat and Manly.

The grammatical features of our three plays undoubtedly stamp them as belonging to a Northern district, most probably—as Prof. Skeat suggests—Yorkshire. The final *en* or *n* of the infinitive, the *i-* prefix of the past participle of strong-verbs and the personal endings of the verb, are all consistently dropped, while the form of the present participle ends regularly in *and. A* for O.E. *ă̆, y* and *i* for O.E. stable *y* and *i, a* for O.E. *ea* before *l* + *consonant,* and other Northern forms also occur quite regularly ; *schal* and *schuld*, however, appear in the place of the more usual Northern forms *sal* and *suld* : such words and phrases as : —*mynnes me, in hy, wil of red, mun, thar, samyn, trayne, nem, bedene, gaynest, mased, apert*, etc., further suggest that the plays belong to the largest of English counties.

It is, however, on the literary, rather than on the linguistic side, that the *Shrewsbury Fragments* are of most interest, since they illustrate a stage in the development of the religious drama, of which examples in French and German manuscripts exist, but which, so far as England is concerned, had remained, prior to their discovery, entirely unrepresented. The now generally adopted theory of the development of the religious drama of the Middle Ages out of the Mass of the Roman Catholic Church, and the carefully collected texts of liturgical plays, edited by such scholars as Lange and Coussemaker,[1] are so well known to literary students as to render any outline of the subject superfluous ; it only remains to be indicated that these fragments from Shrewsbury illustrate a transitional form, linking these Latin liturgical plays to the vernacular religious drama, as later developed and represented by the four great cycles. The secularization, or better, perhaps, popularizing of the liturgical drama involved many changes ; the substitution of English for Latin, the transference of the performance from the interior to the exterior of the church, the introduction of comic characters and scenes, and also of incidents of a non-Biblical origin, the inclusion of lay as well as clerical actors, the change from recitative response to spoken dialogue, and the dissociation of the plays from music and from the liturgical office ; all of which changes, taking place more or less gradually, and in varied combinations, were necessary to give the drama an existence *per se.* The specimens before us represent the stage of development at which the drama is still associated with some particular office of the Church, celebrated on a certain fixed day, is still performed by clerks inside the church—or at least in the churchyard [2]—and has

[1] Lange, C., *die lateinischen Osterfeiern.* 1887.
Milchsack, G., *die Oster und Passionsspiele,* etc. 1880.
Coussemaker, E. *Drames liturgiques du Moyen Âge.*
[2] We can only judge as to the place of performance from a record of a performance of a Resurrection play, at Beverley in 1220, quoted by Mr. Chambers in *The Mediæval Stage,* vol. ii, pp. 108 and 339. The authority is a thirteenth century *Continuator* of the *Vita* of St. John of Beverley, and describes the performance as taking place in the grave-yard of the Minster.

dialogue in the vernacular, in addition to and explanatory of, the conventional Latin sentences of the liturgical plays: the Latin portions, moreover, are still associated with music.

The liturgical character of the plays is placed beyond a doubt: since they are found in a manuscript of Latin anthems; the Latin portions of the plays are noted for voices; the second play is headed, in the manuscript, *Hic incipit Officium Resurrectionis in die Pasche;* the third has the opening words, *Feria secunda in ebdomada Pasche, discipuli insimul cantent;* and several of the Latin verses are found to be identical with those in corresponding portions of liturgical plays written entirely in Latin. The beginning and heading of the first play is lost, but it is no wild conjecture, in consideration of its contents and upon comparison with other liturgical plays, to call it *Officium Pastorum.* It is worthy of note, too, in illustration of our plays' relationship to other liturgical dramas, that three pairs of Latin verses in our *Officium Resurrectionis* are almost identical with a like number in *A Dramatic Office,* published from a fourteenth-century manuscript of a *Processional of the Church of St. John the Evangelist,* in Dublin.[1]   In this Dublin *Office,* to Maria Secunda, is assigned:

> "Heu! Consolacio nostra,
>   Ut quid mortem sustinuit!"   (cf. vv. 1 and 2.)

to the three Marys in chorus:

> "Jam, iam, ecce, iam properemus ad tumulum
>   Ungentes Dilecti corpus sanctissimum!" (cf. vv. 21 and 22.)

and to the third Mary:

> "Surrexit Christus, spes nostra,
>   Precedet uos in Galileam."   (cf. vv. 35 & 36.)

It is extremely probable also that the other Latin verses could be shown to have their origin either in earlier liturgical plays, or in anthems: but the search would not be worth the trouble.

The manuscript of our plays, unfortunately, is an actor's copy, and therefore only gives the parts of the character which he played, and tags—to act as cues—from some of the speeches of some of the other characters; one must therefore attempt to form some idea of what the complete plays were like, by aid of a comparison of other liturgical and mystery plays upon the same subjects.

---

[1] Printed by Manly, vol. i, p. 22, whose text is based on Frere's facsimile of *The Winchester Troper.*

The first fragment, a development of the liturgical *Pastores* play, belongs to Christmas, a season almost equal in significance to that of Easter, in so far as the history of the development of the religious drama is concerned. Its source is a Christmas trope—based upon the Easter *Quem Quaeritis*—which occurs very regularly in tropers of the eleventh and twelfth centuries; in its origin it was an introit trope for the third Mass. At Clermont-Ferrand this Christmas trope followed the *Te Deum* at Matins, and at Rouen an *Officium Pastorum* occupied a similar position. The statutes of Lichfield Cathedral bear witness to its existence on English soil, in the twelfth century, but later, the play seems to have been supplanted by others. In the *Officium Pastorum* the actor whose part our manuscript contains, played the Third Shepherd. The manuscript is incomplete at the beginning, but whether only the heading is lost to us, or some portion of the dialogue as well, it is now impossible to decide. The York play upon the same subject has three twelve-line strophes, preceding the part corresponding to the Shrewsbury play, which are spoken respectively by the three Shepherds in turn. The first Shepherd reminds us of the prophecies of Hosea and Isaiah, the second of Balaam's foretelling of the appearance of "a star in the East," and the third voices the joy which must inevitably be awakened in the hearts of the shepherds upon the fulfilment of this prophecy, following his poetic effort with a matter-of-fact reminder of their duty of sheep-seeking. At this point the star appears and the part of the story corresponding to our play begins. It is therefore possible that a Latin sentence or two, followed by a speech of the third Shepherd, corresponding perhaps to one of the first three stanzas of the York play, as well as the title, have been lost. Professor Skeat assigns all the cues of our play to the Second Shepherd; an arrangement which suggests that the three Shepherds spoke in regular rotation. In the York play the Third Shepherd does not always follow the second, and it is improbable that he did so in the Shrewsbury play; it is a point of quite minor importance, however, and since we have no means of deciding which of the cues represent the speeches of the First Shepherd, and which those of the Second Shepherd, it is a convenient way out of the difficulty to assign them uniformly, with Dr. Skeat, to the Second Shepherd.

Even in its incomplete form, the Shrewsbury *Officium Pastorum* shows unmistakable signs of relationship to the York *Shepherds Play ;* it is very probable also that the indebtedness of the latter to the former would appear still greater if the parts of the First and Second Shepherds had been preserved, and could be brought into the comparison. As far as one can judge, the Shrewsbury play in its complete form would be about equal in length to the York play, probably contained the same ideas a little differently expressed, and—in the text handed down to us—has one stanza almost identical with a stanza in the York play, a coincidence which, in the complete version, may have extended over three stanzas. The York version of the last stanza of our text is :

iii. Pas.   " Now loke on me, my lorde dere,
            þof all I putte me noght in pres,
            Ye are a prince with-outen pere,
            I have no presentte þat you may plees.
            But lo ! an horne spone, þat haue 1 here,
            And it will herbar fourty pese,
            þis will I giffe you with gud chere,
            Slike novelte may noght disease.
            Fare [wele] þou swete swayne,
            God graunte us levyng lange,
            And go we hame agayne,
            And make mirthe as we gange."

Except in respect to one verse, the Shrewsbury version agrees quite closely with the above ; in this one verse, however, it differs from the York version, and gives us an older and truer reading, for it more faithfully preserves the alliteration. The verse in the Shrewsbury version is :

"That may *h*erbor an *h*undreth pese."

The second Shrewsbury play carries us back still nearer to the origin of the drama, since it is an early development of that Easter trope, *Quem quaeritis in sepulcro Christicolae,* the very germ from which the liturgical drama has been developed. The simplest version of this trope, a free adaptation of the Vulgate text, is found in a St. Gaul manuscript and reads as follows :

"Quem quaeritis in sepulchro, O Christicolae ?
Jesum Nazarenum crucifixum, O caelicolae.
non est hic, surrexit sicut praedixerat.
ite nuntiate quia surrexit de sepulcro." [1]

The *Introit,* "Resurrexi et adhuc tecum sum, alleluia : posuisti

[1] *Mediæval Stage,* vol. ii, p. 9.

super me manum tuam, alleluia ; mirabilis facta est scientia tua, alleluia, alleluia," is intended to follow it. The trope itself suggests two scenes, the visit of the three Marys to the Sepulchre and the announcing to the disciples of Christ's Resurrection. In the many extant texts of liturgical plays developed therefrom, however, various other episodes are seen to have been added ; among which, the most usual and most popular were, a scene in which the Apostles themselves visit the tomb, and another in which Mary Magdalene is pictured as remaining at the Sepulchre, after the departure of the other two Marys, and conversing with Christ, mistaking him for the gardener. The Shrewsbury play confines itself to the two scenes of the earlier form of such plays, the form based directly on the simple trope ; whereas the York cycle contains a play of Mary Magdalene, which leads one to suppose that possibly, in an earlier form of the cycle, it was preceded by a Resurrection play, consisting of the same two scenes as the Shrewsbury play.

In this second play, the actor for whom the manuscript was written represented the third Mary, since his part, which has been preserved entire, is rubricated III_a *M.* As already pointed out, three of the Latin couplets are almost identical with those of the Dublin *Easter Dramatic Office*,[1] above referred to ; and the probability is that the remaining Latin portions of the play, of which the verses in the vernacular give a free rendering, also bore a general resemblance to this Dublin *Office*.

Upon what day and at what particular part of the service the *Quem Quaeritis* trope and the dramatic office taking its rise therefrom were celebrated, is somewhat difficult to discover, since the records of the usage of various churches are by no means unanimous upon the subject. In some it was an *Introit* trope at the beginning of the Mass, as was the case in many French churches ; in the Bodleian manuscript of the *Winchester Troper*, dating from the last quarter of the tenth century, it follows the tropes for Palm Sunday, and is immediately followed, under a fresh rubric, by the ceremonies for Holy Saturday, thus being celebrated, apparently, on Good Friday ; in the Corpus Christi College manuscript of the *Winchester Troper*, the Holy Saturday ceremonies are not given, and the *Quem Quaeritis* still precedes the Easter tropes ; the *Concordia Regularis* of Ethelwold, however, describes the

[1] Manly, vol. i, p. 22.

office as forming part of the third Nocturn at Matins on Easter
Morning, and not of the Mass. Our *Officium Resurrectionis* at
present under consideration is headed: " *Hic incipit Officium Resurrectionis in die Pasche,*" which I take to mean that the Mass of
Holy Saturday being at an end, the Paschal solemnity commences.
Originally the *Office of the Resurrection* was said at midnight on
Holy Saturday, but later this practice was discontinued, and it was
said on Holy Saturday itself : our *Officium Resurrectionis*, then,
followed the earlier custom.

The valuable *Concordia Regularis*, above referred to, also gives
us a description of the way in which this Office was celebrated,
which is sufficiently instructive to deserve quotation : [1]

" While the third lesson is being chanted, let four brethren vest
themselves. Let one of these, vested in an alb, enter as though
to take part in the service, and let him approach the sepulchre
without attracting attention and sit there quietly with a palm
in his hand.   While the third respond is chanted, let the remaining three follow, and let them all, vested in copes, bearing
in their hands thuribles with incense, and stepping delicately as
those who seek something, approach the sepulchre. These things
are done in imitation of the angel sitting in the monument,
and the women with spices coming to anoint the body of Jesus.
When, therefore, he who sits there beholds the three approach
him like folk lost and seeking something, let him begin
in a dulcet voice of medium pitch to sing *Quem quaeritis.*
And when he has sung it to the end, let the three reply in
unison *Jhesu Nazarenum.*   So he, *Non est hic, surrexit sicut
praedixerat.   Ite, nuntiate quia surrexit a mortuis.*   At the word
of this bidding let those three turn to the choir and say,
Alleluia ! resurrexit Dominus ! This said, let the one, still sitting there and as if recalling them, say the anthem, *Venite et
vide locum.*   And saying this, let him rise and lift the veil, and
show them the place bare of the cross, but only the cloths
laid there in which the cross was wrapped.   And when they
have seen this, let them set down the thuribles which they
bear in that same sepulchre, and take the cloth, and hold it up
in the face of the clergy, and as if to demonstrate that the
Lord has risen and is no longer wrapped therein, let them sing

[1] We quote Mr. Chambers' English translation from his *Mediæval Stage*,
vol. ii, pp. 14 and 15.

the anthem, *Surrexit Dominus de sepulchro,* and lay the cloth upon the altar. When the anthem is dòne, let the prior, sharing in their gladness at the triumph of our King, in that, having vanquished death, He rose again, begin the hymn, *Te Deum laudamus.* And this begun, all the bells chime out together."

The version of the *Office* preserved in the Shrewsbury manuscript is certainly four centuries later than the time to which the details and description furnished by the *Concordia Regularis* have reference ; but there is every reason to believe that this early fifteenth-century copy preserves plays of a much earlier date, the *scenario* for the performance of which was probably not much more elaborate than that referred to in the above quotation. The fact that the Latin portions of the Offices are set to music, strongly suggests that they were performed inside the church.

The third of the Shrewsbury Fragments is a version of the *Peregrini,* another liturgical drama of Easter Week, already well known early in the twelfth century. Our manuscript is the only known example preserved on English soil ; but France is represented by texts from Saintes, Rouen, Beauvais and Fleury, and by the record of a performance at Lille, and Germany by a text of the play contained in the famous manuscript of the Benedictbeurn Kloster. All these versions contain the two scenes embracing the journey to Emmaus and the supper there, but each of them has received additions peculiar to itself. The simplest version of all is that contained in the Saintes manuscript, the compiler of which apparently found the two scenes just referred to sufficient for his purpose ; whereas at Rouen, the Disciples and Mary Magdalen are introduced, and the *Victimae Paschali* is sung. In the Beauvais and Fleury versions still another expansion of the story occurs, which is of special interest in this connection, since it is a scene in which Christ appears to the unbelieving Thomas. The appearance of Christ in person in the *Peregrini* is explained by Chambers as a reaction of the *Quem quaeritis* upon its less distinguished rival.

Our manuscript does not assign the actor's part which it contains to any of the characters, but Professor Skeat is of the opinion that it belongs to Cleophas : since the manuscript contains the words of the chorus of the disciples, the character for whom the part was intended must have been one of them, and, since tradition and the *Coventry Mysteries* speak of Cleophas as Luke's companion, the part must be assigned to one of the two ; and it is more suitable for Cleophas than for Luke. The play in its complete form, then, consists of scenes embracing the journey of Luke and Cleophas to Emmaus, the appearance of Christ, the supper and Christ's disappearance, the return to the other disciples of Luke and Cleophas singing *Quid agamus vel dicamus*, etc., and then in chorus with the other disciples, *Gloria tibi Domine*, the expression by Thomas of his incredulity and, finally, the completion of the Disciples' Chorus with

> "Frater Thoma, causa tristicie,
> Nobis tulit summa leticie."

The direction, *Feria secunda in ebdomada Pasche*, indicates that the *Office* was intended for celebration upon Easter Monday, and the Gospel regularly appointed to be read on that day contains the story of the journey to Emmaus. At Fleury the *Office* was celebrated on Easter Tuesday, the Gospel for which day deals with the incredulity of Thomas, and was attached, moreover, to the *Processio ad Fontes* which, during the Easter season, formed a regular part of Vespers.[1]

Evidence as to where and when these particular versions of the three dramatic *Offices* were celebrated is entirely lacking. For such testimony one naturally first looks to Shrewsbury, but in this respect the most careful search has proved entirely unsuccessful: not that Shrewsbury was a town without plays and other popular forms of amusement during this period, although its citizens were evidently somewhat deficient in local patriotism, since it was necessary to threaten with fines those who, on the day of the procession, left the town to see the Corpus Christi plays at Coventry. From the year 1495 onwards the names of plays are to be found mentioned in the city's accounts, none of which can be identified however with these liturgical fragments: the titles being of such a character as *The Martyrdoms of Saints Feliciana and Sabina* and *The Three Kings of Cologne*. The Corpus Christi Procession, too, was not in possession of a cycle of plays, as was the case in so many other towns, but had a series of *tableaux* of an emblematic rather than religious character.[2]

In the articles in *The Academy*, which have been referred to above, Professor Skeat suggests that our plays are perhaps remains of the lost Beverley cycle. The reference to Beverley is an

---

[1] *Mediæval Stage*, ii, 37.   [2] *Mediæval Stage*.

exceedingly happy one, although the plays are not to be regarded as belonging to the cyclical type, since their connection with the liturgy is much too close and they illustrate a considerably earlier stage in the development of the mystery play. This statement, however, does not exclude the possibility that the three plays of the lost Beverley cycle, upon the same subjects, performed respectively by the crafts of the Vintners, the Wrights and the Gentlemen, are later forms of the *Shrewsbury Offices;* although the fact of their appearance together in the said cycle is of no value whatever as evidence in support of a theory connecting them with Beverley, since the subjects of these three plays were early dramatically developed, rapidly became popular, and appear with equal regularity in all the great cycles. In a thirteenth-century *continuator* of the *Vita* of St. John of Beverley, the record of a miracle done in the Minster, under the date 1220, informs us, by the way, that a Resurrection play was performed in the graveyard.[1] The Cathedral Statutes of Bishop Hugh de Nonant (1188–98) of Lichfield, provide for the performance of the *Officium Pastorum* at Christmas, and of the *Officium Resurrectionis* and *Officium Peregrinorum* in Easter Week :

" *Item, in nocte Natalis representacio pastorum fieri consueuit et in diluculo Paschae representacio Resurreccionis dominicae et representacio peregrinorum die lunæ in septimana Paschae sicut in libris super hijs ac alijs compositis continentur.*"

On such slight evidence as the above, one cannot make any dogmatic assertions as to the *locale* of the Shrewsbury Fragments ; but, in consideration that a Resurrection play is recorded to have taken place there in 1220, that the customs of Beverley Minster would certainly be very similar to those of Lichfield Cathedral, where we know the three religious subjects under discussion to have been dramatically represented, and that they also were found in the lost Beverley cycle, Beverley still remains the most probable of Yorkshire towns at which the plays may have been performed.

Still two other places in Yorkshire possess records of the performance of liturgical plays, York and Leconfield. "The traditional *Statutes* of York Cathedral, supposed to date in their present form from about 1255, provide for the *Pastores* and the *Stella*," and in the list of customary rewards given by the fifth

---

[1] *Mediæval Stage*, ii, 108, 339.

Earl of Northumberland to his servants, which was made in 1522, occurs the following entry :—

[1] "Them of his Lordschipes Chapell if they doo play the Play of the Nativite uppon Cristynmes-Day in the mornynge in my Lords Chapell before his Lordship. XX·ˢ·

. . . Them of his Lordship Chappell and other, if they doo play the play of Resurrection upon Esturday in the morning in my Lords Chapell, XXˢ·." Beyond the borders of Yorkshire performances of what may have been perhaps similar plays are also recorded. At Yarmouth the churchwardens' accounts between 1462 and 1512 contain items of expenditure which point to the performance of a *Stella ;* at Oxford entries in the Bursar's account of Magdalen College, referring to an expanded *Quem Quaeritis,* occur from 1486 onwards, and at Winchester Cathedral the use of the *Quem Quaeritis* in the liturgy was early established.[2] Reading, Kingston-on-Thames, and New Romney had *Resurrection* plays, and the Digby play of St. Mary Magdalen, of course, has the *Quem quaeritis* and *Hortulanus* scenes. With this we must leave the problem of the localisation of the plays unsolved.

III.

a. CREATION OF EVE AND THE FALL, OR THE NORWICH GROCERS' PLAY.

The Norwich *Grocers' Play* has been twice printed : in 1856, Robert Fitch, a local antiquary, contributed to *Norfolk Archæology* an article containing a somewhat inaccurate transcript of an eighteenth-century manuscript ; itself a copy of certain folios of the *Grocers' Book* which by that time was lost and has unfortunately not been recovered. In 1897 Manly reproduced, in his *Specimens of the Pre-Shaksperean Drama,* this version of Fitch. Since the *Grocers' Book* has been lost or destroyed, the earliest available version of the play is the eighteenth-century transcript made use of by Fitch in 1856, from which time it appears to have remained undisturbed until the summer of 1905, when I collated it with the two printed versions for the purposes of the present edition. For this opportunity to make use of the manuscript transcript I am

---

[1] E. K. Chambers : *Mediæval Stage,* vol. ii, 399.
[2] *idem,* ii, 389, 396, 399.

greatly indebted to Mr. Walter Rye of Norwich ; for he it was who searched for and found it, among the uncatalogued papers in the Record Room of the Castle.

This eighteenth-century copy is written clearly on quarto sheets of paper, and the lines of the verse portions are written undetached as if they were prose. The eighteenth-century copyist evidently strove to represent his original accurately, for the usual manuscript contractions are preserved : the letter *n* is often omitted and indicated by a stroke over the preceding vowel, *es* at the end of words is represented by a flourish, *er, ro,* etc., after *p* are represented by a stroke through the tail of the consonant, and a stroke over *c* serves to indicate a following *i ; ll, h* and *d* are often crossed. In certain cases, the stroke appears over *n*, but that is only intended to prevent this letter from being mistaken for *u*. Mr. Walter Rye, who has an extensive acquaintance with the various handwritings of the Norwich Record-Room manuscripts, cannot say with certainty who wrote the transcript, but thinks that it may have been Sir John Fenn. The said gentleman was born at Norwich in 1739, was a man of strong antiquarian tastes, a member of the Society of Antiquaries, and procured and edited the manuscript of the *Paston Letters :* he also presented the manuscript of a great number of the Paston Letters, elegantly bound, to George III, and, in recognition of the gift and of his services to learning, was knighted by his sovereign : thus, Fenn is a not unlikely person to have made the transcript. On the other hand, Fitch, writing in 1856, refers to his original as "a series of extracts, made early in the last century" : a statement, however, which does not necessarily negative our supposition, since the epithet *early* is delightfully vague, and further, upon other grounds, one is not inclined to place great faith in Fitch's accuracy. The use of capitals and marks of punctuation in the manuscript is highly capricious, and has not therefore been reproduced in the present edition : Latin words and phrases are underlined.

The *Grocers' Book* from which some extracts are taken was begun on June 16, 1533, and opens on the first page with :

"*In dei nomine Amen.* The xvi. day of June in the xxv[th]. yere of þe reygne of ower Souereygne Lorde Kynge Henry the viij[th] and in þe yere of ower Lorde God mcccccxxxiij this booke was made by the hands of John Howerson & Robt. Reynbald, than beynge Wardens of þe crafte of Grocescraft with*h*in þe Cyte of

Norwiche, the whiche boke makyth mencion of þe Story of þe Creacion of Eve with þe expellyng of Adam & Eve oute of Paradyce, the whiche story apparteynythe to þe Pageant of þe Company of þe foresayd craft of Grocery, wherfor thys sayd Booke ys made for the sustentacion and mayntenans of þe same, declaryng & showyng þe name of þe Pageant, with all the Utensylles & necessaryes therto belongyng, all parcelles and charges yerely occupyed to þe same, and also all þe namys of suche men as be Inrollyd in þe sayd craft of Grocery within þe foresayd Cyte of Norwiche, &c." This is interesting as giving us the names of the men who copied the plays and accounts into this new book for the Grocers' Company, but gives us no clue as to authorship. In the accounts for 1534 occurs a further reference :—" It., to Sr Stephen Prowet [1] for making of a newe ballet 12.d. " : if this refers to our play at all, it must refer to the A version, since the other was begun in 1565. The churchwardens' accounts of St. Mary's at Bungay in Suffolk likewise show payments in 1526 for copying the game-book, *and to Stephen Prewett for his labour in the matter.* These three names, then, are all that are mentioned in connection with the composition or copying of the plays.

Immediately following the quotation given above is the version of the play in use in 1533 ; it is incomplete, being deficient from the call of Adam, after the Temptation, to the point where Adam and Eve are expelled from the Garden of Eden. The next extract is taken from the sixth and following folios of the *Grocers' Book*, and contains a second version of the play, the one in use in 1565, and which, with the exception of one slightly-mutilated stanza, is complete. Prefixed to this second version are a prologue or " banns " and a second alternative prologue, the former to be used when the Grocers' pageant was the first one to be performed, and the latter when one or more pageants preceded the Grocers' play. The first stanza of this second, alternative prologue states that it is to be used when *The Creation of the World* and *The Fall of the Angels* [2] have been performed. On some occasions evidently the first pageant or pageants were omitted ; perhaps on account of insufficient funds in some of the guilds. The third extract is a copy of the thirty-

---

[1] " Sir Stephen Prewett was seventh Prebend of the College of St. Mary-in-the-Fields in 1536, and one of the Stipendiary Priests of St. Peter Mancroft Church."—Fitch.

[2] *i. e.* The *Hell Carte* referred to in our list : it is placed third in the list but numbered ii : the Grocers' play is placed second and numbered iij.

fourth and following folios of the *Grocers' Book*, and consists of various entries, many of which give most important and detailed information respecting the manner of performing the play. To this I shall return later.

The two versions of the play have very little in common, the second, " newely renvid & accordynge unto þe Skripture, begon thys yere A° 1565, A° 7. Eliz," being an original piece of work, not at all indebted to the earlier edition. New features appearing in this revised version are, the Prolocutor, Dolor, Misery, the Angel and the Holy Ghost, additions which may be attributed to the influence of the Moralities. To the corresponding plays of the great cycles the Norwich play bears no special resemblance : the *York Plays*, nos. 3 to 6, treat the same subject more at length ; whereas the last twelve pages of the *Towneley* play, *i. e.* from the point where Man is created, are lost, so that the play of *The Creation of Eve and the Expulsion from Paradise*, has not been preserved. Our play, too, appears uninfluenced by the Chester and Coventry pieces upon the same subject.

The metrical construction of both texts of the Norwich play is a seven-line stanza expanded in various ways. The normal form occurs quite frequently and has the rhyme-order *ababcc*, but numerous, very free variations of this form also occur, as for example, *ababb cd cd*, and even *ab abb ccc d cdd ee ; Enjambement*, too, is of frequent occurrence.

The first mention of Corpus Christi celebrations at Norwich, according to Mr. Harrop,[1] is an entry dated 1489, in the Assembly Book of the Corporation ; in which it is ordained that the thirty-one guilds of the town, on Corpus Christi Day, shall go in procession before the pageants "ad Capell in Campis Norwici, modo sequi." The procession was arranged in the following order : the thirty-one guilds, the pageants,[2] *the Shreves clothing, Mr. Shreve, the Mair's clothing, Maister Mair* and *Maister Aldermen with bokes or beads in their hands.* For some time previous to 1527, the St. Luke's Guild, consisting of the pewterers, braziers, plumbers, bell-founders, glaziers, steyners and several other crafts, had apparently been responsible for the entire management of, and outlay in connection with, the Corpus Christi plays ; and in that year, finding themselves, as a result of this, almost in a bankrupt condition,

---

[1] *Norfolk Archæology,* iii, 3. 1852.
[2] Referred to always as *the procession.*

they petitioned the corporation to divide the responsibility and expense among the various guilds. The allotment was made and according to the Assembly Book of the Corporation was as follows :

1. Creation off the World.	Mercers, Drapers and Haberdashers.
2. Helle Carte. . . .	Glasiers, Steyners & Screveners, Parchmynters, Carpenters, Gravers, Caryers, Colermakers with Whelewrights.
3. Paradyse.	Grocers & Raffemen.[1]
4. Abell & Cain. . . .	Shermen, Fullers, Thikwollenwevers, Coverlightmakers, Masons & Lyme brenners.
5. Noyse Shipp. . . .	Bakers, Bruers, Inkepers, Coks, Millers, Vynteners & Coupers.
6. Abraham & Isaac. .	Taillors, Broderers, Reders & Tylers.
7. Moises and Aaron with the Children of Israel & Pharo with his Knyghts.	Tanners, Coryors & Cordwaners.
8. Conflict off David & Goleas.	The Smythes.
9. The Berth off Christ with Sheperdes & iij Kyngs of Colen.	Dyers, Colaunderers, Goldsmiths, Goldbeters, Sadelers, Pewtrers & Brasyers.
10. The Baptysme of Criste.	Barbours, Wexchandelers, Surgeons, Fisitians, Hardewaremen, Hatters, Cappers, Skynners, Glovers, Pynners, Poyntemakers, Girdelers, Pursers, Bagmakers, Sceppers, Wyerdrawers & Cardmakers.
11. The Resurrection. .	Bochers, Fishmongers and Watermen.
12. The Holy Gost. . .	Worsted Wevers.

This, then, appears to have been the complete cycle as it was known in 1527; it is abnormally simple, since it only contains half as many subjects as the Chester, the shortest of the four great cycles. We have seen that the performance of the first two plays was somewhat uncertain and irregular, which may also have been the

---

[1] *i. e.* Rough Tallow-Chandlers. (Fitch.)

case with others; so that it is not impossible that at an earlier date, the Norwich cycle may have been richer, and that all references to the titles of these plays, as well as the plays themselves, have disappeared.

In 1489, a Corpus Christi procession was held, and the pageants were taken in procession *ad capell in Campis Norwici;* but we are not definitely informed whether the plays were actually *performed* at that time and at that place : it is however very probable. The accounts for 1535 and 1536 distinctly refer to the performance taking place on Corpus Christi Day, and, in 1537, we learn, there was no performance, although preparations had been made; but the pageant " went that yere in Octobyr in þe Processyin for þe Byrthe of Prynce Edward." Again in 1538, a performance took place but no details as to time or place are given. In the following year the charges for the pageant were greater than usual, because the Surveyors " bought that yere newe cokelys and many other thyngs þat war in dekaye." In 1540, the Surveyors appear to have contracted for the performance; for, "At thys assembly þe Surveyors toke upon them to set forth þe Pageant & to bere all charges of þe same, to pay þe charges on Corp. Xi day, the house ferme of þe Pageant, & þe Bedell hys fee, & they to have for these foresayd Charges & for thes Labours, 20.s." During the years 1541 to 1543, assessments were made, and so presumably the play was in these years also performed. During the following three years there was no assembly, but, since in 1546 a three years' assessment was levied, we may conclude that during this period, too, the plays had been given. After this date the entries are somewhat irregular, the popularity of the Corpus Christi performances seems to have been on the wane, and the latest mention of the pageant is in 1563, when it was "preparyd ageynst þe daye of Mr. Davy his takyng of his charge of þe Mayralltye"; but in view of the fact that the cost was only one-third of the usual expenditure upon the play, it is probable that the play was not performed but only arrayed as a spectacle or *tableau vivant.*

According to the first paragraph of the first prologue to our play :

> " Lyke as yt chancyd befor this season,
> Owte of Godes scripture revealid in playes,
> Was dyvers stories sett furth by reason
> Of pageantes apparellyd in Wittson dayes,
> And later be fallen into decayes,"

the pageants were performed at Whitsuntide ; in fact on Whit-Monday and Whit-Tuesday :[1] that they also went forth in the Corpus Christi procession is equally certain. The only reference to a place of performance known to us is the somewhat vague one mentioned above in connection with the procession, and, so far as we know, there is no authority for believing that the plays at Norwich went in circuit and were played at "stations" in different parts of the town. Probability is in favour of a stationary place of performance, as was the case with the Coventry plays, the Cornish plays, and the plays at Reading, Shrewsbury and Edinburgh.

Although we are somewhat in the dark about the place of performance, the Grocers' accounts are full of interesting and important details, which render a fairly accurate description of the pageant and its decorations, and of the players and their "make-up" possible. The pageant itself was "a Howse of Waynskott,[2] paynted and buylded on a Carte, *with* fowre whelys," which latter, on stubborn occasions, were lubricated with soap.[3] A square top was fitted to the pageant, and it was ornamented by means of a gilded griffin and a "fane," and with a large iron "fane" at one end and eighty-three smaller "fanes." "*Per*fumes" and "fumygacions" appear occasionally in the accounts, and were presumably for the benefit of the griffin.[4] Another very important stage-property was a tree which it was customary to decorate with oranges, figs, almonds, dates, raisins, plums and apples ; flowers, bound by means of coloured thread, and "a Rybbe colleryd Red," were also required for the performance.[5] During the time the pageant was not needed for the performances, it was stored in some building for which an annual rent of, sometimes two shillings, and sometimes three shillings and four pence was paid. During one period the place of storage was "the Gate howse of Mr. John Sotherton of London." A little of the pageant's history and its final fate is described on folio 66 of the *Grocers' Book*, as follows :—

"Item, yt is to be noted that for asmuch as for þe space of 8 yeris ther was neyther Semblye nor metynge, in þe meane season þe Pageante remaynynge 6 yeris in þe Gate howse of Mr. John Sotherton, of London, untyll þe ferme came to 20 s ; and bycause

[1] Harrop, *Norfolk Archæology*, vol. iii, p. 6.
[2] Entry 1565.　　　[3] 1534 "Item.　Sope to grese þe wheles 1ᵈ."
[4] Entry 1547.　" & *per*fumes for the griffin," etc.
[5] Entry 1557, " for oren*ges*, fy*ges*, allmon*des*, dat*es*, Reysens, preumes, & aples to garnish þe tre with, 10ᵈ," "' for collerd thryd to bynd þe flowers, 2ᵈ."

þe Surveiors in Mr. Sotherton's tyme would not dysburs ani moni therfor, þe Pageante was sett oute in þe Strete & so remayned at þe Black fryers brydge in open strete, when bothe yt was so weather beaten, þat þe cheife *parte* was rotton; wherupon Mr. John Oldrich, then Maior þe yer 1570, together wit*h* Mr. Tho. Whall, Alderman, offred yt to þe Company to sell for the some of 20 .s., and when no pe*r*son wold buy yt for þat price and þat yt styll remayned, & nowe one pece therof rent of & now another as was lyke all to come to nothinge, Nicholas Sotherton, then offycer to Mr. Maior, was requested to take yt in peces for þe dept dewe to hym for þe seyd howse ferm therof for 6 yeres aforesayde, at 3ˢ 4ᵈ. a yer, who accordinglye dyd take downe þe same & howsed yt accordinglye." Such was the pageant and its fate. Other articles upon which money was expended are: "Nayles, firelocks, wyer, whypcord and marham": on one occasion four men were paid 16 d "for their labowrs wayghtyng upon þe Pageant wit*h* lewers."

On the eighth of May, 1534, the Company, in assembly, elected a certain Mr. Robt. Greene as alderman, and chose also, " 2 wardens, 2 Assisters, 4 Surveyors of þe Pageant & 1 Bedell,"[1] and in the same year the following payments were made to actors:

It., to Jeffrey Tybnam playeng þᵉ Father . . 16d.
It., to Mr. Leman's servant playing Adam . . 6d.
It., to Frances Fygot playing Eve . . . . 4ᵈ.
It., to Tho. Wolffe playing þe Angelle . . . 4d.
It., to Edm*u*nd Thurston playeng the Serpent . . 4d :

the names of the actors of Dolor, Misery and the Holy Ghost, are not mentioned. Collecting the scattered details from various accounts we obtain the following impression of the "make-up" of the actors and persons concerned in the performance. God the Father wore a mask, a wig and gloves; the Angel, a wig, a crown, gloves, a coat and "over hosen of Apis skynnis"; Adam, a wig, gloves, and "a cote and hosen steyned"; Eve, a wig, gloves and "two cotes and a pair of hosen steyned"; the Serpent, a wig, a crown, and "a cote with hosen & tayle steyned"; Dolor, "a cote and hosen wit*h* a bagg & capp steyned." Of the stage appearance of Misery and the Holy Ghost no hint is given. The costume of

---

[1] Cf. also, entry 1546 : "Accordyngly were chosen 4 Aldermen & 8 Comyners, who chose Mr. Wyll Rogers for ther Alderman; 2 Wardeyns & 2 Surveyors for settyng forth þe Procession on Corpus Xi day, & for þe Pageant yf it go forth þe next year; & 1 bedell."

the pendon-bearer included a coat of yellow buckram upon which the arms of the Company were painted, while the bearer of the griffin wore a coat, a wig and a crown. Two bearers of the arms, in wig and crown, and streamer-bearers, also accompanied the procession. It is interesting, too, to compare with these details, directions given in connection with the performance of the corresponding portion of the Cornish mysteries, where the stage-directions are given in English: "Meanwhile are got ready 'Adam and Eva aparlet in whytt lether in a place apoynted by the conveyour & not to be sene till they be called & thei kneel & ryse.' Paradise has 'ii fayre trees in yt' and 'a fowntaine' and 'fyne flowers,' which appear suddenly. Similarly, a little later, 'Let fyshe of dyuers sortis apeare & serten beastis as oxen, kyne, shepe & such like.' Lucifer incarnates as 'a fyne serpen made with a virgyn face & yolowe heare vpon her head.' Presently comes the warning, ' fig leaves redy to cover ther members,' and at the expulsion, 'the garmentis of skynnes to be geven to adam and eva by the angell. Receave the garmentis. Let them put on the garmentis and shew a spyndell and a dystaff.'" [1]

The performance was undoubtedly accompanied by music, the text of which unfortunately has not been preserved, but was probably of a similar nature to that accompanying some of the plays of the York cycle, part of which is reproduced in Miss Toulmin-Smith's excellent edition of that collection. In the first version of the Norwich play, music appeared twice; firstly, immediately after the large *lacuna*, where the stage-direction is simply "music," and secondly, at the end, where Adam and Eve are to sing the last couplet, "walkyng together about the place, wryngyng ther hands"; which verses, the eighteenth-century transcript of the *Grocers' Book* informs us, in the original were set to music twice, and then again for a chorus of four parts. At the end of the second version of the play appears the note:—"Old Musick, Triplex, Tenor, Medius, Bass," [2] which apparently applies to the

---

[1] The materials required for the play at Beverley are given as :—j karre, viij hespis, xviij stapels, ij visers, ij wenges angeli, j fir-sparr, j worme, ij paria caligarum linearum, ij paria camisarum, j gladius." Beverley, *Great Guild Book* cited in *Med. Stage*, ii, p. 339.

[2] Triplex or Triplum—the name given to a third part when added to two other parts, one of which was a *canto fermo*, the other a counterpoint. It was generally the upper part, hence triplex came to mean canto-primo (treble). *Medius* is the tenor part. The music thus appears to have been male-voice quartet : or, as now expressed, alto, 1st tenor, 2nd tenor, bass.

Te Deum immediately following. The singing had also an organ accompaniment, since in 1534 a certain John Bakyn received a payment of sixpence for "playeng at the organs," which were borrowed for the occasion ; because in the same account appears an item of fourpence spent upon a present given to the person who lent the instrument in question. Such are the most relevant details to be drawn from the Grocers' accounts. The remaining entries are of a more general nature such as are to be found in similar accounts in connection with other Corpus Christi processions and performances, consisting mainly of a very liberal expenditure upon beer and victuals (at this period, apparently very necessary for the successful performance of religious plays) and for the transport of the same, but add nothing of historical value to a description of the Norwich performance.

In addition to the four great cycles, which of course all contain a play on the same subject, and the Cornish plays, performances of plays of *Adam and Eve* are on record at Beverley, Reading, and Aberdeen, the texts of which, however, have been lost, and about which very little information has been preserved.[1]

b. Noah's Ship, or the Newcastle Play.

The earliest version of the *Newcastle Shipwrights' Play* now available, is that printed by Henry Bourne, M.A., a curate of All Hallows in Newcastle, in a book entitled *The History of Newcastle-upon-Tyne ; or, the Ancient and Present State of that Town,*[2] issued in 1736, four years after the death of its author. Bourne's text is very far from being satisfactory, and therefore was probably based upon some manuscript original, itself very incorrect or else offering textual difficulties which Bourne, in consequence of insufficient grammatical knowledge, failed to overcome. In 1789, in the second volume of John Brand's *History and Antiquities of Newcastle-upon-Tyne,*[3] appeared a reprint of Bourne's text, and a second reprint in 1825, in T. Sharp's *Dissertation on the Coventry Mysteries.*[4] In volume III of *Göteborgs Högskolas Arskrift,* 1897, F. Holthausen printed a critical and

[1] Reading had an *Adam and Eve* play in 1507 on "the Sunday afore Bartylmas-tide, in the Forbury : a 'schapfold' and pagentts are mentioned." *Med. Stage,* ii, 392.
[2] The play in question is printed on page 139 *et seq.* in double columns. All the substantives have capital letters.
[3] Page 369 *et seq.*   [4] Page 223 *et seq.*

emended text based upon that of Bourne, along with a score pages of criticism and historical discussion; while two years later, R. Brotanek turned his attention to the play, and printed in vol. xxi of the *Anglia*, Sharp's text, together with a restored text, representing the play in its original dialect, *i. e.* the Northern dialect of the second quarter of the fifteenth century. The present edition is a reproduction of Bourne's version with a minimum amount of correction and emendation; all the other versions have been consulted and all variants of real importance in any of these have been given in the footnotes. I believe such a method to be in harmony with the aims of the E. E. T. S.'s editions, and have therefore not given a hypothetical, reconstructed text, for which I must refer readers to the extremely clever and skilfully executed restoration of Mr. Brotanek, in the *Anglia*.

Bourne, in his transcript, with the best of intentions no doubt, modernised the spelling throughout; but apparently he did not understand his original very well, since, in very many instances, he has put down verses which are incapable of bearing any meaning at all, and has left them in such a state that it is extremely difficult to conjecture what his original gave him. Three lines he has omitted, and states the fact, but other places in the play seem to have suffered from the same process, although he has not acknowledged it.

In spite of all the ill-treatment, however, which his copy received, there are sufficient traces of original forms to establish the fact that it belonged to a Northern district, and probably to the first half of the fifteenth century. Holthausen is of the opinion that Bourne used a sixteenth-century copy of a still earlier version. The same editor has carefully collected and arranged the grammatical peculiarities of the piece, from which we select the following most important:

1. *In rhyme position: laith, skaith*, 118, 119; *wayns, baynes*, 152, 154; *die, fee*, 32, 34; *you wends, friends*, 161 and 163.
2. *Spelling*: long *a* represented by *ai* or *ay*, e. g. :—*fair*, 194; *fayre*, 140 and 173; *wayns*, 152; *skaith*, 119; *baynes*, 154.
3. *weet*, 131, 133; *atour*, 145; *whunt*, 114; *tent*, 39.
4. *Inflexion: thou has*, 195.
5. *Vocabulary: bewschere*, 116; *hoothe*, 8; *atour*, 145.

The spelling *whunt* for the word *quaint* points to the fact that the original had the Northern spelling *qu* or *quh* in such words as *what* and *when*, for which the copyist systematically substituted *wh*. The rhymes, with two exceptions (*do, go*, 5 and 7 ; *boat* and *sprot*, 84 and 86), too, are impossible if we do not assign to the rhyming words a Northern pronunciation. The genitive and plural inflections, in certain cases, function as syllables in respect to the metre, and therefore a fairly early date in the fifteenth century for the play is extremely probable.

In the case of a work so badly handed down to us it is somewhat difficult to discover in what strophic forms it was at first composed ; but the following at least seem to have been in the original. A four-line strophe with the rhyme-order *abab* occurs the most frequently, and consists generally of all four verses with three stresses, but occasionally of all four verses with four stresses. The next most usual stanza is a six-line strophe, sometimes entirely of verses with three stresses, sometimes entirely of verses with four stresses, and less frequently containing a mixture of three-stress and four-stress verses ; the rhyme-order is uniformly *ababab* in the first two cases, and *aab ccb* in the third case. The irregularity of the strophic arrangement becomes distinctly pronounced upon the entrance of the Devil. Was this intentional on the part of the writer, and so designed in order to be in keeping with the ranting and unruly behaviour conventionally assigned to this popular stage-figure ? In some instances, too, four-line stanzas are connected by the repetition of the same rhyme, and stanzas with a *cauda* are not infrequent. The whole play—the speeches of the Devil in particular—is rich in examples of alliteration. In dividing the play into stanzas I have sought to obtain, wherever possible, one or other of the four, six or eight-line stanzas, which however left some portions still undivided ; these have been treated upon their merits.

Our play only concerns itself with the former part of the Noah story, the building of the Ark ; but one of the crafts, the titles of whose plays are not now ascertainable, was very probably responsible for a play dealing with the second part of the story. In the York cycle each half of the story has its own play : in the Towneley cycle the whole story is given in one. Brotanek thinks that the Newcastle play is indebted to the two York plays, which opinion he thinks is justified by the fact, that at Newcastle the subject seems to have been divided between two plays in the same manner as at York, and by certain other, not very strong parallelisms. In view of the close connection known to exist between some of the plays of the Towneley and York cycles respectively, it is by no means improbable that a third Northumbrian cycle may have also borne some close resemblance, at least in parts, to these two extant collections;[1] thus, while not negativing Brotanek's opinion, we feel the evidence to be too slight to satisfactorily substantiate it, and would prefer to leave the question among the many other doubtful ones which seem to be inevitable when considering the early history of the stage.

In comparison with the first York play and the first part of the Towneley play, the Newcastle version is arranged on a considerably more elaborate scale, without much alteration in point of length. The extension consists of the superfluous introduction of the Angel in addition to God, the appearance of Noah's Wife already in the first part of the story, and the presence of the Devil. The introduction of the Angel was doubtless intended to increase the spectacular effect—the chief consideration in the early fifteenth century—although at the same time it increased the dramatist's difficulties, since it necessitated God's command appearing twice : this the writer obviated somewhat, by making the Angel address to Noah much that was not in his original message, and omitting very much that was ; in the Coventry Noah-play an angel is also introduced. The popularity of Noah's wife as a comic character was sufficient to induce the writer to introduce her into the first part of the story as well as the second, and would also warrant the repeating of much of the *vis comica* connected with her appearance. The inclusion of the Devil in the Noah story is, as far as I know, an idiosyncrasy of the Newcastle version. His Infernal Highness looking back with pleasure upon the success of his methods in the Garden of Eden, repeats the experiment with Noah's wife, this time substituting "a drink" for "the apple" : the anachronism involved is, of course, to the fourteenth and fifteenth-century dramatist, a mere trifle. Professor Brandl,[2] in speaking of the play, remarks, that by the introduction of the Devil the construction of the play approaches one step nearer to the form of the Morality. To the Devil, too, is entrusted

---

[1] The Beverley plays were also probably indebted to the York cycle.
[2] Paul's *Grundriss*, II. 711.

the part of speaking the Epilogue, and he concludes the play in a spirit quite in harmony with the comedy that has preceded. In the York play of the Temptation,[1] and in one of the Chester plays, the Devil is likewise made to address the spectators.[2] The description of the shipwrights' tools and materials goes exhaustively into details and shows that the author had an intimate knowledge of the trade, or else was assisted by one of the members of the craft; while the realism and comedy displayed in the piece indeed compare not unfavourably with that of the plays attributed to the author of the Towneley *Second Shepherds Play*, whose ability Mr. Pollard has so highly, but not too highly, praised.

External evidence of the date and manner of performance of the play is, fortunately, comparatively plentiful, and is to be found in the records of the various craft-guilds. The earliest mention of Corpus Christi performances is a notice, dated Jan. 20th, 1426, in the Coopers' " ordinary " ; they are also mentioned, in 1436, in the books of the Smiths and Glovers, in 1442 in those of the Barbers, in 1451 by the Slaters', in 1459 by the Sadlers', and in 1447 by the Fullers' and Dyers'. Other references, too, are to be found. In the " ordinary " of the Millers, *e. g.* under the date 1578, occurs the following minute :—" Whensoever the generall plaies of the towne shall be commanded by the mayor, &c.," the guild shall play, "the antient playe of their fellowship, the Deliverance of the Children of Isrell out of the Thraldome, Bondage and Servitude of King Pharo." From this it seems probable that at this date the plays had lost some of their popularity, and that the guilds did not consider them worth the expense and trouble which performance involved ; at least it is clear that by this date they had ceased to be performed annually.

It is also clearly established by the records that at Newcastle there was a cycle of plays. The names of twelve plays with the crafts performing them are known, and are as follow :—

1. " The Creation of Adam." Bricklayers and Plasterers.
2. " Noah's Ark." Shipwrights.
3. " The Offering of Isaac." Slaters.

---

[1] v. 175.
[2] Noah also addresses himself directly to the spectators. Cf. vv. 93 and 96, 200 and 201.

4. "The Deliverance of the Children of Israel out of the Thraldom, Bondage and Servitude of King Pharao." Millers.

5. "The three Kings of Cologne." Goldsmiths, Plumbers, Glaziers, Pewterers and Painters.

6. "The Flying of our Lady into Egype." Bricklayers and Plasterers.

7. "The Baptizing of Christ." Barbers (and) Chirurgeons with Chandlers.

8. [The Last Supper.][1] Fullers and Dyers.

9. "The Bearing of the Cross." Weavers.

10. "The Burial of Christ." House-carpenters.

11. "The Descent into Hell." Tailors.

12. "The Buriall of our Lady Saint Mary the Virgin." Masons.

In addition to this, we know that the Merchant Venturers Company were responsible for five plays, one of which was to be performed by the Ostmen and paid for by the town; the plays of the remaining five guilds (exclusive of the Joiners) are not known. In the Joiners' "ordinary," dated 1589, is the instruction, "whensoever it shall be thought necessary by the mayor, &c. to command to be sett forth and plaied or exercised any generall playe or martial exercise, they shall attend on the same and do what is assigned them"; the interpretation of which seems to be that they were not responsible for the performance of any particular play, but rather expected to give assistance of a general character. Allowing one play to each of the five guilds whose plays are unknown, the total number in the cycle would be twenty-two; but it is possible that one or more of these crafts performed two plays, as the Bricklayers and Plasterers did, in which case the total number of plays may have been anything between twenty-two and twenty-seven. Holthausen includes in his list the play *Hogmagoge*, mentioned in the accounts of the Merchant Adventurers under the date 1554, but Mr. Chambers is of the opinion that it is a Spring or Summer folk-feast that is here referred to; an explanation which, in my opinion, seems more plausible.

It rested with the Corporation to decide when the plays were

---

[1] The title is not mentioned, but it is clear from the items of expenditure what the play was.

to be given, but the cost was to be defrayed by the various craft-guilds, who made a definite levy upon each of their members for that purpose; *e. g.* "in 1536, the Taylors required three-pence from each hireling, and seven-pence from each newly-admitted member, whereas the Fullers and Dyers paid nine shillings for the 'play lettine' to four persons."[1] The time of the performance is generally said to have been afternoon or evening, a judgment based upon a deposition made by Sir Robert Brandling of Newcastle, in 1569, who said that on Corpus Christi Day, 1562, "he would after his dinner draw his will, and after the plays would send for his consell, and make it up." This how-ever does not necessarily imply that the plays *began* in the evening.

A good deal of difference of opinion exists as to whether the Corpus Christi plays at Newcastle were taken round in circuit and played at certain chosen street-corners, or before the houses of distinguished citizens, or, as was the case at Edinburgh, given at some fixed place.

The supporters of the latter theory base their opinion upon two facts. It is known that the Procession commenced at 7-0 a.m., and yet Sir Robt. Brandling refers to the plays in the evening; this deposition, however, is in no respect irreconcilable with the sup-position that the plays were cyclical, beginning in the morning and extending until towards evening : even the twelve plays the names of which have been preserved would be sufficient to occupy this length of time, since we must not forget that cases are on record where more than one day was required for the performance of some of the larger cycles. The second fact partly responsible for such an opinion is a phrase in the closing speech of the Devil, " All that is gathered in this stead "; a phrase which, to my mind, cannot function as a crucial instance at all, since the delight-fully indefinite word " stead " applies equally well to an enclosed place of performance, or to a stopping-place at some street-corner, or market-place, one of the " stations " of the procession through the town. On the other hand, payments for the car, and for " them that bear the car," are fairly numerous in the accounts of the various crafts, and also relatively large, a fact which makes a second, alternative solution of the difficulty, that offered by Miss Toulmin-Smith, viz. that the pageants were taken to the place of

[1] E. K. Chambers, *Med. Stage*, vol. ii, p. 385.

performance before the play, also appear somewhat unlikely: and, finally, an entry to be met with in the books of the Fullers and Dyers, appears to place the matter beyond a doubt :—

> " Item, for the care and banner berryng 20*d.* Item, for the carynge of the trowt and wyn *about the toun.*" [1]

The pageant used for the performance of plays dealing with the story of Noah was made in the form of a ship or ark, and was probably larger than the usual form of pageant in use for other plays ; for we find in some accounts at Lincoln that three times as much was charged for "housing" the Noah pageant as for the others,[2] and, moreover, the one in possession of the Trinity Guild of Master Mariners and Pilots of Hull in 1421, was valued at the sum of £5 8*s.* 4*d.*[3] In the Digby play of St. Mary Magdalena a practicable ship appears to have been moved about the *platea*,[4] and the trench so often referred to in connection with the mystery plays at Perranzmabulo, is explained by some authorities as having been used for the purpose of floating Noah's ship.

There is little to be said about the arrangements of the ship and the make-up of the actors. The accounts at Hull make it clear that there at least, the pageant was on wheels and went about the town, and also had a rigging; that Noah had a coat made of three skins, a pair of mittens and a "pyleh," and that he and his children made their beds of straw. The pageant was afterwards hung in the church. In the Newcastle play the actor who played *Diabolus* apparently wore a mask, which gave opportunity for the expression :

> " I swear thee by my crooked snout." [5]

In addition to Newcastle and the four great cycles, the series of plays performed at Beverley and that at Norwich, each possessed a Noah-play, the texts of which, unfortunately, have not been preserved. At Hull, as at many other sea-ports, English as well as Continental, the Plough-Monday Festival had taken on such a maritime character that the usual plough was replaced by a boat. Although at Hull there is no trace of Corpus Christi plays, there are incontestable records of the performance of a Noah-play, which took place in connection with the Plough-Monday procession

---

[1] E. K. Chambers, *Mediæval Stage*, vol. ii, 385.   [2] *Idem* 379.
[3] *Idem* 371.   [4] *Idem* ii, 136.   [5] v. 127.

and celebrations.[1] Bristol in 1486 did honour to Henry VII by the performance among others of the "shipwrights' pageant," and Dublin had a performance in 1498, but these were probably in dumb-show.

c. ABRAHAM'S SACRIFICE, DUBLIN AND BROME VERSIONS.

Two non-cyclical plays upon the Abraham-and-Isaac story have been preserved, the so-called Dublin and Brome plays. The former has been edited twice : in 1836, by J. P. Collier, in his volume entitled *Five Miracle Plays*, and in 1899, by Rudolf Brotanek, in vol. xxi. of the *Anglia*, whereas the latter has appeared in four editions ; in 1884, Miss E. Toulmin-Smith published it in vol. vii. of the *Anglia*, and in 1886 in *A Commonplace-Book of the Fifteenth Century ;* in 1887 it was printed by Mr. Walter Rye in the third volume of the *Norfolk Antiquarian Miscellany*, and lastly by Professor Manly from Miss Smith's two editions, in 1897, in *Specimens of the Pre-Shakesperean Drama.* In the preparation of the present edition all the above have been consulted.

In a collection of manuscripts, the gift of Bishop Ussher to the library of Trinity College, Dublin, is one marked D. iv. 18, containing one of our two plays. It is a small, quarto, paper manuscript, clearly and beautifully written, entitled *Tractatus Varii* and containing pieces of a somewhat miscellaneous character. The first fourteen pages, which are written in a larger hand than the remainder of the manuscript, contain satiric, religious, didactic and political pieces. Folios fifteen *recto* and sixteen give us an enumeration of the Christian kings of the world, including those of England, and state the duration of each reign, except in the case of the last, Henry VI. It is therefore clear that this list was made between 1422 and 1461, and since the same hand continues to the end of the manuscript, the whole of this part, from folio fifteen onwards, must have been written down during that reign. On the back of the next leaf, our play, which is without a title, begins. Folio seventeen has clearly been stitched in the wrong place, since it contains a continuation of a poem found on folio fourteen *verso*, and since folio eighteen takes up the continuation of our play. Folios eighteen

---

[1] Cf. In 1529 we read, "item, Nicholas Helpby for wrytg the play vij^d " ; and 1483, "To a man clearing away the snow 1^d ":--this latter reference is more likely to refer to Plough Monday than to Corpus Christi day, also Hadley, who gives the items, refers to them as extracted from "the expences on Plough day."

verso and nineteen *recto*, being filled with heraldic designs, also interrupt the play under consideration, which folios nineteen *verso* to twenty-three *recto*, bring, without interruption, to a close. Two pages are then left entirely blank, after which follows a register of the mayors and bailiffs of Northampton : " Hic sunt Majores et Ballivi de Northampton a primo anno Regis Ricardi usque in hunc diem " : then follow another empty leaf and a very badly-mutilated one, which appears to have contained a calendar. Following these pieces come some prose tractates written in another hand : " How men þat ben in hele schulden visite sike folk and how a man shulde be comforted aȝens grucchinge in sikenesse, þe secunde chapter," which is then followed by a sermon beginning—" Capitulum Primum—Tary not for to turn the to God ne drawe not a leyte fro day to day for sodenly he takes wrecches in sharpnesse of deeth," while at the end comes the inscription : " Here enden the XII Chapitres of Richard, heremyte of Hampole," after which follow Latin manuscripts. The next piece is the short Latin Chronicle extending as far as the thirty-sixth year of Henry the Sixth's reign, immediately preceding, and written with the same ink, and in the same hand as our play ; which latter is then followed, still in the same hand but written with different ink, by a bailiff's register, extending as far as the first year of Edward the Fourth's reign. The probability, then, is that the two former pieces were written down at about the same time, and the last-named piece somewhat later ; so that 1458, the thirty-sixth year of Henry the Sixth's reign, seems a very probable date for the compilation of this Dublin version of the play of *Abraham and Isaac.*

Until challenged by Davidson and Brotanek, the opinion that this play was one of a lost cycle performed at Dublin, had been general. The former scholar has, however, pointed out that the evidence upon which the supposition is based, a memorandum in the Chain-Book of the City for 1498, is far from convincing. The entry in question is as follows :—

" Corpus Christi day a pagentis :—
        The pagentis of Corpus Christi day, made by an olde law and conformed by a semble befor Thomas Collier, Maire of the Cite of Divelin, and Juries, Baliffes and commones, the iiij^th Friday next after midsomer, the xiii. yere of the reign of King Henry the VIIth.

Glovers: Adam and Eve, with an auter and the ofference. Peyn xl. s.

Corvisers: Cayn and Abell, with an auter and the ofference. Peyn xl. s.

Maryners, Vynters, Shipcarpynderis, and Samountakers: Noe, with his shipp, apparalid acordyng.   Peyn xl. s.

Wevers: Abraham [and] Ysaak, with ther auter and a lamb and ther offerance.   Peyn xl. s.

Smythis, Shermen, Bakers, Sclaters, Cokis and Masonys: Pharo, with his hoste.   Peyn xl. s.

Skynners, House-Carpynders, and Tanners and Browders: for the body of the camell, and Oure Lady and hir Chile well aperelid with Joseph to lede the camell, and Moyses with the children of Israel, and the Portors to berr the camel. [Peyn] xl. s.

[Goldsmy]this: The three Kynges of Collynn, ridyng worshup-fully, with the offerance, with a sterr afor them.   Peyn xl. s.

[Hoopers]: The shep[er]dis, with an Angill syngyng Gloria in excelsis Deo.   Peyn xl. s.

Corpus Christi yild: Criste in his Passioun, with three Maries, and angilis berring serges of wax in ther hands.   Peyn xl. s.

Fisshers: The Twelve Apostelis.   Peyn xl. s.

Marchauntes: The Prophetis.   Peyn xl. s.

Bouchers: tormentours, with ther garmentis well and clenely peynted.   [Peyn] xl. s.

The Maire of the Bulring and bachelers of the same: The Nine Worthies ridyng worshupfully, with ther followers accord-yng.   Peyn xl. s.

The Hagardmen and the husbandmen to berr the dragoun and to repaire the dragoun a Seint Georges day and Corpus Christi day.   Peyn xl. s.

A second list, almost identical with this one, immediately fol-lows, and is headed "The Pagentys of Corpus Christi Procession."

The general impression to be derived from a careful considera-tion of the phraseology, the irregular order of the pageants and the inclusion of profane subjects, is that they were simply dumb-show accompaniments of a Corpus Christi Procession, an opinion with which both Davidson and Chambers are in full agreement. The former scholar, basing his opinion upon a comparison of the Dublin

and Aberdeen pageants with those of Bethunia, thinks that the
two former were of the character of *tableaux vivants ;* but whether
this be the case or no, it is very difficult to regard them, on the
occasion here referred to, as a cycle of Corpus Christi plays. On
the other hand, it is not improbable that each of the crafts had
acted, or perhaps still acted, a play on the subject assigned to it
in this record. It is also not improbable that the religious plays
alone had been performed in their proper order in a cycle. The
explanation of the irrational order of the pageants as here recorded
is, to my mind, that there was no intention of arranging them as
to subject, but according to the rank of the guilds in question, each
of which, no doubt, jealously saw to it that it received a place in
the procession worthy of its dignity.

Again, we have later records of performance in Dublin which
undoubtedly have reference to plays :—" Tho. Fitzgerald, Earl of
Kildare and Lord Lieutenant of Ireland, in the year 1588, was in-
vited to a new play every day in Christmas, Arland Uster being then
mayor, and Francis Herbert and John Squire bayliffs, wherein the
taylers acte the part of Adam and Eve ; the shoemakers represented the story of Cri[s]pin and Crispianus ; the vintners acted
Bacchus and his story ; the Carpenters that of Joseph and Mary ;
Vulcan, and what related to him, was acted by the Smiths ; and
the comedy of Ceres, the goddess of corn, by the Bakers. Their
stage was erected on Hoggin Green (now called College Green),
and on it the priors of St. John of Jerusalem, of the blessed
Trinity, and All Hallows caused two plays to be acted, the one
representing the passion of our Saviour, and the other the several
deaths which the apostles suffered." [1] In this case, however, there
is no mention of an Abraham-and-Isaac play. These are clearly
single plays, independent of any cycle, and Davidson regards the
religious plays among them at least as having been very similar in
character to our play, for he says, " if now the play of the Priors
of St. John of Jerusalem or that of the Carpenters were extant,
wherein would it differ from the play of Abraham and Isaac ? " It
is not impossible that on some similar occasion to the above the
last-named play was performed.

Brotanek, however, in his article in the *Anglia* assigns the play
not to Dublin, but to Northampton, or near by. His arguments
in support of his opinion are indeed weighty, and if sometimes a

[1] Quoted by Chambers from Harris, *History of Dublin*, p. 147.

little fanciful, are for the most part convincing. One has pronounced above in favour of the date 1458 for the manuscript : the
play could not have taken its rise much before this, and at the
earliest at the beginning of the fifteenth century. In so late a
specimen, too, it is somewhat difficult to arrive at a very definite
opinion upon the dialect of the piece, but what traces are to be
found, as Brotanek points out, are certainly characteristic of the
English Midlands rather than of the district around Dublin. All
characteristically Northern forms, as well as the known peculiarities of Dublin manuscripts of the period, such as the confusion of
th with *t* and *d*, of *w* with *u*, and the omission and erroneous inser-
tion of the aspirate, are entirely absent ; whereas, the interchange
of *i* and *e*, which is a peculiarity of the East Midlands, and *us* as
the plural form of the substantive, which is a West Midland peculiarity, occasionally occurring in East Midland manuscripts, both
appear and are further assured by being present in rhyme-position
(*e. g.* vv. 330-334, and v. 205). In addition, the grammatical
features of the play approach very closely those of the *Ludus
Coventriae*, and therefore one must infer that our specimen belongs
to the borders between the East and West Midlands. So much is
certain with respect to the *locale* of the play : a more definite
assignation of it to a particular town or district cannot be very
certain, but must very largely be a matter of more or less justi-
fiable conjecture. The appearance in the same manuscript, in the
same handwriting, of the register of bailiffs of Northampton, certainly makes that town appear far from improbable ; but as yet
no records of any performances of plays there have come to light.
Negative evidence of course in this respect is always of very small
value, and, as Brotanek points out, since the dramatic activity of
Coventry was at this time very great, the not-far-distant town of
Northampton is certain to have been under the same influence.
The same authority further suggests that in the famous quotation
from the Coventry Plays :

> " A Sunday next if that we may,
> At VI of the belle we gynne oure play
> In N —— towne, whereof we pray, &c.,"

the N —— would more probably stand for some particular name
rather than for the generic term *nomen*, since the day and time
are definitely stated ; and, therefore, why not Northampton ? The
arguments are worth considering, and with that we must leave them.

MYSTERY PLAYS.   *d*

The play is written in strophes the form of which is varied
with a good deal of skill and taste. The most common form is
a stanza of eight verses, with the rhyme-order *a a a b c c c b*, but
sometimes with only two rhymes, as for example, in the stanzas
72–79, 193–200 and 295–302. The stanza is not foreign to the
mediæval religious drama ; it is, in fact, the dominant strophic
form in the Chester cycle, and the Towneley and Coventry cycles
also have page after page written in the same form. Longer
strophes of nine, twelve, thirteen and seventeen verses, always
used with a definite purpose, also frequently occur : thus, for example, the opening speech of Deus is cast in two of these seventeen-
line strophes, while other long speeches demanding dignity, and the
prayer at the end, are also written in one or other of these longer
stanza forms. This stanza, in its normal construction, consists of
thirteen verses with the rhyme order *a b a b a b a b c d d d c*, a form
to be found in the *Towneley* and *Coventry* cycles, and also in *The
Castle of Perseverance ;* the other varieties are formed by an
extension of the *cauda*. The metrical structure within the verse
itself is also varied, since septenars, alexandrines, verses of three
and of four stresses, and here and there a verse of five stresses, are
all to be found. The septenar only appears in the long strophes at
the beginning and end of the play. Alliteration as an additional
adornment frequently appears, but not as a metrical principle,
although certain time-honoured, conventional, alliterative pairs
still remain, as, for example, *truþe for to tell* 5, *ouþer mete or mele*
24, *in wele and wo* 265, and sometimes a verse is alliteratively
linked to the next, but whether intentionally or accidentally, it is
difficult to say.[1]

The Brome play of *Abraham and Isaac* is contained in a
manuscript commonplace-book of the fifteenth century, made for
the owners of the Manor of Brome, in the County of Suffolk. The
manuscript was accidentally found among other papers relating to
the same family, by Dr. G. H. Kingley, in the muniment room
belonging to the land-agent's office at Brome. The late Sir
Edward Kerrison, owner of the manuscript, accorded Miss Toulmin-
Smith permission to print from it *ad libitum*, with the result
that two editions of our play appeared, to which we are indebted for our text, and the following details descriptive of the

[1] Cf. vv. 39, 40 ; 359, 360.

manuscript.[1] "The manuscript of paper, five-and-a-half inches wide by eight long, is bound in a parchment cover with a flap turned over, somewhat injured by damp. It contains eighty-one leaves. The book seems to have been originally intended for a collection of poems, moral or religious; these occupy the first part of the volume, written in a fine neat hand of the second half of the fifteenth century. Following these (in one case written between two poems) are several interesting accounts for sale of corn and barley, lists of church dues, common rights, etc., and a few miscellaneous items, together with a kind of chartulary embracing deeds from 3 Edward III to 30 Henry VI, each given with an English translation following the Latin. All these are in two or three different hands. On the last leaf but one is a poem in the same hand as those at the beginning of the book.

The principal poems are as follows :

Twenty-six lines, beginning, "Man in merthe has meser in Mynde" (fo. 1), also cipher puzzles and sayings (fo. 1. v⁰).

Predilections of fortune by the cast of dice (fos. 2 and 3). On one page the dice are drawn. Another copy of this, differing in some particulars, is found in Sloane 513 (fo. 98).

Adrian and Epotis (fos. 5–14) resembles the version in Ashmol. 61 and Cott. Calig. A. II. At the end of this is a pretty design in red and black of the sign I.H.S., with a spear and heart.

Play of *Abraham and Isaac* (fos. 15–22).

Fifteen Signs of Doom (fos. 23–26).

Owayn Miles (fos. 28–38). This belongs to the type of the Cotton (Calig. A. II. fo. 89) version, not to that of the Auchinleck manuscript. Life of St. Margaret and Sir Olybryus (fos. 39–44). A fragment of the fifteenth-century version printed by Horstmann. Lydgate's stanzas on Prudence, Justice, Temperance and Fortitude (fo. 80).

The local entries in the manuscript chiefly refer to the village of Stuston, attached to the Manor of Brome, and date from the fifteenth year of Henry VII (A.D. 1499).

This version of *Abraham and Isaac* thus dates from the second half of the fifteenth century, but that it is by no means the original manuscript of the play is clearly evident from the variety and irregularity of its metrical form. By far the greater portion of

---

[1] Editions : (*a*) 1884, *Anglia*, vol. vii ; (*b*) 1886, *A Common-place Book of the Fifteenth Century.*

the play is written in a four-verse stanza usually with verses of
four stresses, but sometimes of five, and the rhyme-order *a b a b*.
The strophe next to this in frequency of occurrence is one of five
similar verses and rhymed *a b a a b:* but the number of stanzas of
the former kind is more than double that of the latter. The
greatest probability is, then, that the original was written in this
four-line stanza above named, and that a copyist intending to
transcribe it into another stanza-form, the five-line stanza rhymed
a b a a b, did this in the case of the first five stanzas and in eleven
other cases, but for some reason or other did not carry his original
plan to completion. A copyist introducing a new stanza would
naturally do it at the beginning, and here it is noticeable that in
the first five strophes, the third or the fourth verse can be omitted
without damaging the sense of the piece. Further irregularities
and corruptions are doubtless to be explained as being due to later
copyists ; and, perhaps, at some stage in the history of the play's
transmission, to oral communication ; while the many exclamatory
phrases which so much interfere with a really systematic division
into strophes, are perhaps to be regarded, like similar passages in
the York plays, in the light of prose. The original was clearly
much anterior in date to the present copy, being at least as old as
the fourteenth century.

No story in the whole dramatic repertoire of the Middle Ages
was more popular than that of *Abraham and Isaac*, which is
testified to by the fact that no less than six such plays have been
handed down to us. The story apparently enjoyed the same
popularity on the Continent, since there dramatic versions are
equally numerous. In France a separate copy of the play existed
in addition to the portion of the *Vieil Testament* dealing with the
subject. The question then naturally arises, how are our two
plays related to each other, to the corresponding play in each of
the four great cycles, and to the two French plays ?
The Midland play preserved in the Dublin manuscript, which
for convenience will be referred to as the Dublin *Abraham and
Isaac*, appears to be very largely independent of the five other
English plays on the subject, but to bear a general resemblance to
the French versions of the story. It is also the only one of the
English Abraham-plays in which Sara appears as a speaking
character, and in which the thought of her, in the minds of father

and son, stands out so prominently. The mention of the mother does certainly occur in the Chester and Brome versions, but in a much less marked degree, and here Sara does not appear as a character of the play. Further, it remains to be mentioned, that the Dublin play has one or two verbal resemblances in parts, to passages in the Towneley play, but with this its relationship to the other English plays ceases. On the other hand, its general resemblance to the French play, especially in respect to scene arrangement, is certainly striking. In the edition issued for the *Société des Anciens Textes Français*, under the editorship of Baron Rothschild, two versions of the play are given ; the A B C version, where it is part of the cycle, and the E F version, which is to be regarded as a detached play. The latter was printed in 1539, and it is not impossible that the printer then made use of manuscripts other than those from which the A B C version was compiled, and which have since been lost.[1] It is with this 1539 printed version that our play most closely corresponds, a comparative table of which we subjoin from the twenty-first volume of the *Anglia :* [2]

Scene.	VT (ABC).	VT (EF).	Dublin.[3]
1.	Dieu. Misericorde. Justice. 9610-9686.	Dieu. 195-221.	Deus. 1-21.
2.	Dieu. Ceraphin. [Misericorde. Justice] 9687-9712.	Dieu. Raphael. Misericorde. 222-242	Deus. Angelus. 22-34.
3.	—	—	Habraham : 35-47.[4]
4.	Ceraphin. Abraham. 9713-9782.	Raphael. Abraham. 243-277.	Habraham. Angelus. 48-67.
5.	Abraham. 9783-9800.	Abraham. 278-291.	Habraham. 68-83.
6.	Sarra. Abraham. 9801-9820.	Sarra. Abraham. 292-311.	Sara. Habraham. Isaac. [Servant]. 84-136.
7.	Abraham. Isaac. Ismael. Eliezer. 9936-10,022.	Abraham. Isaac. Ismael. Eliezer. 609-704.	Habraham [Isaac]. [Servant]. 137-144.
8.	Abraham. Isaac. 10,023-10,441.	Abraham. Isaac. 705-1434.	Habraham. Isaac. 145-260.
9.	Ceraphin. [Abraham. Isaac]. 10,442-10,455.	Raphael. [Abraham. Isaac]. 1435-1452.	Angelus. [Habraham. Isaac]. 261-273.

[1] Cf. Brotanek. [2] Brotanek, *Anglia*, xxi, 28.
[3] Brotanek calls this the Northampton Play.
[4] In the corresponding place in the French play, there is a conversation between Sarra, Abraham and Isaac.

Scene.	VT (ABC).	VT (EF).	Dublin.
10. ⎫		Abraham. Isaac. 1453–1538.	Habraham [Isaac]. 274–268.
11. ⎪	Abraham. Isaac. 10,456–10,526.	Raphael. Abraham. [Isaac]. 1539–1564.	Deus. [Habraham]. [Isaac]. 287–302.
12. ⎬		Abraham. [Isaac]. 1565–1590.	Habraham. [Isaac]. 303–307.
13.	Abraham. Isaac. Ismael. [Eliezer]. 10,535–10,548.	Abraham. Isaac. Ismael. Eliezer. 1619–1632.	Habraham. Isaac. [Servant]. 308–318.
14.	Sarra. Abraham. Isaac. 10,549–10,598.	Sarra. Abraham. Isaac. 1633–1698.	Sara. Habraham. [Isaac]. 319–370.

The difference in construction between the French and English plays is slight : the Dublin drama omits the character *Misericorde*, to which in the French version two short speeches are allotted, and in the English play the two servants, Ismael and Eliezer,[1] who in the *Vieil Testament* (EF) are speaking characters, are not named. The French drama, it is true, is nearly four times as long as the Dublin play, but that is at least quite a normal proportion when considering English and French religious plays of the fifteenth century. But Brotanek presses the point still further, and cites a number of verses which he believes to have been directly suggested by corresponding verses in the French play : here I must confess that the influence has been too subtle for me to trace. In spite of this, however, the strong possibility, or perhaps even probability, that the author of the Dublin play knew some version or other of this detached French edition (*Vieil Testament* EF) still remains.

The relation of the Brome play to the French Mysteries and to the Chester plays has already been carefully considered by scholars in connection with a study of the latter cycle, and has led to various theories. Ungemach, in his *Quellen der ersten fünf Chester Plays*, maintains that the Chester and Brome Abraham-plays both go back to the same French original, and that, at the time when the Chester cycle underwent revision, the Brome version was used by their reviser. I must, however, agree with Hohlfeld, when he says that Ungemach, in reference to the Brome play's indebtedness to a French original, has not proved his case ; since I have carefully considered his lengthy and skilfully-selected extracts, selected, too, sometimes from the A B C, and sometimes from the E F version, as each suited his purpose best, and cannot find any

---

[1] According to the *Cursor Mundi*, a son of Abraham.

resemblances whatever which support a theory of indebtedness, but only a general similarity between the two plays, which is quite capable of being completely explained by the fact that they both go back to the Vulgate version of the Biblical story. Of Ungemach's contentions as to the indebtedness of the Chester Plays to the *Vieil Testament*, this is not the place to speak.

The similarity, however, between the Brome play and a part of the Chester play upon the same theme, leaves no question as to the indebtedness of one play in some form to the other : the question to be considered is, how was the influence exercised ? In the first place, it is to be noted that the similarity refers to a part of the play only. Up to the point where Isaac declares his readiness to go with his father, there exists no striking likeness whatever between the two versions, and the same applies to the concluding portions ; but the central part, the main scene, is very similar in both versions, a resemblance not only of general construction and plan, but also of details of expression and words in rhyme-position, both of which will readily be seen upon a comparison of our text with the portions of the Chester play printed below it. (Cf. pp. 40–49 of text.) These coincidences and similarities have, moreover (even Ungemach admits this, or rather asserts it), no resemblance whatever to anything in the French Mystery : what, then, is their explanation ? I have tried to show that the present form of the Brome play is a revision of an earlier, probably fourteenth-century version ; we know that the Chester plays at the time of their being formed into a cycle, probably the turn of the fourteenth and fifteenth centuries, underwent revision, and further, that unlike the Brome compiler, the Chester poet, in this instance, could not choose his stanza ; therefore, the solution is that the Chester compiler then made use of the earlier version of the East Anglian play, an opinion with which both Hohlfeld and Ungemach, although of contrary opinions in respect to the French influence, are in complete agreement.

The mystery plays which have been handed down to us do not often offer scope for satisfactory literary criticism, and indeed, in most cases, it would be most unfair to their compilers to indulge in it, for their aim was directed towards the production of a grand spectacular effect rather than towards the compilation of a text of literary worth and beauty. Portions of the mass of mediæval drama, however, have attained a standard worthy of being designated literary works, as, for example, those plays of the Towneley cycle from the pen of the author of the *Secunda Pastorum*, of which Mr. Pollard has so rightly sung the praises, while parts at least of our two Abraham-and-Isaac plays, the best of the six upon this subject, are by no means to be despised. In the York play, Isaac is represented as a man of thirty years of age, while Sarah is not mentioned, and thus disappears of necessity any opportunity for introducing those beautiful touches of pathos to be found in the Dublin and Brome texts. The incomplete Towneley play, the shortest of them all, introduces the Deity in person, but in its treatment of the strife in Abraham's soul between paternal affection and his duty to his God, the real point of interest, it is very dull and lifeless. The Coventry copy is a bald narrative, equally prosaic. The Chester, like the Brome play, which in essentials it closely resembles, closes with the speech of an expository character, somewhat shorter, and placed in the mouth of a "Doctor." The Dublin text, the only one which introduces Sarah in person, develops very well indeed the capabilities of the story on the side of domestic affection, especially in relation to the mother. In the Dublin version, too, a somewhat prominent part is also assigned to the Deity. Both plays treat the struggle in Abraham's mind between fatherly love and obedience to God extremely well.

That both the Dublin and Brome plays were performed as single plays and not as parts of cycles I have attempted to show earlier in this short introduction, but evidence as to the particular manner, place, and time in and at which they were performed, is unfortunately not to hand ; therefore, it is to be supposed that the stage was the usual pageant, and the mode of performance practically identical with what we do certainly know about the performance of other plays on the same, and similar subjects.

IV.

THE PLAY OF THE SACRAMENT.

The *Play of the Sacrament*, or, as it is often called, the *Croxton Play*, has been twice edited : in 1861 by Whitley Stokes in *Transactions of the Philological Society* (Appendix), and in 1897 by Prof. Manly in his *Specimens of the Pre-Shaksperean Drama.* In the preparation of the present edition, the latter has been collated with the manuscript, and with Whitley Stokes' version.

The play in question is contained in a quarto paper, manuscript (F. IV. 20), preserved in the library of Trinity College, Dublin, marked *Irish Historical Pieces*, and in the new catalogue scheduled No. 652. The contents of the manuscript, of a somewhat miscellaneous character, and written in various hands, are as follow :

1. Lee, Thos. Declaration of the Government of Ireland, discovering the discontents of the Irishry.
2. French. (Nic. titul. Bp. of Ferus.) *Apologia pro se et aliis Catholicis.*
3. Davis (Sir John). Argument upon Impositions.
4. Cambden (Wm.). Genealogy of the English, with some of their arms ; also lives and effigies of the Popes (in his own hand).
5. Informations exhibited to the Committee of the Fire of London, 1667.
6. Miracle play of the conversion of Jonathas the Jew by the miracle of the Sacrament.
7. Poems by Sir John Davis and others.
8. Map of Cabra and neighbourhood, in pencil.

The handwriting of our portion of the manuscript is that of the latter half of the fifteenth century, and is occasionally difficult to decipher, especially the first page, which, before its inclusion in the present binding, was apparently at some time or other the unprotected outside sheet of the manuscript, and thus became much more stained and faded than the remaining leaves. Two scribes were at work upon the manuscript, which divides itself into four sections ; the " banns " with verses 1 to 246 and 405 to 566, being written by one scribe, and verses 247 to 404 and 567 to the end, by the other. The writer of sections one and three marked off the speeches of the different characters by means of horizontal black lines, drawn in ink across the page, and the stanzas by means of bracketing the lines which were intended to rhyme together ; while the scribe of sections two and four contented himself with a division of the speeches, and left the stanzas unmarked. Both scribes make a free use of the usual contractions of the period, but the latter perhaps shows a rather more consistent use of the double *l* with a stroke, and wrote a somewhat larger hand than his colleague : in the fourth section of the work he appears to

have used paler ink, or at least ink more inclined to rapidly fade;
in point of carelessness it is difficult to discover which of the two
was the more accomplished. (Cf. e. g. *boylde*, Prol. 42; *obouyn*,
Prol. 46; *ys*, copied a verse too early, v. 603; *dysaved*, 467;
pyxys lockyd, 846, etc.) That the former scribe was an Irishman
seems highly probable from the frequency with which he confuses
u, w and *v*, and *t* and *th*, a peculiarity which appears very rarely in
the rest of the play. (Cf. e. g. *hat*, 2, 437, and 532; *spekyt*, 491;
waytheth, 40 (Prol.); *amatystis*, 81; *awoyd*, 420; *sawe* for *save*,
77 (Prol.); *walew*, 210; etc.)

The Irish peculiarities of the manuscript are clearly due to
the scribe, and not to the writer of the play, which was certainly
written in England, and most probably in the East Midlands.
The manuscript is so late, falling well after the time at which
the *Schriftsprache* (as the German scholars call it) had certainly
established itself, and the poet handles his rhymes either so care-
lessly, or so freely, that no very definite conclusions as to its
original locality are to be drawn. 'Unfortunately the name
Croxton, occurring in the "banns" of the play, is no very great
help, since at least seven such places are known, any one of which
is possibly the one meant. In consideration that five of the
seven are in the East-Midland district, that there is nothing in the
poem to disprove an East-Midland origin, and that the dramatic
activity of that district is well ascertained, until a better solution
can be found, the above must serve as a general indication.[1]

Although there is ample and convincing evidence that miracle-
plays were performed in England, the *Play of the Sacrament* is—
with the exception of the *Play of Mary Magdalene*, a combination
of Miracle, Mystery and Morality, in which the first element pre-
dominates—the only text of this class which has been preserved.
Many scholars would deny that the *Play of the Sacrament* has a
claim to the title of miracle-play because its subject matter is not
drawn from the Lives of the Saints; this is however clearly un-
justified, for although many of the miracle-plays in England and
France did derive their inspiration from such a source, this is by
no means the essential feature of the miracle-play. In France,
indeed, the subjects of the miracle-plays were drawn from the
greatest possible variety of sources, sacred and profane, of early
and of almost contemporary date. The essential feature of the

---

[1] Cf. pp. lxiii and lxxiv.

miracle play is that the action centres round some miraculous event : that is clearly true of our play, for the comic element is purely episodic.

The story which forms the main subject of the *Play of the Sacrament* is only one of a very large number, the popularity of which was due to the strong anti-Semitic feeling prevailing in the West of Europe during the Middle Ages, and which is still recognisable, expressed in other ways in many parts at the present day. The most famous of all such stories perhaps is that of Hugh of Lincoln. The miracles alleged to have taken place in connection with Jewish outrages upon sacred wafers, were held to prove the doctrine of the Real Presence, and that communion under both kinds was unnecessary ; while a third and less spiritual result was, that the stories served as an excuse for the murder of wealthy Jews and the confiscation of their property. Continental versions of the story are numerous from the year 1290 [1] until the seventeenth century, but in the great majority of cases they differ from the English version in that the torturers of the Host as a reward for their pains are burnt alive. Dramatic versions of the story, too, are numerous in France, Italy, and the Netherlands ; thus, for example, in 1473, as part of the festival at Rome held in honour of Leonore of Aragon, certain Florentine players performed plays of *Susanna, John the Baptist* and the *Miracle of the Host* [2] ; in or about the year 1500, a Dutch play of more than a thousand verses in length upon *The Miracle of the Host*, was written by a certain Smeken and performed in Breda ; and a French play of a similar nature is preserved in two printed editions of the sixteenth century, the former of which bears the title: " *Le jeu et mystère de la sainte hostie,* par personnages." The *motif* of this play, which introduces twenty-six characters and is fifteen hundred and ninety verses in length, is somewhat similar to that of the Croxton play, but the details are not the same.

A woman oppressed with poverty has pawned a portion of her clothing with a Jew money-lender, which she beseeches him to restore to her when the Passover Feast comes round. This the Jew promises to do, but only on condition that she brings to him the consecrated Host which she is to receive in communion at church ; the poor woman agrees to the conditions and the Jew obtains the holy

---

[1] Villani, *Croniche*, Ao. 1290. (Cited by Stokes.)
[2] Creizenach, I, 332.

wafer. He then cuts it savagely with a knife, whereupon it bleeds
profusely. The Jew's family beg of him to desist, but he refuses
and unsuccessfully tries to destroy the Host by every means of
which he can think ; after this his son reveals the circumstances
to a Christian woman, who takes the wafer back to the priest ; and,
since the news of the sacrilege has spread all over Paris, the Jew
is seized, brought before the judges, convicted, and burnt to death,
while the members of his family are baptized. The woman who
betrayed the Host commits the crime of murdering her illegitimate
child in order to conceal her guilt, likewise repents, and is burnt
at the stake; which miracle was supposed to have taken place in
the thirteenth century, and in memory of which the Church of
Carmelites was founded.

That the story upon which this play is founded is by no means
to be counted among the more unimportant Parisian legends, is
testified to by the frequency with which the incident is referred to
by French historians. Further, in 1664, a certain Fr. Leon, of
the Order of Carmelites of the Holy Sacrament, published under
the patronage of the Bourbon arms, a duodecimo, bearing the title:
*L'Histoire de l'Hostie Miraculeuze, arrivé au Convent des Religi-
euses Carmes du Saint Sacrement, des Billetes*, wherein this tradition is referred to as three hundred and seventy-four years old,
again giving us as date the year 1290.

Thirty-one years earlier, certain members of the University of
Paris had turned their attention to the story and issued a report as
follows : " We, the undersigned Doctors of the Faculty of Theology,
of Paris, certify that we have seen and closely examined this
History of the Miraculous Host of Paris, in which we have not
found anything contrary to the Faith nor to morals. Given at
Paris, this second day of August, 1633.

N. PIGNAY. [1]

F. DAMOURETTES."

To return to a consideration of the English play, it is to be
remarked that its source is undoubtedly this French legend, dating
from 1290, varied in certain details. The Jew's treatment of the
Host is essentially the same in the Parisian legend and the English
play ; but the English dramatist has selected certain incidents and
omitted others. According to the Parisian legend, the Jew treats
the Host in the following manner. First he lays it upon the table

[1] W. Hone, *Legend of the Miraculous Host.*

and stabs it several times with his penknife, with the result that blood gushes from it freely, after which he further mutilates it with a hammer and nails. It is next hung upon a stake and scourged as often as the body of Christ received lashes by the scourging, and then thrown into the fire, where it is seen moving about untouched. The Jew, becoming mad, attacks it with a large carving-knife, but this proves unsuccessful, so " he hangs it up in a place deemed the vilest in the house," and pierces it with the point of a spear. Finally, it is thrown into a cauldron of boiling water, whereupon the water turns to blood, and a crucifix with a figure of the dying Saviour rises up above it. At this the Jew is terrified and hides himself in the cellar ; the church bell is ringing for Mass, and a child of the Jew's runs from the house crying out, " Where do you go to seek your God? to the Church? Has not my father, then, after having inflicted so many tortures on Him, has he not yet killed Him?" Upon hearing this, a woman, a neighbour of the Jew, went to the house feigning to ask for a light, and beholding the affecting picture of the Passion of Christ there re-enacted, prostrated herself and made the sign of the Cross. The body of Jesus Christ returned to the form of the Host, and placed itself in a vessel which she held in her hand, which she then carried to the Church of St. John en Grève, where it was received by priests. The story was told, the Jew and the betrayer of the Host were arrested and condemned to be burnt ; King Philip and his Queen, Jane of Navarre, commanded that the Jew's house should be converted into a temple, and that there should be kept the Jew's penknife and cauldron, and the dish in which the Host was taken to the church. On the Sunday before Easter, the Chapter of St. John carried in procession the evidences of the miracle, which for four centuries were preserved, and then, on the first Sunday after Easter, a festival was held in celebration of the event.

The alterations which the English dramatist has made in the story are many and important. In the English play a Christian merchant is substituted for the poor woman as the betrayer of the Host, the Jew is a wealthy merchant and not a money-lender, and has moreover four Jewish accomplices, and the stock comic characters of the doctor and his man are added, while the *dénouement* is, contrary to continental custom, the absolution of the Jews from their sins, and their subsequent baptism.

To modern taste the greater part of the play is extremely gro-
tesque and almost loathsome, while even the comic and satiric
touches are uncommendably broad. The passages in which
Brundyche, *Magister Physicus*, himself makes merry over the
manner in which he treats his patients, as well as the comic
ejaculations and remarks of his boy Colle, are well calculated to
please the ignorant and rustic crowds which thronged to the market-
places of small towns and to village greens in search of amusement.

The incident, too, is of additional interest in that it serves as
an example of the influence of the Spring folk-drama upon the
miracle play. The inveterate quack-doctor who so frequently
appears in the former has been bodily imported into the latter.
In the folk-drama, it is true, the doctor was an essential element
of the story,[1] while in the miracle-play he has become an episodic
character, introduced for the sake of the comedy supplied ; but
that is quite the normal development in such cases.

The various outrages exercised upon the consecrated wafer and
the miraculous appearance of Jesus as a speaking character, appear
now, deprived of their mediæval *milieu* of belief, somewhat puerile
and paltry ; this was, however, not so when the play was performed, but exactly what portion the fifteenth-century audience
treated as comic, and how much as serious and reverent, is now
difficult to determine.

The metre in which the play is written is considerably varied,
the purpose of which, however, is not always apparent. The
commonest of all used, is a four-line stanza, rhymed *abab*, in which
the normal verse has four accents, with considerable freedom of
construction in the unstressed portions ; verses of five and three
accents also often occur. In the majority of instances, the last
verse of the stanza rhymes with the first verse of the stanza
immediately following, thus giving an eight-line strophe, with the
rhyme order *a b a b b c b c ;* but since the scribe betrays irregularity in marking off the stanzas, and since the above construction
is not adhered to throughout, we have preferred to divide the play,
in these portions, into stanzas of four verses each.[2] The next stanza
in order of frequency used, is one of eight verses rhymed *a a a b c c c b*,
and is found from verse 409 to 520 with slight interruptions, and
again in verses 542 to 572. Other more irregular stanzas also occur,

---

[1] Cf. E. K. Chambers, *Mediæval Stage*, vol. i, 185, 207, 213.
[2] Manly arranges in eight-line stanzas.

e. g., in verse 172, with the appearance of Clericus, verse 198, in the part of Jonathas, verses 247 and 296 of Aristorius, where a five-line stanza *abbba* is used, while in verses 440 to 444, the rhyme-order is *ababb*. But the metrical form is most markedly interrupted, and quite naturally too, upon the entrance of the two comic characters, Master Brundyche, and Colle, his boy. As far as verse 517, they are kept within the bounds of the eight-line stanza, *aaab cccb*, but after this, the greatest freedom is used. The speech of Brundyche, for example, consists of seven verses, the first six of which have as rhyme-syllable—*acyon*, and the seventh does not rhyme at all : after which follow seven couplets, and then the eight-line stanza is again resorted to. Verses 655 to 660 form a stanza with the rhyme-order *abbbba*, and then the four-line stanza construction is continued to the end of the play. We have previously referred to the carelessness, or unsatisfactory choice of the rhymes, which points to a poet of inferior merit : the merest glance at the rhythm leads to the same conclusion. Alliteration, although not present as a consistent principle, is very much in evidence, and more so at the beginning of the play than towards the end. Where alliteration was easy to use, there the poet has made the most of it, but where it was difficult, he has apparently largely abandoned it. Thus, for example, when he introduces a list of places, which he obviously drew from some geographical manual, probably alphabetically arranged, the alliteration shines forth in all its glory, the names appearing even in alphabetical order :

" In *A*ntyoche and in *A*lmayn *m*och is my *m*yght,
    Iu *B*raban and in *B*rytayn I am full *b*old,
In *C*alabre and in *C*oleyn ther *r*ynge I full *r*yght,
    In *D*ordrede and in *D*enmark I be the chyffe *t*old.

In *A*lysander I have *a*bundawnse 'in the *w*yde *w*orld ;
    In *F*rance and in *F*arre *f*resshe be my *f*lowers,
In *G*yldre and in *G*alys have I bowght and sold,
    In *H*amborowhe and in *H*olond *m*oche *m*erchandyse is owris."

That the author considered such a profusion of alliterative forms in keeping with the character of Aristorius' boastful speech, may have been the case, for the corresponding boast of the Jew merchant has the same peculiarity; certain it is, however, that it is largely confined to the former part of the play.

After the list of *dramatis personae* given in the manuscript at the end of the play, is the remark, " IX may play it at ease." A study of the structure of the play, makes it clear that none of the actors who played the parts of Aristorius, Jonathas, Jason, Jasdon, Masphat and Malchus, could possibly take another part ; and it is equally certain that if the company be limited to nine actors, the parts of Clericus and Colle must be played by the same person. The *rôle* of Magister Physicus could only be taken by one of the actors who played the parts of Presbyter and Episcopus respectively. It only now remains to decide how the figure of Jesus, which speaks a considerable number of verses, and to which the stage-direction applies the words, "an image with woundis bledyng," was actually represented. The person who spoke as the image, must have been an actor who in this scene does not otherwise appear ; the choice therefore rests between the actors of the parts Aristorius, Presbyter, Episcopus, and the boy who played Colle and Clericus. Of these, the last-named is the most probable, since in verse 724, the image seen is referred to as "a chyld apperyng with wondys blody," the explanation of which is difficult apart from the above supposition.

The somewhat crude character of the play itself, the fact that some of the actors take more than one part, and the evidence of the " banns " all point to the play as being one of those interludes[1] so popular in the fourteenth century, which were taken from village to village, and town to town, and played at the market-place and village-green. Everything goes to prove that it is a play of this class, short enough to be performed in an hour or a little more, in which the simplest scenic arrangements suffice, and suitable alike for performance at a baronial banquet, in the guildhall of a town, perhaps even in a church, or in the courtyard of some then oft-visited inn. The doubling of parts is entirely unknown to the mystery play, and common to this latter class, the records of which are numerous ; thus, *e. g.*, Bale's *Three Laws* required five players, and *Lusty Juventus*, four.

The announcement of the play by means of " banns " was common to the regular mystery-plays as well as occasional plays, but was probably even more necessary in the latter case than the former, which were well-established and well-known municipal events : however, Chester and Beverley both had their " banns," and they

---

[1] The term interlude was certainly held to include miracle-play, as Mr. Chambers points out, *Mediœval Stage*, ii, 182, 183.

are also on record at New Romney. The Croxton Play is announced beforehand by two banner-bearers, *vexillatores*, accompanied by a minstrel, who speak in turn, briefly outlining the story of the play, and finally giving their hearers an invitation to the performance in the following terms :

> "And yt place yow, thys gaderyng þat here ys,
> At Croxston on Monday yt shall be sen ;
> To see the conclusyon of þis lytell processe
> Hertely welcum shall yow bene.
>
> Now Jhesu yow sawe from treyn and tene,
> To send vs hys hyhe ioyes of hevyne,
> There myght ys withouton mynd to mene !
> Now, mynstrell, blow vp with a mery stevyn ! "

As we remarked above, the name Croxton alone does not help very much in locating the place where the play on this occasion was performed, since it occurs in Cambridgeshire, Leicestershire, Lincolnshire, Norfolk, Cheshire, and other counties. Mr. Chambers in his *Mediæval Stage*, assigns it to Norfolk, but puts a mark of interrogation after his note. One of the many Croxtons which is far from being improbable is on the road from Oxford to Cambridge ; it is a parish in the Union of Caxton and Arrington, in the county of Cambridge, three-and-a-half miles W.N.W. of Caxton. A second Croxton, which is also not improbable, is in the Union of Thetford, in the Western Division of Norfolk, two miles north from Thetford. Other Croxtons are :

A parish (St. John the Evangelist) in the Union of Glandford-Brigg, East Division of the Wapentake of Yarborough, Lincoln : seven miles N.E. by E. of Glandford-Brigg.

A chapelry in the parish of Fulmodeston in the Union of Walsingham, Western Division of Norfolk : four miles E. by N. of Fakenham.

A township in the parish of Eccleshall, Union of Stone, in the Northern Division of the Hundred of Pikehill, Staffordshire : three and three-quarter miles N.W. by N. of Eccleshall.

Croxton South : a parish (St. John the Baptist) in the Union of Barrow-upon-Soar, in the Northern Division of Leicestershire : nine-and-a-quarter miles N.E. by E. of Leicester.

A township in the parish of Middlewich, Union and Hundred of Northwich, Cheshire : one mile W.N.W. from Middlewich.[1]

---

[1] Lewis : *Topographical Dictionary of England.*
MYSTERY PLAYS. *e*

Two other place-names occur in the play, the latter of which, near Bury St. Edmunds, having been well known because of a settlement of Franciscan friars there; they occur in verses 540 and 541 :

> "Inquyre to the Tolkote, for ther ys hys loggyng,[1]
> A lytylle besyde Babwelle Mylle."

V.

THE PRIDE OF LIFE.

The Pride of Life, although fragmentary, is a particularly interesting specimen, because of its early date and the light which it throws upon the early history of the drama ; the *Paternoster* and *Creed Play* being lost, it is thus the earliest extant Morality. The text of the above play has twice been ably edited. In 1891, Mr. Mills, of the Record Office, Dublin, first printed a copy of the manuscript in the *Proceedings of the Royal Society of Antiquaries of Ireland,* while seven years later, Professor Brandl, in his *Quellen des Weltlichen Dramas vor Shakspere,* issued an edition based upon Mr. Mills' *editio princeps,* a collation of the manuscript made by the Rev. Prof. Skeat, and a second collation made by Mr. Mills. For the purposes of the present edition I have collated Mr. Mills' text with the manuscript and compared it with that of Prof. Brandl.

The poem in question has been preserved in a parchment roll, belonging to the canons of Christ Church, Dublin, a religious house which, unlike many other communities of a like nature, escaped suppression in the sixteenth century. The roll is in some respects quite a palæographical puzzle. It consists of a body of accounts extending from 1333 to 1346, which have been stitched together to form a roll eleven feet eight-and-a-half inches in length, and varying from eight-and-a-quarter to eleven-and-a-quarter inches in breadth, the four different documents of which were probably stitched together not more than a century after their compilation. They were first noticed about the middle of the eighteenth century by Dr. Loyd, during the preparation of his *Novum Registrum,* who, however, did not copy them, but simply referred to them under the title, "Accounts of the expenditure of the Prior and his Chamber." The reverse side of the second account in its original state had been

---

[1] See also Index of Places, p. 105 *et seq.*

left unoccupied, and here, between certain groups of expenditure items, the *Pride of Life* was later, most probably in the former half of the fifteenth century, added to the manuscript. First are four crowded columns giving us respectively verses 1 to 38, 127 to 160, 161 to 196, and 197 to 234 of the play, where the continuity is broken by the appearance of items already upon the parchment, after which are four more columns containing respectively verses 39 to 126, 235 to 326, 327 to 416, and 415 to 502.[1] After verses 126 and 136 are *lacunæ*, while the close of the play is also missing; the explanation of which is, that originally another skin was attached to the roll and has unfortunately since disappeared.

Two scribes of different ability and peculiarities, speaking different dialects, have clearly been at work upon the manuscript. The one, an old man, writing somewhat shakily and as if out of practice, wrote a professional, clerkly hand, and contributed verses 5 to 32, 83 to 126, 155 to 326 and 439 to 502 : the other, apparently an unpractised hand, unaccustomed to the copying of English manuscripts—since he utterly confuses þ, y and ȝ—wrote a running hand, and is responsible for verses 1 to 4, 33 to 82, 127 to 154 and 327 to 438.[2] That the scribes had a written original to follow, and did not write the poem down from dictation or from memory, is clearly evident from the blunders which they made, all of which are mistakes of the eye and not of the ear, such as the confusion of *f* with long *s* (*sort* for *fort*, v. 42 ; *fot* for *sot*, v. 360), of *t* with *c*, and the omission of the stroke above the line for *n* (*gocyl* for *gentyl*), v. 333.[3] The work appears to have been divided between them entirely without reference to the contents or strophic divisions.

The way in which the two scribes did their work and treated their original, has been so admirably set out at considerable length by Prof. Brandl,[4] whose book is not so readily accessible on English library shelves as it should be, that nothing can be more satisfactory than to give the substance of it here. The scribe to whom we have referred to as a professional, Professor Brandl designates by B, his colleague by A.

    1. A makes use of numerous abbreviations which he uses in Latin as well as English words : B confines himself to

---

[1] vv. 415 and 416 appear twice in the MS. : at the bottom of col. 3 and top of col. 4.
[2] Mills.   [3] Brandl, *op. cit.*   [4] *idem.*

the use of the horizontal stroke above the line to denote
m or *n*, and þᵘ for *thou*.

2. A carefully distinguishes between *e* and *o*: B often confuses
the two vowels, cf. vv. 132, 50.

3. A writes always *com*: B always *cum*.

4. A invariably represents O.E. *á* by *o*: B often has *a*, e. g.
yam v. 73, *baldli* 127, *sa* 358, *halt* 359, etc.

5. A represents O.E. *eo* before *r* by *e*: B has twice *a*, e. g.
smartli 138, *far* 357.

6. A represents O.E. *y* by *i* or *e*, e. g. *lesten* 118, *listen* 471,
siche 317 : B has *u*, e. g. *mucil* 37, 38, *churg* 423, *suc* 35,
148, 328.

7. A preserves a final *e* after *v* or *i* : B drops it, e. g. *leu* 57,
liu 145, *hau* 151, 354, etc.

8. In A the vowels of unaccented syllables are no longer
preserved intact : cf. *wolte* (for *wolþou*) 218, *vndir* 213,
sikir 493, etc.   B is still more advanced in this respect :
cf. *horkynt* 1, *trecri* 335, *uileni* 337.   A has *messager*
263, 280, 307, etc. : B has the *later* form *messengere* v.
75.

9. A sometimes denotes consonant-sharpening : *flessch* 19,
florresschist 277, *bisschop* 309, 323, 449, etc. : B never.

10. A writes *w* quite regularly : B often replaces it by *u*: cf.
79, 128, 132, 134, etc.

11. A regularly has *qwh* for *wh* : B generally *w* or *u*.

12. Initial *h* is only occasionally wrongly inserted by A :
oftener by B. e. g. *heme* 83, *hal* 1, 70, *hold* 2, *hend* 52,
etc.   B shows an inclination to drop initial *h* in particles
or to substitute *y* or ʒ.   (This latter feature is only seen
'at the beginning of the poem, later he reserves *y* and ʒ
for þ.)   Final *h* before a word beginning with þ appears
in two instances as *t* : cf. *þayt þe* 381, *þot þou* 437.

13. A generally preserves þ, sometimes in this form and at
other times as *th*.   At first B seldom writes a clear þ,
but takes it up after v. 391 : in the middle of a word he
generally puts *y* or ʒ and in final position *t* (occasionally
þt or *yt*).   B has also occasionally, in initial position,
y instead of þ.

14. For final *d*, B often writes *t*.   Cf. *lerit* and *leut* 4, *warnit* 70,
irerit 342, *touart* 369.   On the other hand, B sometimes

omits it after *n*, or introduces it wrongly after this consonant. Cf. *underston* 77, *wand* 73.

15. The palatals ʒ and *y* do not change with *g* : on the other hand, in B, in the initial position in particles, they are dropped. Final ʒt and *ght* are simplified by B to *t*, corresponding to the fifteenth-century pronunciation : A has regularly ʒt.

16. B has *c* instead of *ch*, especially after an accented vowel : e. g. *mucil* 37, 38, *precit* 69, *trecri* 335, etc. The reverse in initial position, is also found in B, viz. *ch* for *c* or *k*, *charp* 53, *chont* 68, *cham* 69, *chong* 130, etc.

17. For *sh* B puts occasionally *c* : (*bicop* 67, 73, *ficis* 361 ; still more seldom *ss*, *bissop* 407). Initial *s* appears as *sch*, e. g. *schir*, 391, 435.

18. *K* after an accented vowel in connection with *n* or *l* often appears as *g*, in B, e. g. þing 365, 391, 399, etc. ; an initial *g* sometimes as *c*, e. g. *can* 65, *wyl cot* 425.

19. In the conjugation of the verb, A has : in Pres. Indic. Singular 2 and 3, occasionally the Northern ending *is*, e. g. 192, 266, 276 : otherwise *ist* and *it(h)* and once or twice, in the plural, no ending, e. g. 259, 284. In the Pres. Indic. the Northern form þou *schal*: cf. vv. 165, 190, 297 and 299, but also þou *schalt*. B has always the latter form. A has sometimes a Northern peculiarity never found in B, the preservation of final *n* in the perfect part. of strong verbs : 244, 443, etc.

The conclusion clearly to be drawn from such a systematic study of the work of the two scribes, is that A spoke the Northern dialect, and B a special variety of the Northern dialect, peculiar to Dublin, the special features of which are :—the confusion of *w* and *u* and of *w* and *v*, the occasional representation of O.E. *y* by *yu*, the frequent dropping and misplacement of initial (sometimes of medial) *h* [1], the interchange of þ and *t* (occasionally þt), the appearance of *t* instead of final *d*, *sh* for *s*, and *ss* for *sh*.

The only guide which can be of any value in attempting to determine the date of the poem and the locality in which it was

---

[1] This, as well as the sharpening of consonants, is of course not peculiar to Dublin alone ; but in conjunction with the other criteria is of value : the Dublin dialect is best studied in *The English Conquest of Ireland*, 1425, E.E.T.S. 107. MS. (undoubtedly a Dublin MS.) Trin. Coll. Dub. E ii, 31.

originally written, is the rhyme; and since the author appears to
have been far from fastidious in this respect (cf. v. 106, *kaʒte, lafte*,
247, *bronde, wronge*), the conclusions which can be drawn are not
very definite or certain. The peculiarities, however, which dis-
tinguish the language from the written, London dialect, in the
opinion of Professor Brandl, point to a poet of the South, before the
end of the fourteenth century. What kind of a person the author
was is somewhat difficult to exactly decide : in all probability a
cleric of one of the simple orders ; a conclusion which is suggested
by the fact that he makes use of Latin stage-directions, French
exclamations, and satire of a character befitting such a personality.
The manuscript had also probably passed through Northern hands
before arriving in Dublin, since both scribes preserve many
Northern peculiarities in common.

External evidence as to the time and place of composition has
as yet not been discovered, but two references within the poem
itself have an important bearing upon the subject. The first is a
reference to the Earldom of Kent in verse 42, as follows :

> (to Nuncius.) "þou schalt have for þi gode wil
> to þin auauncement,
> þe castel of gailispire on þe hil
> and þe erldom of Kent."

From 1407 to 1462 the Earldom of Kent was vacant; did this influence the poet in his choice of this particular bounty as Mirth's
reward ? If so, the date of composition must be brought into the
first half of the fifteenth century ; the case is at least worthy of
consideration.[1] In verse 285 occurs a reference to Berwick-on-
Tweed :[2]

> "I am mirth—wel þou wost,
> þi mery messagere ;
> þat uostou wel withoute bost
> þer nas neuer my pere ;
>
> doʒtely to done a dede
> þat ʒe haue ffor to done ;
> hen to berewik opon twede
> & com o-ʒein ffull sone ;"

which, of course, would have much more effect and point when
spoken in the South of England : a Northerner would more
probably have selected Land's End and a Dublin man some
extreme point in the East of England.

---

[1] Mills first drew attention to this.   [2] Brandl, *op. cit.*

Unfortunately, *The Pride of Life* has not been preserved intact, which is still more regrettable when we consider that it is the earliest Morality which has been handed down to us. It is possible, however, with the help of the prologue, to form out of the fragments, which roughly represent the first half of the original play, some idea of what it was like in its entirety. The King of Life, a character closely related to the Herod of the Mystery-cycles, opens the play with a boasting speech descriptive of the infiniteness of his powers, is gently rebuked by his queen, of whose speech the last stanza alone is preserved, and is flattered and supported in his vaunting behaviour by two of his soldiers, Fortitudo and Sanitas. This is followed by a long dispute between the King and Queen, after which the former proclaims his powers again, and appeals to his soldiers, who, of course, support his views. Mirth, the messenger, who appears to have acquired some of his master's vaunting capabilities, is next sent for, and makes a speech of a like character: the King then desires rest, and commands one of his soldiers to draw the curtain of his *tentorium*. The Queen then makes her appearance, and sends Mirth, the messenger, to fetch the Bishop. The former, willingly going on the Queen's errand, departs singing:

> " Madam, i make no tariyng
> With softe wordis no ;
> For I am solas, i most singe,
> Ouer al qwher i go."   et cantat.

He finds the Bishop " on his se," but the conversation which there ensued is lost to us, for here we have another *lacuna* in the manuscript. After this follows, addressed to the audience, the Bishop's monologue, expressing a somewhat pessimistic view of mankind and attacking the rich, powerful and aristocratic, in the usual fourteenth and fifteenth-century satiric way. At the close he addresses himself to the King, who scoffingly replies, and after saying adieu to the Bishop,

> " Fare wel, bisschop, þi way,
> And lerne bet to preche,"

sends out his messenger, Mirth, with a challenge of combat to all and sundry, even to the King of Death himself. The messenger declares his readiness to go, and commences his proclamation, which, however, is cut short by another break in the manuscript. In the last part, according to the authority of the prologue, the King of Death appeared in response to the challenge, conquered the King of Life, who then appeared before the Judgment, and whose soul was finally saved "throgh priere of oure lady mylde." [1]

Such is the outline of the play in its entirety as far as reconstruction is possible, and its importance in the history of the Morality plays is, that it forms a connecting link between plays, resembling more or less the dramatic Dance of Death, *i. e.* the first plays in the vernacular into which allegory entered as an essential feature, and the Moralities of the later form and construction. The application of allegory to the drama clearly gave us the Morality play, and the only disputed question is where the exact point of departure was. Professor Seelmann, of the Royal Library in Berlin, has proved beyond a doubt that the *Lübecker Totentanz* and *La danza general de la muerte* are older than any other extant forms of the Dance of Death, and further that both (the former by way of a Netherlands intermediate form) are based on a French original of the fourteenth century, later worked up, but considerably altered, into *la danse macabre*. He has also conclusively proved that the text and not the picture was the original : further, that the text was a drama.[2] The performance took place in the church upon a stage, erected for the purpose, which was capable of being approached from both sides, one of which represented a tomb. A priest takes his place in the pulpit, which is immediately in front of the stage, and warns the clerks assembled, who form the audience, that no one can obtain exemption from death, and that they who have done much good during their earthly life, and cared for their flocks, will receive a rich reward in Heaven. After this, Death comes on the stage, calls all creatures to follow him and to prepare themselves by means of good works. First, he calls the Pope, who was regarded as the highest potentate on earth, and is therefore honoured with the chief place. The Pope, complaining, steps up to Death, who moves with him in dance-step to the grave, and at the same time answers his complaints. The Pope then disappears into the grave, or through a doorway, which is regarded as the entrance to the grave, and Death calls upon in turn, and treats in a similar manner, Emperor, Cardinal, King, who all appear decorated in the

---

[1] Verse 97.

[2] The following description of the performance is a free translation from Seelmann, *Die Totentänze des Mittelalters*, p. 17. Norden and Leipzig.

full splendour of the insignia of their respective orders, while Death is clad in a tight-fitting, canvas suit, painted so as to make him look like a corpse. The dance was accompanied by music and the text delivered as song or recitative, while it is also probable that at a previous stage in its development it was given with dumb show. Numerous accounts of performances of the *Dance of Death*, about the dramatic character of which there can be no doubt, are to hand : it is sufficient to mention one of July 10th, 1453, in Besançon, and one of 1449 in Bruges.

With the *Pride of Life* the *Dance of Death* has many points of connection. The central idea in the two pieces is the same, that it is impossible for any one to escape death ; but this idea is differently treated in the *Dance* and in the play. In the *Dance*, it is given forcible expression in that Death dances in turn with a representative of each rank from Pope and Kaiser to the poorest priest and peasant ; in the *Pride of Life* we see that even the King of Life himself cannot withstand Death. The Judgment, too, is definitely referred to in the priest's prologue, where he advises his hearers to see to it that they have done good deeds before Death seizes them. In the later Moralities this idea of Death and Judgment does not play so prominent a part, for the interest centres rather in the struggle between good and evil forces for man's soul, but the beginning of this development is seen in the *Pride of Life ;* and still more in *Everyman*, the other Morality belonging to this group of Death and Judgment. The allegorising in the play, and the plot-structure, too, are very modest indeed compared with that of the later Moralities. The choice of the King of Life and the King of Death is only a variation of their relationship in the *Dance of Death ;* the addition of Queen and Bishop is not very daring, since the personifying of various ranks had already taken place in the *Dance of Death ;* the Devil and the Virgin were certainly regarded as historical figures and not personifications ; while the inclusion of the two soldiers and Mirth is perhaps a reminiscence of some Pilate play : [1] the personifications of ethical subtleties came later. In addition to this Prof. Brandl points out that the *Pride of Life* has certain verbal resemblances to the *Lübecker Totentanz* and to the Spanish *Danza General :* these, however, are of such a general character that I prefer not to definitely attribute

---

[1] York Plays, xxx. Pilate has two soldiers, a comic bailiff and a wife who is anxious about him.

them to the influence of the fourteenth-century French original
of the two above-mentioned Dances of Death. That plays of the
Dance-of-Death type existed on English soil in the English tongue,
and that the poet of the *Pride of Life* was conversant with some
such, or at least with some similar French play, is not improbable;
since the existence of the type, at least upon the Continent, stands
beyond a doubt. Thus the origin of the Morality is in certain
respects very similar to that of the Mystery; it had its origin in
the cloister, was performed in the church, and was accompanied
by music, recitative and song.

It would not be strictly fair perhaps to the author of the *Pride
of Life* to criticise his work too closely, since less than half of it
has been preserved, and even that portion has been very badly
handled by careless or incompetent scribes, damp and other dis-
turbing conditions. The only extant English Morality bearing
a resemblance to the *Pride of Life* is *Everyman*, which is certainly
its superior in every respect. *The Cradle of Security*, a sixteenth-
century Morality, of which we only know the outlines, also appears
to have borne some resemblance to these two plays.

In pursuance of their purpose, the driving home of the lesson
that death is inevitable, these two early Moralities, the *Pride of
Life* and *Everyman*, in common with classical tragedy, select the
end of mortal man as their central theme. Thus, for example, in
the *Pride of Life*, the King is introduced to us just before his
pride brings about his fall, consequent upon his challenge to the
King of Death; while, on the other hand, the later Moralities, such
as *The Castle of Perseverance* and *The World and the Child*, in addition to man's death and judgment, and the salvation of his soul, as
given in these earlier Moralities, depict man's journey through life,
subject to various influences, good and bad. Instead of the consistent, dignified earnestness of *Everyman*, the *Pride of Life*
contains a good measure of somewhat primitive, not very high-class,
comedy, which may have been commensurably greater, if the second
portion in which the Devil played a part had been preserved. The
boasting of the King of Life, his rude, rough answers to the Queen
and the Bishop, and his coarse witticisms directed against them,
with the behaviour of Mirth, who must always go singing and no
doubt knew other clownish stage-tricks for provoking laughter, all
provided the audience with somewhat hearty, if very coarse fun.
On the other hand, this comedy is balanced by the serious earnest

entreaties of the Queen and the preaching and satiric monologue of the Bishop, the gentle arguments of the former being far from unskilfully treated, and the satire of the latter certainly forcefully expressed. Here Mirth is a comic character but yet cannot be called the Vice, since he is only a secondary character and does not fulfil the functions of the orthodox Vice. In addition to being the King's messenger or herald, he is a kind of court-fool, loved by the King, but at the same time by his flattery (if we can call it flattery) encouraging the King in his pride. An intentional seducer of the King he is certainly not, since he readily goes on the Queen's errand in search of the Bishop.

The metrical structure of the *Pride of Life* consists throughout of a four-line stanza similar to ballad-verse, with the rhyme order *abab*, the verses containing generally four stresses, but sometimes only three, the unstressed portions being freely handled. The poem is very rich in alliteration, but the rhymes are not always quite satisfactory. On the whole, the metrical features of the poem proclaim the poet to be anything but a great master of verse.

From verse 10 it is clear, irrespective of the way we fill up the gap there occurring, that the performance took place in the open air, and that at any rate the audience was fully exposed to the weather. It is evident, too, that at least two of the characters, the King of Life and the Bishop, had fixed seats upon the stage. That of the former appears to have been a canopied couch with a curtain in front of it, for in verse 303 the King commands one of his soldiers to draw the curtain :

> " Draw þe cord sire streynth,
> Rest I wol now take,"

et tunc, clauso tentorio, dicet Regina secrete nuncio. Thus, when out of the action the King remained upon the stage, which is quite in accordance with the custom of mediæval stage-management. The Bishop also had his place as we learn from verse 323, spoken by Mirth, who has been sent by the Queen to call the Bishop :

> " Sire bisschop, þou sitest on þi se,
> With þi miter on þi heuede."

The other characters were also probably upon the stage from the beginning of the piece. Perhaps Mirth was an exception to this, since in verse 263 the King says :

" Qwher is mirth my messager," but it would be in no way

inconsistent with mediæval custom for the King to say this, even if the *nuncius* were already on the stage. The stage-arrangement for which, however, evidence in case of the *Pride of Life* is entirely lacking, would probably be somewhat similar to that sketched for us in the Macro manuscript of *The Castle of Perseverance*, which is so well known as to render superfluous any description of it here.[1]

---

[1] Prof. Brandl sees in verses 9, 109 and 474 a reference to the crowd pressing round the players, and in verse 269 an indication that Mirth sprang now and then over a ditch surrounding the place of performance: I confess that these indications are too subtle for me.

The Non-Cycle Mystery Plays.

[THE SHREWSBURY FRAGMENTS.]

[*Officium Pastorum.*]¹

Pastores erant i*n* regione eade*m* uigila*n*tes *et* custodi-
entes grege*m* suu*m*. Et ecce angelus D*o*m*i*ni astitit
iuxt*a* illos *et* timueru*n*t timore magno.²

[*II. Pastor.*]³	We, Tib !	
III. Pastor.	Telle on !	
[*II. Pastor.*]	. . . . þe nyght.	
III. Pastor.	Brether, what may þis be,	4
	þus bright to man & best ?	
[*II. Pastor.*]	. . . . . . at hand.	
III. Pastor.	Whi say ʒe so ?	
[*II. Pastor.*]	. . . . . warand.	8
III. Pastor.	Suche siʒt was neu*er* sene	*The star appears.*
	Before in our*e* Iewery ;	
	Su*m* merueles wil hit mene	
	þat mu*n* be her*e* in hy.	12
[*II. Pastor.*]	. . . a sang.	
III. Pastor.	ʒe lye, bothe, by þis liʒt,	
	And raues as recheles royes !	
	Hit was an angel briʒt	16
	þat made þis nobulle noyes.	*The voice of an angel is heard.*
[*II. Pastor.*]	. . . . . of pr*o*phecy.	
III. Pastor.	He said a barn schuld be	*A child shall be born in*
	In þe burgh of Bedlem born ;	20 *Bethlehem ;*
	And of þis, my*n*nes me,	
	Our*e* fadres fond beforn.	

---

¹ MS. contains no heading.   ² Noted for voices.
³ The speaker's name, within square brackets, is that supplied by
Dr. Skeat.

[*II. Pastor.*] . . . . . . Iewus kyng.

III. Pastor. Now may we se þe same   24
               Euen in oure pase puruayed ;
               þe angel nemed his name,—
"Crist, Saueour," he saied.

[*II. Pastor.*] . . . . not raue.   28

III. Pastor. ȝone brightnes wil vs bring
               Vnto þat blisful boure ;
               For solace schal we syng
               To seke oure Saueour.   32

Transeamus usque Bethelem et uideamus hoc verbum
quod factum est, quod fecit Dominus *et* ostendit nobis.[1]

[*II. Pastor.*] . . . . to knawe.

III. Pastor. For no-þing thar vs drede,
               But thank God of aH gode ;
               þis light euer wil vs lede   36
               To fynde þat frely fode.

[*II. Pastor.* Now wat ȝe what][2] I mene.

III. Pastor. A ! loke to me, my Lord dere,[3]
               AH if I put me noght in prese !   40
               To suche a prince without[en][4] pere
Haue I no presand þat may plese.
               But lo ! a horn-spone haue I here
               þat may herbar an hundrith pese : 44
þis gift I gif þe with gode chere,
               Suche dayntese wil do no disese.
Fare-wele now, swete swayn,
               God graunt þe lifyng lang !   48

[*I. Pastor.* And go we hame agayn,
               And mak mirth as we gang ![5]]

---

[1] Noted for voices in MS. ; after this Manly inserts the direction, *They follow the star.*
[2] Supplied by Dr. Skeat.
[3] Before this verse in the MS. there is an asterisk referring to the
words *Saluatorem, Christum, Dominum, infantem pannis inuo-
lutum, secundum sermonem angelicam.* They are written in a later
hand, and belong to a Christmas trope (Manly).
[4] Dr. Skeat supplies [en].
[5] Dr. Skeat says, in the *Academy:* "I supply these two lines
from the York Mysteries, and assign them to the first shepherd,
instead of the third, because the MS. has here two blank lines,
showing that the third shepherd did not speak them."

[*Officium Resurrectionis.*]¹

Hic incipit Officium Resurreccio*n*is i*n* die Pasche.

*III. Maria.*² Heu ! Redemcio Is*r*ael,
   Ut quid morte*m* sustinuit !

[*II. Maria.*] . . . . . payne.

III. Maria. Allas ! he þat me*n* wend schuld by   4
   A$\dashv$ Israel, bothe knyght & knaue,
   Why suffred he so forto dy,
    Sithe he may a$\dashv$ sekenes saue ?
   Heu ! cur ligno fixus clauis   8
   Fuit doctor tam suauis ?
   Heu ! cur fuit ille natus
   Qui p*er*fodit ei*us* latus ?

Alas ! that He who could cure all ills should have suffered death.

[*II. Maria.*] . . . . . . is oght.   12

III. Maria. Allas, þat we suche bale schuld bide
   þat sodayn sight so forto see,
   þe best techer in world wide
    W*it*h nayles be tacched to a tre !   16
   Allas, þat eu*er* so schuld betyde,
    Or þat so bold mo*n* born schuld be
   For to assay oure Saueo*ur* side
    And open hit with-oute pite !   20

Alas ! that we should have seen Him on the cross.

[*All Three*].³ Iam, Iam, ecce, iam properem*us* ad tumulu*m*,
   Vngentes Dilecti corpus sanctissimum !

Let us to the sepulchre.

*Et approp*ri*antes sepulcro cantent :*

[*All Three.*] O Deus, quis reuoluet nobis lapidem
   Ab hostis monumenti ?⁴   24

Who shall roll away the stone ?

[*II. Maria.*] . . . . . . him leid.

III. Maria. He þat þus kyndely vs has kend
   Vn-to þe hole wher*e* he was hid,
   Su*m* socour*e* sone he wil vs send,   28
   At help to lift away þis lid.
     . . . . .⁵

He Himself will send us help.

---

¹ Title supplied from the next line.   ² MS. has iija M.
³ Noted for voices.
⁴ It is clear from the direction *cantent*, that the second couplet was sung by all three Marys : the probability is that this was also the case with the first couplet. The second couplet is of very common occurrence in the texts of liturgical plays.
⁵ "They find the stone rolled away, and learn from the angels that Christ is risen."—Manly.

    III. Maria. Alleluya schal be our*e* song,

      Sithe*n* Crist, our*e* Lord, by angell*us* steuen,

Schew*us* him as mon her*e* vs among   32

And is Goddis Son, heghest i*n* heue*n*.

. . . .[1]

[*II. Maria.*] . . . . . . was gon.

[*III. Maria.*] Surrexit Christus, spes n*os*tra

Precedet vos i*n* Galilea*m*.[2]   36

    III. Maria. Crist is rysen, wittenes we

By tokenes þ*a*t we haue sen þis morn !

Our*e* hope, our*e* help, oure hele, is he,

And hase bene best, sithe we wer*e* born !   40

Yf we wil seke hi*m* for to se,

Lettes noght þis lesson be for-lorn :

    " But gose eue*n* unto Galilee ;

þere schal ȝe fynd hi*m* ȝow beforn ! "   44

[*Officium Peregrinorum.*][3]

Feria secunda i*n* eb*do*mada *Pasche discipuli insimul* cant*en*t :

[*Chorus.*] Infidelis incursum populi

Fugiamus, Ihesu[4] discipuli !

Suspenderu*n*t Ihesum patibulo ;

Nulli p*ar*cent eius discipulo.[5]   4

. . . .[6]

    [*Luke.*][7] . . . . fast to fle.

[*Cleophas.*] But if we flee, þai wil vs fang,

And full felly þai wil vs flay ;

[1] "The Marys return and announce the Resurrection to the disciples."—Manly.

[2] Skeat assigns these two lines to the Angel : Manly to III. Maria.

[3] There is no heading in the MS. : the above is supplied by Manly. Skeat gives as the title : "The two Disciples going to Emmaus."

[4] Skeat's emendation of the MS., *Ihesum :* the scribe in copying was probably led astray by *Ihesum* in the following line.

[5] Since the words of this chorus appear on this actor's copy he must have been one of the disciples.

[6] "The disciples depart, Luke and Cleophas go together."—Manly.

[7] The MS. of the play does not name the speakers. Skeat assigns the part to Cleophas, and the cues to Luke. Cf. Introduction, pp. xxiii and xxiv.

Agayn to Emause wil we gang, 8 Let us go the quickest way to Emmaus, remembering Christ's Passion.
And fonde to get þe gaynest way.
And make *in* mynd eue*r* vs amang
Of our*e* gode Maister, as we may,
How he was put to paynes strang,— 12
On þat he tristed con hi*m* be-tray !
[*Iesus.*] . . . . . . but agayn.[1]
[*Cleophas.*] By wy*m*men wordis wele wit may we From the women we
Christ is risen vp in gode aray ; 16 know He is risen :
For to our*e*-self þe sothe say[d][2] he, He foretold His death and Resurrection,
Where we went in þis world away,
þat he schuld dye & doluen be,
And rise fro þe dethe þe thrid day. 20
And þat we myȝt þat siȝt now se, and will direct us
He wisse vs, Lord, as he well may ! to Himself.
[*Jesus ?*] . . . . resou*n* riȝt.
[*Cleophas.*[3]] Et quonia*m* tradideru*n*t eu*m* summi sacer-
dotes *et* pr*incipes* nostri *in* da*m*pnacio*n*e[*in*][4]
mortis *et* crucifixeru*n*t eu*m*.

Right is þat we reherce by raw 24 Let us remember how He was condemned and led to Calvary.
þe maters þat we may on mene,
How pr*estis and princes of our*e lawe
Ful tenely toke hi*m* hom be-twen,
And dampned hi*m*, wit*h*-oute*n* awe, 28
For to be dede wit*h* dole,[5] be-dene ;
þai crucified him, wele we knaw,
At Caluary, wit*h* caris kene.
[*Cleophas and Luke.*][6] Dixeru*n*t etia*m*[7] se visione*m*
angelor*um* vidisse, q*u*i dicu*n*t eum uiuer*e.*
[*Luke.*] . . . . wraist. 32
[*Cleophas.*] The wy*m*men gret, for he was gon ; The women mourn, for He is gone. Yet they say
But ȝet þai told of meruales mo :

---

[1] A red line in the MS. Skeat suggests that Jesus entered at this point. Manly gives the stage-direction : "Jesus enters and talks with them."
[2] Skeat's emendation of the MS. *say.*
[3] Manly assigns both the Latin and English to Cleophas : Skeat only the English.
[4] Supplied by Skeat.   [5] Skeat *dole :* Manly *dele.*
[6] Skeat does not assign this Latin portion to any one. Manly assigns it to Cleophas and Luke, and then suggests that each gave the sense of it, in English, emphasizing different features.
[7] Manly : *eciam.*

þai saw angell*us* stondyng on þe ston,

And sayn how he was farne hom fro.   36

Sithen of oures went ful gode wone

To se þat si3t, & said ri3t so.

Herfore we murne & mak*is* þis mon ;

Now wot þou wele of aꝉ our*e* wo.   40

[*Luke.*]¹ . . . . . . in pese.

[*Cleophas and Luke.*²] Mane nobiscum, quonia*m* adues-

perascit et inclinata est iam dies.   Alleluya !³

[*Iesus.*] . . . . . . wight.⁴

[*Cleophas.*]⁵ Amend our*e* mournyng, maister der*e*,

And fond our*e* freylnes for to feꝉ !   44

Herk, broþ*er* ! help to hold hi*m* here,

Ful nobel talis wil he us teꝉ ?

[*Luke.*] . . . . lent.

[*Cleophas.*] And gode wyne schal vs wont non,   48

For þer-to schal I take entent.

[*Luke.*] . . . . . . he went.⁶

[*Cleophas.*] Went he is, & we ne wot how,

For her*e* is no3t left in his sted !⁷   52

Allas ! where wer*e* our*e* wittis now ?

With wo now walk we, wil of red !

[*Luke.*] . . . . . [he brak]⁸ our*e* bred.

[*Cleophas.*] Our*e* bred he brak & blessed hit ;   56

On mold wer*e* neu*er* so mased me*n*,

When þat we saw him by vs sit,

þat we couthe noght consayue hi*m* þen.

[*Luke.*] . . . . ay.⁹   60

[*Cleophas and Luke.*] Quid agam*us* vel dicam*us*,

Ignorantes quo eam*us*,

Q*ui* doctorem sciencie

---

¹ It is impossible to decide whether to assign this to Luke or to
Jesus.

² Thus assigned by Manly : Skeat does not give them to any
character.

³ In the MS., noted for voices.

⁴ Manly inserts the direction : "They approach Emmaus."

⁵ Manly : omitted by Skeat.

⁶ Manly inserts before this verse the direction : "Jesus breaks
the bread, and, after giving it to them, vanishes."

⁷ Skeat's emendation of MS. *stid.*   ⁸ Supplied by Skeat.

⁹ Manly supplies the direction : "Cleophas and Luke return to
the other disciples, saying : "

Side notes:

that angels
told them
that He
was risen.

Master,
dispel our
mourning
and remove
our frailty.
Brother, help
to stay Him
here.

He is gone,
and we know
not how.

He broke and
blessed our
bread :
we were
astonished
and could not
comprehend
His being in
our midst.

Et patrem consolacionis   64
Amisimus?[1]

[*Luke.*] . . . . gode state.

[*Cleophas.*] We schal home teH, w*ith*-oute*n* trayn,   We shall tell
Bothe word & werk, how hit was,   68   of it at home.
I se hom sitt samyn i*n* a playn.
Forthe in apert dar I not pas !

[*Luke.*] . . . . . . & wife.[2]

[*Cleophas.*] We saw hi*m* hoH, hide & hewe ;   72   We saw Him,
þerfore be still, & stint ȝoure strife !   therefore
                                            be still.
þat hit was Crist ful wele we knewe,   We know it
                                           was Christ ;
He cutt oure bred w*ith*-oute*n* knyfe.[3]   He cut our
                                           bread with-

[*Chorus.*] Gloria tibi, Domine,   76   out a knife.
Qui surrexisti a mortuis,
Cu*m* P*a*tre *et* Sancto Spiritu,[4]
In Sempiterna secula ; Amen.[5]

[*Chorus.*] Frater Thoma, causa tristicie,   80
Nobis tulit summa leticie !

[Explicit.][6]

---

[1] Noted for voices, in the MS.
[2] Manly supplies the direction : " They join the other disciples."
[3] Manly supplies, after this speech, the direction : " All the disciples sing."
[4] Noted for voices.
[5] Here Manly supplies the direction : " Enter St. Thomas, who refuses to believe until convinced by the appearance of Christ."
[6] Supplied by Manly.

[THE NORWICH PLAY.]

[*Text A.*]

The Story of þe Creacion of Eve, wi*th* þe expellyng of Adam & Eve out of Paradyce.

Pater. *Ego principiu*m *Alpha* et O [1] *in altissimis habito ;*
  In þe hevenly empery I am resydent.

It is not good
for man to
be alone :

  Yt ys not semely for man, *sine adjutorio,*
   To be allone, nor very convenyent.   4
  I have plantyd an orcheyard most congruent
  For hym to kepe and to tylle, by contemplac*i*on :

let us make
him a helper :

  Let us make an adjutory of our formac*i*on   7

   To hys symylutude, lyke in plasmac*i*on.
    In to Paradyce I wyll nowe descende
   Wi*th* my mynysters angelicall of our creac*i*on
    To assyst us in ow*er* worke þat we intende,
    A slepe in to man be soporac*i*on to sende.   12

I take a rib
out of his
side and
make a
woman for
his mate.

  A rybbe out of man*n*ys syde I do here take ;
   Bothe flesche & bone I do thys creatur blysse ;
  And a woman I fourme, to be his make,
   Semblable to man ; beholde, here she ys.   16

O my Lord
God, thy
magnificence
is incompre-
hensible.

Adam. O my Lorde God, Incomprehensyble, withowt
  mysse,
  Ys thy hyghe excellent magnyficens.

This creature
I call virago
and give
Thee praise
and honour.

Thys creature to me ys *nunc ex ossibus meis,*
  And *virago* I call hyr in thy presens,   20
  Lyke on to me in natural preemynens.
Laude, honor and Glory to the I make.
Both father and mother man shall for hyr forsake. 23

---

[1] MS. & ω. The Latin quotations are underlined in the MS.

Pater. Than my garden of plesure kepe thou suer.[1]   Eat of all the
trees except
the tree of
knowledge
of good
and evil.
  Of all frutes & trees shall thou ete & fede,
  Except thys tre of connyng, whyle ye bothe indure ;
  Ye shall not touche yt, for that I forbede.

Adam. Thy precept, Lorde, in will, worde and dede 28   I will observe
Thy com-
mandment.
  Shall I observe, and thy request fulfyll
  As thou hast commandyd, yt ys reason & skyll.

Pater. Thys tre ys callyd of connyng good & yll ;   The day ye
eat of the
tree of know-
ledge of good
and ill ye
shall die.
  That day that ye ete therof shall ye dye,
  Morte moriemini, yf that I do you aspye : 33

  Showe thys to thy spowse nowe bye and bye.
  I shall me absent for a tyme and space ;
  A warned man may live : who can yt denye ? 36
  I make the lord[2] thereof ; kepe wyll my place ;
  If thou do thys, thou shall have my grace ;   If thou obey
thou shalt
have my
grace.
  In to mortalite shall thou elle*s* falle.
  Looke thow be obedyent whan I the calle. 40

Adam. Omnipotent God and hygh Lord of aℍ,   Omnipotent
God,
  I am thy servante, bownde onder thyn obedyens,
  And thou my creatour, one God eternall ;   my Creator,
  What þou com*m*andest, I shall do my dylygens.   I obey Thy
commands.
  Pater. Here I leve the, to have experyens, 45   I leave thee,
  To use thys place in vertuse occupac*i*on,   and will
return to my
habitation.
  For nowe I wyll retorne to myn habitac*i*on.

Adam. O lovely spowse of God*es* creac*i*on,   O lovely
spouse, I
  I leve the here alone, I shall not tary longe, 49   leave thee
here and
will walk a
while for my
recreation.
  For I wyll walk a whyle for my recreac*i*on
  And se over Paradyce, that ys so stronge.
  No thyng may hurt us nor do us wronge ;   Nothing can
hurt us,
God is our
protector.
  God ys ower protec*t*our & soverayn guyde ;
  In thys place no*n* yll thyng may abyde. 54

Serpens. O gemme of felicyte and femynyne love,   Why has God
forbidden
thee to eat
of this tree ?
  Why hathe God under precept p*r*ohybyte thys
    frute,
  That ye shuld not ete therof to your behofe ?
  Thys tre ys plesant wit*h*owten refute. 58   The tree is
pleasant.

[1] MS. had first *sure,* and then *suer* has been written above.
[2] MS. has Lord : but the MS.'s use of capitals is manifestly
capricious : we have therefore not followed it.

Lest we
should die :
we may not
touch it by
God's com-
mand.
Ye shall not
die, but be
as gods.

Eva. Ne forte we shuld dye, & than be mortall ;
  We may not towche yt, by God*es* comm*a*ndement.
Serpens. Ne quaquam, ye shall not dye perpetuall,
  But ye shuld be as God*es* resydent,
  Knowyng good & yll spyrytuall ;
  Nothyng can dere you þat ys casuall.   64

What is the
best to be
done ?

Eva. For us than nowe what hold you best,
  That we do not ow*er* God*e* offende ?

Eat of the
apple.
God sent me
to thee.
I take of it,

Serpens. Eate of thys apple at my requeste.
  To the, Almyghty God dyd me send.   68
Eva. Nowe wyll I take therof ; and I entend
  To please my spowse, therof to fede,

to know good
and ill.

  To knowe good & ylle for ow*er* mede.   71

Adam. I have walkyd abought for my solace ;

How do you,
My spouse ?
An angel
came and
gave me an
apple from
this tree.

  My spowse, howe do you ? tell me.
Eva. An angell cam from God*es* grace   74
  And gaffe me an apple of thys tre.
  Part therof I geffe to the ;

Eat of it.

  Eate therof for thy pleasure,
  For thys frute ys God*es* own treasure.   78

Adam! where
art thou ?

Pater. Adam, Adam, wher art thou thys tyde ?
  Byfore my p*r*esens why dost thou not apere ? 80

  [*Gap in MS.*]

Musick.

*Aftyr that Adam & Eve be drevyn owt of Paradyse they
schall speke thys foloyng :*

Adam. O wit*h* dolorows sorowe we maye wayle & weepe !

Alas! why
were we so
presumptu-
ous!

  Alas, alas, whye ware we soo bolde ?
  By ow*er* fowle presumpsyon we are cast full deepe,
  Fro pleasur to payn, wit*h* carys manye fold.   84

Eva. Wit*h* wonderous woo, alas ! it cane not be told ;
  Fro Paradyse to ponyschment and bondage full
    strong.

O wretches
that we are,
let us wring
our hands in
doleful song.

  O wretches that we are, so eu*er* we xaⱨ be inrollyd ;
  Therfor ow*er* hand*es* we may wrynge wit*h* most
    duⱨfuⱨ song.   88

And so þei xaH syng, walkyng together about the place,
wryngyng ther handes.

Wythe dolorous sorowe, we maye wayle & wepe
Both nyght & daye in sory, sythys fuH depe.   90

N.B. These last 2 lines set to musick twice over and
again, for a chorus of 4 parts.

[TEXT B.]

The Storye of þe Temptac*i*on of Man in Paradyce,
being therin placyd, & þe expellynge of man & woman
from thence, newely renvid & accordynge unto þe
Skripture, begon thys yere A*nn*o 1565, A*nn*o 7. Eliz.

Item. Yt ys to be notyd þat when þe Grocers' Pageant
is played withowte eny other goenge befor yt then doth
the Prolocutor say in þis wise.

[First Prologue.]

[*Prolocutor.*] Lyke as yt chancyd befor this season,
  Owte of Godes scripture revealid in playes,
Was dyvers stories sett furth, by reason
  Of Pageant*es* apparellyd in Wittson dayes;   4
  And lately be fal[l]en into decayes;
Which stories dependyd in theyr orders sett
By severall devices, much knowledge to gett.   7

God's scripture used to be set forth in plays at Whitsuntide.

Begynny[n]g in Genesis, that story repleate,
  Of God his creac*i*on of ech lyvynge thynge,
Of heaven & of erth, of fysh smalle & greate,
  Of fowles, herbe & tre, and of aH best*es* crepynge,   11
  Of angeH, of man, w*h*ich of erth hath beynge,
& of þe faH of angeH[s], in þe Apocalips to se;
W*h*ich stories w*ith* the Skriptures most justly agree.   14

The story commenced with the Fall of the Angels and the Creation,

Then followed this ower pageant, w*h*ich sheweth to be
  þe Garden of Eden, w*h*ich God dyd plante,
As in þe seconde chapter of Genesis ye se;
  Wherin of frutes pleasant no kynde therof shulde
    wante;   18

and was followed by our pageant of man in the Garden of Eden.

In w*hi*ch God dyd putt man to cherish tre & plante,[1]
To dresse & kepe þe grounde, & eate what frute hym lyste,
Ex[c]ept þe tre of Knoweledge, God*es* high wytt to
    resyste.   21

The story
shows the
Creation and
Temptation
of Eve:

The story sheweth further, that, after man was blyste,
    The Lord did create woman owte of a ribbe of man ;
W*hi*ch woman was deceyvyd with þe Serpentes darkned
    myste ;
By whose synn ow*er* nature is so weak no good we can ;

expulsion
from
Paradise.

Wherfor they were dejectyd, & caste from thence than
Unto dolloure & myseri & to traveyle & payne
Untyll God*es* spright renvid ; & so we ende certayne. 28

*Note that yf ther goeth eny other pageante*s *before yt,* þe
Prolocutor sayeth as ys on þe *other syde & leaveth owte
this.*

[Alternative Prologue.]

The Prolocutor. As in theyr former pageantes is sem-
    blably declared
Of God*es* mighty crea*ci*on in every lyvyng thynge,
As in þe fyrst of Genesis to such it is prepared
    As lust they have to reade to memory to brynge   4
Of pride & fawle of angells that in Hell hath beinge :
In þe seconde of Genesis of mankynde hys crea*ci*on
Unto this Garden Eden is made full preparacion.   7

Our pageant
begins with
man in
Paradise,

And here begyneth ow*er* pageant to make þe declaracion,
    From þe letter C. in þe chapter before saide,
How God putt man in Paradyse to dresse yt in best
    fassion,
    And that no frute therof from hym shuld be denayed,
Butt of þe tre of lyffe þat man shuld be afraide
To eate of, least that daye he eat þat he shuld dye ;
And of woman*es* crea*ci*on appering by & bye ;   14

telling of
the serpent's
deception.

And of þe deaville*s* temptacion, diseaivinge w*ith* a lye
    The woman, beinge weakest, þat cawsed man to tast.
That God dyd so offende, that even contynentlye
    Owte of þe place of joye was man and woman caste,

---

[1] Manly's emendation of Fitch's [*hem*] *taute* and MS. *taute.*

And into so great dolloure and misery browght at last ;
Butt that by God his spright was comforted ageyne.
This is of this ower pagent þe some & effect playne.　21

[Creation and Fall.]

God þe Father. I am *Alpha et homega,* my *Apocalyps*
　　doth testyfye,
That made aH of nothinge for man his sustentacion ;
And of this pleasante garden þat I have plant most goodlye
　　I wyH hym make þe dresser for his good recreacion.
Therfor, man, I gyve yt the, to have thy delectacion.
In eatyng thou shalt eate, of every growenge tre,　　6
Ex[c]epte þe tre of knowledge, þe which I forbydd the ;

I have made all things, and give this garden into the care of man.

For in what daye soever thou eatest thou shallt be
　　Even as the childe of death ; take hede : & thus I saye,
　　I wyH the make an helper, to comforte the aHwaye.
Beholde, therfore, a slepe I bryng this day on the,
　　& oute of this thy ribbe, that here I do owte take,　12
　　A creature for thy help behold I do the make.
Aryse, & from thy slepe I wyH the nowe awake,
& take hyr unto the, that you both be as one
To comfort one thother when from you I am gone.　16

I make thee a helper.

&, as I saide before when þat thou wert alone,
　　In eatying thow mayst eate of every tre here is,
Butt of þe tre of knowledge of good & evyH eate non,
　　Lest that thou dye the deth by doenge so amysse.
I wyll departe now wher myne habytacion is.
I leave you here　.　.　.　.　.　.　.　.　.　.　.[1]
Se þat ye have my woordes in most high estymacion.　23

Thou mayest not eat of the tree of knowledge of good and evil.

Then man & woman speke bothe.

[*Man and Woman.*] We thanke the, mighty God, & gyve
　　the honoracion.

Man spekethe.

[*Man.*] Oh bone of my bones & flesh of my flesh eke,　25
　　Thow shalte be called Woman, bycaus thow art of me.
Oh gyfte of God most goodlye, þat hast us made so lyke,
　　Most lovynge spowse, I muche do here rejoyce of the.

Thou shalt be called woman.

[1] *Lacuna* in the MS.

Woman. And I lykewyse, swete lover, do much reioyce
of the.

God therefore be praised, such comforte have us gyve

That ech of us with other thus pleasantly do lyve.   31

I will walk
about this
garden,
farewell.

Man. To walke abowt this garden my fantasye me meve ;

I wyłł the leave alone tyll that I turne ageyne ;

Farewełł myn owne swete spouse, I leave þe to
remayne.

Farewell.

Woman. And farewełł, my dere lover, whom my hart
doth conteyn.   35

The Serpent Speketh.

[*Serpent.*] Nowe, nowe, of my purpos I dowght nott to
atteyne ;

I can yt nott abyde, in theis joyes they shulde be.

I will tempt
them to sin.

Naye, I wyłł attempt them to syn unto theyr payne ;

By subtyllty to catch them the waye I do wełł se ;

Unto this, angell of lyght I shew mysylfe to be ;   40

With hyr for to dyscemble, I fear yt nott at ałł,

Butt that unto my haight some waye I shall hyr całł.

Oh lady of felicite, beholde my voyce so małł !

Why has God
commanded
you to eat
not of every
tree in this
garden?

Why have God sayde to you, " Eate nott of every tre

That is within this garden ? " Therein now awnswere
me.   45

Woman. We eate of ałł the frutte that in the grounde
we se,

Ex[c]epte that in the myddest wherof we may nott
taste,

For God hath yt forbydd, therfor yt may not be,   48

Lest we die
the death, etc.

Lest that we dye þe deth and from this place be caste.

The Serpent. Ye shałł not dye þe deth ; he make you
butt agaste ;

If ye eat,

Butt God doth know fułł wełł þat when you eate of yt,

Your eys shałł then be openyd & you shałł at þe last

ye shall be
as God.

As God[1] both good & evyłł to knowe ye shal be fytt.   53

Woman. To be as God[1] indede and in his place to sytt,

Thereto for to agre my lust conceyve somewhatt ;

---

[1] MS. *Godȝ.*

Besydes the tre is pleasante to gett wysedome & wytt,   That were indeed pleasant.
And nothyng is to be comparyd unto that.

The Serpente. Then take at my request, and eate, and   Then take, eat.
fere yt natt.   58

Here she takyth and eatyth, and man cumyth in and
sayeth unto hyr :

Man. My love, for my solace, I have here walkyd longe.
Howe ys yt nowe with you? I pray you do declare.

Woman. In dede, lovely lover, the Heavenly Kyng most
stronge
To eate of this apple his angell hath prepare ;   Take, eat this apple among other fruits.
Take therof at my hande thother frutes emonge,
For yt shall make you wyse & even as God to fare. 64

Then man taketh & eatyth and sayethe :

[*Man.*] Alack ! alacke! my spouse, now se I nakid we ar;   Alas, I see, we are naked :
The presence of ower God we can yt nott abyde.

We have broke his precepte, he gave us of to care ;   we have broken God's command.
From God therfor in secrete in some place lett us hide.

Woman. With fygge leavis lett us cover us, of God we be
nott spyede.   69

The Father. Adam ! I saye Adam ! Wher art thou nowe   Adam, where art thou ?
this tyde,
That here before my presence thou dost nott nowe
apere ?

Adam. I herde thy voyce, Oh Lorde, but yett I dyd me
hide.   72
For that which I am naked I more greatly dyd feare.   Because I am naked I did fear.

The Father. Why art thou then nakyd ? Who so hath
cawsyd the ?

Man. This woman, Lord & God, which thou hast gyven   This woman gave me to eat.
to me.

The Father. Hast thou eat of þe frute þat I forbyd yt the?
Thow woman, why hast thou done unto him thys   Why hast thou done this trespass ?
trespase ?   77

Woman. The Serpente diseayvyd me with that his fayer   The serpent deceived me.
face.

The Father. Thow Serpente, why dydst thou this wise   Why didst thou, Serpent,
prevente my grace,

My creatures & servant*es* in this maner to begyle?

The Serpente. My kind is so, thou knowest & that in
     every case,—

     Clene oute of this place theis per*s*ons to exile.   82

The Father. Cursed art for causynge my com*m*andement
     to defyle,

     Above aȴ catteȴ & beast*es*. Remayne thou in þe fylde,

Crepe on thy belly & eate duste for this thy subtyȴ wyle;

     The womans sede shall over*c*ome the, thus þat have I
     wylde.   86

Thou, woman, bryngyng chyldren w*ith* payne shaȴ
     be dystylde,

And be subiect to thy husbonde, & thy lust shall per*t*ayne

To hym : I hav determynyd this ever to remayne.   89

And to the, man, for þat my voyce thou didst disdayne,

     Cursed is þe erth for ever for thy sake;

Thy lyvyng shaȴ thou gett with swett unto thy payne,

     Tyll thou departe unto the erth [whereof]¹ I dyd the
     make.

Beholde, theis letherin aprons unto yo*u*rselves now
     take.   94

Lo! man, as one of us hath bene, good & evyȴ to
     knowe;

     Therfor I wyȴ exempt hym from this place to aslake,

Lest of the tre of lyfe he eate & ever growe.

Myne angeȴ, now cum furth & kepe þe waye & porte,

     Unto þe tre of lyffe that they do not resorte.   99

The Aungeȴ. Departe from hence at onys from this place
     of comforte,

     No more to have axcesse or ell*es* for to apere.

From this place I exile you, that you no more resorte,

     Nor even do presume ageyne for to com here.   103

Then man & woman departyth to þe nether parte of þe
     Pageant and man sayeth :

[*Man.*] Alack! myn owne sweteharte, how am I stroke
     w*ith* feare,

¹ Suggested by Manly : not in MS.

Marginal notes (left column):

beguile my creatures?

It is my nature.

Cursed art thou.

Creep on thy belly and eat dust.

Thou, woman, shalt bring forth children with pain. Obey thy husband.

Thou, man, shall get thy living with sweat.

Take these aprons.

Angel, come forth and guard the way to the Tree of Life.

Depart from hence.

That from God am exiled, & brow*gh*t to payne & woo.

Oh! what have we lost! Why dyd we no more care, Alas, and what have we lost!

And to what kynde of place sha₦ we resort & goo?

Woman. Indede into þe worlde now must we to and fro, We must into the world.

And where or how to rest, I can nott say at a₦.

I am even as ye ar, what so ever me befa₦.   110

Then cumeth Dolor & Myserye & taketh man by both armys & Dolor sayeth.

[*Dolor.*] Cum furth, O Man, take hold of me! Man, thou must always have me, Dolor, in sight.

Through envy hast lost thy heavenly lyght

By eatinge : in bondage from hence shall be.

Now must thou me, Dolor, have allways in sight. 114

Myserye. And also of me, Myserye, thou must taste And also me, Misery.
    & byte,

Of hardenes & of colde & eke of infirmitie ;

Accordinge to desarte thy portion is, of right,

To enjoy that in me that is withoute certentye.   118

Adam. Thus troublyd, nowe I enter into dolor & miserie.

Nowe, woman, must we lerne ower lyvyng*es* to gett We must learn to get our living; with labour.

With labor & with trave₦ ; ther is no remedye,

Nor eny thyng therfrom we se that maye us lett. 122

    Then cumyth in þe Holy Ghost comforting man & sayeth :

[*Holy Ghost.*] Be of good cheare, Man, & sorowe no more. Be of good cheer, and sorrow no more.

    This Dolor & Miserie that thou hast taste,

Is nott in respect, layd up in store,

    To þe joyes for the that ever shall last.

    Thy God doth nott this the away to cast,

But to try the as gold is tryed in the fyer ;

In the end, premonyshed, shalt have thy desyre.   129

Take owte of the Gospe₦ þat yt the requyre, Take from the Gospel Faith in Jesus Christ and Grace shall follow.

    Fayth in Chryst Ihesu & grace sha₦ ensewe.

I wyl be thy guyde & pay the thy hyer

    For a₦ thy good dylygence & doenge thy dewe.   133

    Gyve eare unto me, Man, & than yt ys trewe,

Thou shalt kyll affect*es* þat by lust in the reygne

And putt Dolor & Mysery & Envy to payne.   136

MYSTERY PLAYS.   C

Theis armors ar preparyd, yf thou wylt turn ageyne

To fyght wyth, take to the, & reach woman the same ;

Take the
breastplate
of Righteous-
ness,
the shield of
Faith

The brest plate of rightousnes Saynte Paule wyH the
retayne ;

The shylde of faythe to quench, thy fyrye dartes to
tame ;　　　　　　　　　　　　　　　　　　140

and the
helmet of
Salvation.

The hellmett of salvacion the devyl*es* wrath shall lame ;

And þe sworde of þe Spright, w*h*ich is þe worde of God,—

All theis ar nowe the offred to ease thy payne & rodd.

Adam. Oh ! prayse to The, Most Holye, þat hast w*ith*
me abode,　　　　　　　　　　　　　　　　144

In mysery premonyshynge by this Thy Holy Spright.

Holy Ghost,
I feel great
comfort.

Howe fele I such great co*m*forte, my syns th*e*y be unlode

And layde on Chrystes back, w*h*ic*h* is my joye and
lyght.　　　　　　　　　　　　　　　　　147

This Dolor & this Mysery I fele to me no wight ;

Death is
overcome.

No ! Deth is overcu*m* by forepredestinacion,

And we attayned wyth Chryst in heavenly consolacion.

Therfor, myne owne swett spous, withouten cavylacion,

Together lett us synge, & lett o*u*r hart*es* reioyse,

& gloryfye ower God wyth mynde, powre & voyse. 153

　　　　　　　　　　　　　　　　　Amen.

Old Musick, Triplex, Tenor, Medius, Bass :

With hart and voyce

Let us reioyce

Let us praise
the Lord. ˙

　　　And prayse the Lord alwaye

　　　For this o*u*r joyfull daye,

To se of this o*u*r god his maiestie,[1]

Who the hath given himsellfe ov*er* us to raygne &
to gov*er*ne us.

Lett all o*u*r harte reioyce together,

And lett us all lifte up our voyce, on of us with
another.

---

[1] The manuscript here appears corrupt : perhaps originally it
was a regular stanza.

[THE NEWCASTLE PLAY.]

NOAH'S ARK; OR, THE SHIPWRIGHTS' ANCIENT PLAY OR DIRGE.

Deus incipitur :

[*Deus.*] Fre[1] was this world that I have wrought ;
   No marvel (it is) if I it [destroy][2] ;
Their folk in earth I made of nought ;
   Now are they fully [growen][3] my foe.   4

I will destroy this world which I have created,

Vengeance now will I do
   Of them that have grieved me ill ;
Great floods shall over them go
   And run over hoothe and hill.   8

and take vengeance on offending mankind.

All mankind dead shall be
   With storms both stiff and steer,[4]
All but Noah, my darling free,
   His children and their wives dere.   12

Mankind shall be destroyed except Noah and his family,

Evermore yet they trow'd in me,
   Save therefore I will their lives.
Henceforth, my angel free,
   Into earth look that thou wind ;[5]
Greet well Noah in this degree,
   Sleeping thou shalt him find ;   18

who have always trusted in me.

Bid him go make a ship
   Of board stiff and great ;[6]

Angel, go bid Noah make a ship.

---

[1] Emended by Holthausen. Bourne has *Ere.*
[2] Bourne has: *No marvel it is if I do show.* Brotanek as above. Holthausen *if I dos how.*
[3] Supplied by Brotanek.
[4] Brotanek : *With storms that both steer and stiff is.* Holthausen : *Steer and stiff.* Bourne concludes the verse with *wiues.*
[5] Bourne has *would* instead of *wind* and *what* instead of *that.*
[6] Bourne : *of stiff board and great.* Holthausen inserts *both* after *board.* Brotanek has *bordis.*

Although he be not a wright,
    Therfore bid him not lett ;   22

He shall have wit at will,
    Be that he come therto ;
All things I him fulfill,
    Pitch, tar, seam and rowe.[1]   26

Bid him in any manner of thing,
    To ship when he [2] shall walk,
Of alkin beast [and fowl with wing][3]
    The male and female with him he take.   30

Bid him go provey, say so,
    In ship that they not die ;
Take with him hay, corn and straw,
    For his fowl and his fee.   34

Henceforth, my angel free,
    Tell him this for certain ;
My blessing with thee be,
    While that thou come again.   38

Angelus dicat. Waken, Noah, to me take tent !
    Noah, but [4] if thou hear this thing,
Ever, whilst thou live, thou shalt repent.

Noah respondit. What art thou, for Heaven's King,   42
    That wakens Noah of [5] his sleeping ?
Away I would thou went.

Angelus dicat. It is an angel to thee sent,
    Noah, to tell thee hard tiding ;   46

For every ilk a wight, for warkis [6] wild,
    And many fouled in sins sere,[7]
And in felony fouly [8] filled ;
    Therefore, a ship thou dight to steer,   50

Of true timber, highly railed,
    .   .   .   .   .   [9]

Side notes:
He shall have the necessary knowledge.

Bid him take into his ship male and female of all beasts and fowl,

and provender as well.

Give him My blessing.

Waken, Noah !

What art thou ?

An angel.

Thou shalt make a ship,

---

[1] Holthausen : *Pitch and tar, beam and towe.*
[2] Holthausen inserts *and his.*
[3] Bourne: *Of all kine kind of beast and fowl.* Brotanek: *Of alkin best, bird with wing.* Holthausen : *Of alle-kine kind of beasts living.*
[4] Bourne: *bid.*   [5] Bourne: *Off.*   [6] Bourne: *warks.*
[7] Bourne : *fowled, sair.*   [8] Bourne : *fowly.*
[9] A hiatus of two verses.

. . . .
With thretty cubettis ; in defence,   54

. . . . . . .¹
Look that she draw when she is drest,
And in her side a door thou shear,   with a door,
                                                        and windows
With fenesters full fitly fest ;   and cham-
                                                        bers,
And make chambers, both less and more,²
For a flood that up shall brest.³   60   for there shall
                                                        come a flood.

In earth shall be such a flood,⁴
That every ilke ⁵ life that hath life form,⁶   All shall be
                                                   destroyed
Beast and body with bone and blood,
They shall be stormed through stress of storm.⁷ 64

Albeit thou, Noah, and thy brood,   except thou
                                                   and thy
And their three wives in your hand—   family.
For you are full righteous and good—
You shall be saved by sea and land.   68

Into ship ere you are bent,⁸   Take with
                                                   you male an
You take with you both ox and cow ;   female of all
                                                   living things
Of ilk a thing that life has lent,
The male and female you take with you ;   72

You fetch in fother for your freight,   and fodder
                                                   also.
And make good purveiance for you prove,⁹
That they perish not in your sight :
Do, Noah, as I have bidden thee now.   76

Noah respondit. Lord, be then [present]¹⁰ in this stead, Lord, I am
                                                            not fitted for
That me and mine will save and shield.   the task,
I am a man no worth at need,
For I am six hundred winters old.   for I am six
                                                   hundred
                                                   winters old.

¹ Hiatus of one verse or possibly more. Holthausen's reading
is : *Of thirty cubits* [*hight*], *but feare.*
² Originally *mair.* Bourne, *both more and less.*
³ Holthausen omits this verse. Bourne, *burst.*
⁴ Bourne : *Such a flood in earth shall be.*
⁵ Bourne : *every like.*
⁶ Bourne : *life-ward.* Holthausen : *that is livand.*
⁷ Holthausen : *They shall be stroied* [*in water and sand*].
⁸ Brotanek's reading. Bourne has : *Into ship ere you enter out.*
Holthausen : *entent.*
⁹ Brotanek suggests *prow.*   ¹⁰ Holthausen.

Unlusty I am to do such a deed,
Worklooms for to work and weeld.   82

I have never
handled
a boat.

For I was never, since on life,[1]
Of kind of craft to burthen a boat;
For I have neither ruff nor ryff,[2]
Spyer, sprund, sprout, no sprot.

Christ be the
maker of this
ship.

Christ be the shaper of this ship,
For a ship need make I must.   88

Alas, for sin!

Ever[3] wo worth the, fouled sin,
For all too dear thou must be bought.

God regrets
He made
mankind.

God forthinks[4] he made mankind,
Or with his hands that he them wrought.   92

O men, mend
your lives.

Therefore, [good men,] or ever you blind,
You mend your life and turn your thought,[5]

I will begin
my work.

For of my work I will begin.
So well were me were all forth brought.   96

Out, out,
harro.

Deabolus intrat. Out, out, harro,[6] and welaway,
That ever I uprose this day,
So may I smile and say;
I wene[7] there has been none alive,   100
Man, beast, child nor wife,
But my servants were they.

I hear that a
ship is to be
made by
Noah and
his crew.

All this I have heard say,
A ship that made should be,
For to save withowten nay,
Noah and his meenye:

They lie.

Yet trow I they shall lie.[8]   107

Therto I make a vow:

I trust to
confound
them.

If they be never so slee,
To taynt them yet I trow

I'll to Noah's
wife.

To Noah's wife will I wynd,

---

[1] Brotanek's emendation of Bourne's *since I was born.* Holthausen has: *in all my life.*   [2] Bourne: *ryff nor ruff.*
[3] Brotanek's emendation of Bourne's *Even wo worth thou.* Holthausen: *Ever wo worth, thou fouled sin.*
[4] Bourne: *for thanks.*   [5] Bourne: *You mind your wife.*
[6] Sharp: *Put out harro.* Holthausen and Bourne: *Put off.*
Sharp's version: *Put out* seems originally a mis-copying of *Out,
out.*   Manuscript capitals are often troublesome.   Bourne has:
wele away.   [7] Bourne: *went.*
[8] Holthausen: *Yet trow [bled] they shall be.* Bourne: *yet trow I
they shall be.*

Gare her believe in me;
In faith she is my friend : 113

She is both whunt[1] and slee.
Rest well, rest well, my own dere dame![2]

Uxor Noah dicat. Welcome, bewschere;[3] what is thy
name?

Tyte that thou tell me! 117

Welcome, good sir. What is thy name?

Deabolus dicat. To tell my name I were full laith,[4]
I come to warn thee of thy skaith,
I tell thee secretly;
And thou do after thy husband read,
Thou and thy children will all be dead,
And that right hastily. 123

That is secret.

If thou followest thy husband's advice thou and thy children shall be dead.

Uxor dicat. Go, devil! how say, for shame![5]
Deabolus dicat. Yes, hold the still, le dame,[6] 125
And I shall tell thee how.
I swear thee by my crooked snout,
All that thy husband goes about,
Is little for thy prow.[7] 129

Go, devil!

Be still, and I will tell thee how.

Yet shall I tell thee how
Thou shalt weet all his will?
Do as I shall bid thee now,
Thou shalt weet every deal. 133

Do as I bid thee, and thou shalt know all.

Have here a drink full good, [iwis],[8]
That is made of a mightfull main :
Be he hath drunken a drink of this,
No longer shall he lain.[9] 137

Have a drink of this.

Believe, believe, my own dame dere,[10]
I may no longer bide;
To ship when thow shall fayre,[11]
I shall be by thy side. 141

When thou goest to ship, I shall go with thee.

Noah dicat. This labour is full great
For like an old man as me;

This labour is too great for an old man like me.

---

[1] Brotanek suggests as emendation *quaint.*
[2] Brotanek's emendation. Bourne has *Dereday.*
[3] Bourne : *fewsthere.* [4] Bourne : *loath.*
[5] Holthausen repeats *for shame.*
[6] Holthausen [*and stab*] *le dame.* [7] Bourne : *profit.*
[8] Brotanek. [9] Bourne has *learn.* [10] Bourne : *dere dame.*
[11] Brotanek : Bourne has *sayre.*

I sweat.

Lo, lo, [how] fast I sweat,
    It trickles atour myn ee.   145

I will go
home to rest
my bones.

Now home [then] will I wende,
    My weary bones for to rest:
For such good as God hath[1] sent
    There I get of the best.   149

Rest well [good] day, what chear with thee!

Welcome,
Noah.

Uxor dicat. Welcome, Noah, as might I thee,
    Welcome to thine own wayns!
Sit down here beside me,   153
    Thou hast full weary baynes.

Eat, and I
will give thee
a drink.

Have eaten, Noah, as might I thee,
    And soon a drink I shall give thee,
Such drank[2] thou never afore.   157

What the
devil is it!
I am almost
mad.
If thou dost
not tell me
where thou
goest we shall
not be friends.

Noah dicat. What the devil, what drink is it!
    By my father's soul, I have nere lost my wit!
Uxor dicat. Noah, bot[3] you tell me [now],
    Where about you wends,
I give God a vow,
    We two shall nere be friends.   163

Noah dicat. O yes dame, could thou stint,[4]
    I would tell thee my wit,

God ot
Heaven sent
to bid me
make a ship.

How God of Heaven an angel sent,
    And bad me make a ship.   167

He will
destroy the
world except
thee and me
and our
children.

This world he will fordo
    With storms both stiff and steer,[5]
All but me and yow,[6]
    Our children and wives [dere].[7]   171

Who the
devil made
thee a
wright?

Uxor dicat. Who, devil, made thee a wright—
    God give him evil to fayre—
Of hand to have such slight,
    To make ship less or mare![8]

[1] Brotanek suggests *will*; but is emendation necessary?
[2] Bourne: *such drink thou never none afore.*   [3] Bourne: *bode.*
[4] Holthausen's suggestion: Bourne gives *layne*, and Brotanek adds *trewely* and *fra hie* to verse 164.
[5] Bourne: *both stiff and steer fell.*
[6] Brotanek's suggestion—Bourne: *me and thee.*
[7] I suggest *dere* has been omitted.   [8] Bourne: *more perfect.*

When you began to smite,
Men should have heard wide where.   177

Noah dicat. Yes, dame, it is God's will :   It is God's will.
Let be, so thou not say.
Go make an end I will
And come again full thray.[1]   181

Uxor dicat. By my faith, I no rake,
Whether thou be friend or foe :
The devil of hell the take,[2]   The devil take thee
To ship when thou shalt go.   185   when thou shalt go to ship.

Noah dicat. God send me help in hy [3]
To clink yon nails twain ;[4]
God send me help in hy [3]   God send me help in my task.
Your hand to hold again ;
That all well done may be,[5]
My strokes be not in vain.   191

Angelus dicat. God hath thee help hither send,   God has sent thee help.
Thereof be thou right bold ;
Thy strokes shall fair be kend,
For thou thy wife has told.[6]   195

Noah dicat. Now is this ship well ginned,[7]   Now the ship is ready,
Within and without thinks me :
Now home then will I wend,   and I will go to fetch my money.
To fetch in my money.
Have good day, both old and young,   Young and old,
My blessing with you be.   201   Good-day.

Deabolus dicat. All that is gathered in this stead,
That will not believe in me,
I pray to Dolphin, prince of dead,   I pray Dolphin, Prince of the Dead, to scald
Scald you all in his lead,   you all in his lead.
That never a one of you thrive nor thee.   206

Finis. Amen.

[1] þra, i. e. *throng* (as given by Bourne).
[2] Bourne : *thee speed.* Brotanek suggests as above. Holthausen
has *thee speed*, rhyming with *I take no heed* in verse 182.
[3] Bourne : *high.* Brotanek : *hie.*   [4] Bourne: *yon Nail too.*
[5] Bourne : *That all may well be done.*
[6] Brotanek and Holthausen : *cold.* Bourne : *cowld.*
[7] Bourne has : *made.* Brotanek suggests the above. Holthausen
has *gare* instead of *ginned* and *fare* instead of *wend.*

[TWO PLAYS OF ABRAHAM AND ISAAC.]

[*Abraham and Isaac.*   Dublin MS.]

[¹ leaf 16, bk.]

I have created all :

[*Deus*] ¹ Of all þing þe<i>r</i> eve<i>r</i> was I am þe begynner<i>e</i>,
Boþe hevenly & erþely, & of he<i>m</i> þat ben in hell ;

but Adam has displeased me.

At my bidding was wrought boþe goode man & synner<i>e</i>,
All in ioy to have dwellid, tyl ada<i>m</i> to syn fell.   4
His unkindnes haþe displesid me, truþe for to tell,
For many a þing made I for his ioy·& daliaunce.
Whi sholde he displese me þat I loued so well,
& comaunded hy<i>m</i> but on þyng, & ȝit be forfetid my
    plesaunce.   8
But ȝit siþ he haþ displesid me, I have made p<i>ur</i>-
    viaunce

Another of his kind shall please me ;

þ<i>at</i> a nodr<i>e</i> of his kynd shal plese me a yeyne,
þe which haþe ever be my servaunt in al manere
    obse<i>r</i>uaunce :

Abraham is his name.

Abraham is his name, my man þat cannot feyne, 12
    But evyr hathe be trewe.
    Here before he requyred me hye
    To have a childe of his body,

To him I granted a child, Isaac.

    & I g<i>r</i>auntid hy<i>m</i> & [he] haþe on redely,   16
    Isaac ful feyr<i>e</i> of hewe.²

He loveth Isaac of all things the best :

Of al þing erþely, I wot wel, he loueþ him best ;
    Now he shuld loue me moste, as reson wold & skylle,
& so, I wot well, he doþe, I dyd it neu<i>er</i> mystrest. 20
But ȝit, for to pr<i>eu</i>e hym, þe truþe wol I fele.

I will prove his love for me. Angel, go tell him he

Myne aungel, go to Abraham þat I loue riȝt wele,
    & say þat I comaunded & charged hy<i>m</i> aboue all
    þinge,

must make sacrifice of Isaac.

The furst dede þat he doþe, ouþer mete or mele,   24
    To make sacrifise vnto me of Isaac his son ȝynge.

² Written at the side in the MS.

Angelus. O, blessid lord, I am redy at þi bidding

   To do þat shal plese þe in hevyn, erþe & helle ;

   For all þese owen to þe obedience aboue all þing.

   þis message vnto Abraham þi servaunt I wol go

     telle.¹   [leaf 18]

Deus. Then hye the þat þou were on grounde.   30

   I do not but to assay hym,

   & if he do it I wol not dismay hym ;

   Of his sorow I shal delay hym,

     & for on childe encrease hym a þusunde.²   34

   Et vadit angelus ad terram et expectat usque dum

     Habraham dicit.

[*Abraham.*] O gret god on hye þat al þe worlde madest,

   And lendist vs oure leving here to do þi plesaunce,

   Wiþ swete counfort of þe erþe all oure hertys gladest,

   To þe be honoure, to þe be ioy & all dewe obesaunce ;

   & hily, lord, I þank þe þat so makest my purviaunce

   To purvide or I dye a childe of myne owne body.

   To reioyse þat þou gaue me in erþe to my daliaunce

   & to plese þe, souereigne lord, I shall charge hym

     perfitly,   42

     Isaac, my son so dere.

   I have ben out all day :

   Now shal I go home & to my wif & say,

   þere shal I fynde bothe tway,

     Sara & Isaac in fere.   47

   Et vadit et in eundo obruat ei angelus et dicit.

Angelus. Abraham, Abraham !

Abraham. Alredy, who calleþ ? lo, here, I am.

   Who is þere, in þe hye lordes name,

     þat al þing shope of nought ?   51

Angelus. I am here, a messangere

   Of þat souereigne lord entere,

   þerfore herkyn now & here

     What message I haue brought.   55

   þe goode lord of al hevenes hye

   Comaundeþ þe to take & sacrifye,

Marginal notes:

I am ready, O Lord.

Go. I only do it to prove him.

O Lord,

to Thee be honour.

I thank Thee that Thou hast given me Isaac, my son.

Now I go home.

Abraham !

Ready, who calleth ? Here am I.

The good Lord commandeth

¹ After this in the MS. there is an acrostic.   ² MS. .m.

to sacrifice
Isaac thy son.
Isaac þi son þat þou louest so hertlye
To his souerente & plesaunce blyve.   59
Fare wele, for my message I haue þe sayde. [leaf 19, back]

Angel, I will
not refuse
God;
*Habr*aham. Aungel, as God wol, I am right wele payde ;
For of me his wille shal neu*er* be w*ith*nayde
Whil I am on lyve ;   63

And hardly, aungell, trust ther*e* to,
it shall be
done.
Farewell.
For doughtles it shal be do.
Angelus. Fare wele þan, for I wol go
To bringe our*e* lord relacion.   67

Lord, grant
me heart to
do it.
*Habr*aham. Now, goode lord, graunt me hert þer*e* tylle,
þat I may do that is thy wille :
& be my trouþe, I shal it fulfille
W*ith*out fraude outher cauelacion.   71

Et vadit angelus et dicit Habraham.

O Lord,
what is best
to be done?
A good lord, what is now best to do ?
Home to my wif I most nedis go
For þer is Isaac & I trowe she wol be ful wo,
If she knew þe case.   75

For she hathe hy*m* & no mo,
I must needs
tell my wife.
& if I telle her þat it is so,
þ*at* god wol have hy*m* to deþe ido,[1]
She faileþ not of sorowes trase.   79

I had rather
she were
displeased
than God.
No forse, I haue levyr þat she displesid be,
Than þat god be wroth with me.
Now doughtles I shal go and se
How prevely that I can it do.   83

Who is here?
Undo þese yates ! hey, who is here ?
None but I
and my son;
welcome, my
Lord.
Sara. None but I & my son dere.
Welcom my lord, welcom my fere,
Welcom my counfort also.   87

A, ye haue walkid ferr*e* aboute !
How have ye
fared while
ye have been
out?
How3 haue ye fare whil ye have be oute ?
W*ith*out fayle, I haue had gret doute
Last any thinge did you grevaunce.   91
*Habraha*m. Nay, I thanke the goode lorde,
All things
are well.
All thing & I done wel acorde,

[1] MS. *I do.*

Saving þis ; my goode lord haþ sent me worde,
That I moste nedis go do his plesaunce : 95

I most do sacrifyse upon þat hille on hye.
& þerfore, sirs, makeþ myne asse redye,
& Isaac, son, þou never ȝit me sye
Do no such obseruaunce. 99
þerfore aray the & go with me,
& lerne how god shuld plesid be ;
For, son, and euer þou þenke to the,
Put euer god to honowraunce. 103

Isaac. So shal I, fadir, & euer haue do,
As ye haue taught me & my moder also.
Loke, when euer þat ye wol go,
I shal not be behynde. 107
Sara. Ye, but I pray you, gentil fere,
As euer ye haue loued me dere,
Lat Isaac abide at home here,
For I kept not he went in þe wynde. 111

Habraham. Peese dame, lat be, do way.
þou wost wele, I wax ryght gray,
& þis child neuer ȝit say
How god shuld be plesid ; 115
& þerfore now he shal go with me
& þer he shal boþe know & se,
How þat god shal plesid be
& myn hert i-esid. 119

Sara. Then, siþe ye wol haue forthe my childe,
Goode, loke þat his horse be not so wilde,
&, sirs, wayte on hym, þat he be not defilde
With neiþer cley nor fen. 123
& loke wele þat his horse go rownde
& þat he stumbel not for no pownde.
Now, goode hert, god send þe home sownde,
þi fadir & all his men ! 127

Habraham. Gete hidre oure horses & let vs go hen,
Boþe I & Isaac & these two men ;

Marginal notes:

I must go sacrifice. Make mine ass ready ;

and Isaac, come thou with me and learn how God should be pleased.

So shall I do.

I pray you, let Isaac remain at home.

Peace, dame. Thou knowest I am old, and this child never yet saw sacrifice.

Look that he take no harm.

Let us go hence, Isaac, with two men.

& loke we haue fyre & stikke*s* to bren!

Lepiþ vp, haue ido,[1] anon!   131

All things are ready, *Sara.* All þing is redy, I you say;

But, gentil hert, I you pray,

but tarry as little as ye may. Tary as litel while out as ye may,

Because of Isaac, my son.   135

Et equitat et *equitando Habraham dicit:*

Habraham. Now, sirs, abide here ye two,

Takeþ here my horse & Isaac also:

For he & I most a litel farþer go

To do þis sacrifyse.   139

Abide here while Isaac and I go yonder. & I charge you þat ye abide here in deede,

& þ*at* ye remeve not from þis stede,

Whil Isaac & I go do þis dede

To god in our*e* best wise.   143

Come, Isaac. Come hidr*e*, Isaac, my son goode,

Take up þ*i*s fyre & þis wode,

Spar*e* not þ*i* cloþes, geue me þ*i* hode,

I shal not combre the sore.   147

Isaac. Now gawe, fader, þat þis dede were hyed,

For þis wode on my bak is wel tyed.

But where is the beast that shall be sacrificed? But where is þat quyk best þat shal be sac*ri*fied

Be hynde vs, or a fore?   151

Habraham. Son, care not þerfore on neu*er* a side,

Let God provide for us, my son. But let god alone þerw*ith* þ*i*s tyde,

& for our*e* wey he shal p*ur*vyde

& defend vs from fere.   155

A, son, I haue aspyed þe place,

þat god haþe p*ur*vided vs of his gr*a*ce.

Come on, son, a riȝt goode pace

And hye vs þat we were þere.   159

Now, Isaac, must I tell thee the truth. Now Isaac, son, I may no lengr*e* refrayne,

But I most tell þe truth certayne,

& þerfore loke þou be not þer agayne,

But do it w*ith* all þi wille.   163

---

[1] MS. *I do.*

þe hye god, þat all haþe wrought,
Comaunded me þat hidre þou shuldest be brought,
& here þi body shal be brouȝt to nought
Unto sacrifise on this hille.   167

God has commanded me to sacrifice thee here.

Lay downe þat wode on þat auter there,
& fast delyver þe & do of þi gere.

Isaac. Alas, gentyl fader, why put ye me in þis fere?
Haue I displesid you any thing?   171
Ȝif I haue trespast, I cry you mercy ;
&, gentil fader, lat me not dye !   [leaf 21]
Alas, is þer none oþer beste but I
þat may plese þat hy king?   175

Alas! father! Have I displeased you?

Is there no other beast but I?

Habraham. Nay, son, to me þou hast do no trespas,
But þou hast my blessing in euery place ;
But I may not forfet þat lordes grace,
þat al þing haþe me sent.   179
For & it shuld be affter me,
I had leuer haue slayne al my bestes þan þe.
But his wille nedys fulfilled most be,
& truly so is myn entent.   183

Nay, His will must needs be fulfilled.

Isaac. Alas, what have I displesid þis lord of blisse,
þat I shal be martyred in þis mysse?
But, gentil fader, wot my modre of þis,
þat I shal be dede?   187
Habraham. She? mary, son, crist forbede !
Nay, to telle her it is no nede :
For whan þat euer she knoweþ þis dede,
She wol ete affter but litel brede.   191

Have I displeased this Lord of Bliss?
Does my mother know of this?

She? Christ forbid!

Isaac. In feiþe, for my moder I dar wel say,
And she had wist of þis aray
I had not riden out from her þis day,
But she had riden also.   195
Habraham. Ye, son, god most be serued ay,
þi modre may not haue hir wille all way.
I loue þe as wele as she doþe, in fay,
& ȝit þis dede most be do.   199

Had she known of this I had not ridden out to-day.

God must always be served.

I love thee as well as she.

Isaac. A, fader, þen do of my gowne,
Vngirde me & take hem with you to towne ;

Then, father, ungird me.

I cannot.

For I may not.   I falle in swowne,
Depe hap enbrasid myn hert.   203

But I pray
thee let my
mother never
see my
clothes.

But on þing, fader, I pray you þus :
Let neuer my moder se my cloþus ;
For & she do, withouten oþus,
It wol greue her to smert.   207

Ah, me, what
shall I do!

Habraham. A, dere hert, what shal I do by þe ?
Wo is me þat shal sle þe !
With all my goodes I wold by þe,
& god wold assent þer to.   211

Father, do
what ye
please.

Isaac. A, fader, do now what euer ye lyst,
For of my modre, I wot wel, I shal be myst.   [leaf 21, back]
Many a tyme haþ she me clipt & kyst,
But fare wel nowe, for þat is do.   215

She was wont to calle me hir tresoure & hir store ;

Farewell, my
mother.

But farewel now, she shal no more.
Here I shal be dede & wot neuer wherefore,
Saue þat god most haue his wille.   219
Fader, shal my hed of also ?

Yea, son, it
must needs
be done.

Habraham. Ye, forsoþe, son, þat most nedis be do.
Alas, goode hert, þat me is wo,
þat euer I shuld þe þus spille !   223

Father, bind
my hands
and give me a
great stroke.

Isaac. þen, fader, bynde myne handes & my legges fast,
& yeue me a gret stroke, þat my peynes were past ;
For last I shrinke, I am riȝt sore agast,

Strike me but
once.

& þan ye wol smyte me in a noþer place :   227
Then is my peyne so moche the more.
A, soffte, gentil fader ; ye bynde me sore.

Woe is me,
my mind is
worse than
ever.

Habraham. A, dere hert, wo is me therefore,
My mynde is worse than evyr it was.   231

Lay me down
softly and
fairly.

Isaac. A, fadir, ley me downe sofft & feyre
& haue ido nowe, & sle youre eyre.
For I am hampred and in dispeyre
& almost at my lives end.   235
Habraham. A, fayre hert rote, leue þi crye !
þi sore langage goþe myne hert ful nye.

No man is in
such woe as I.

þer is no man þerfore so wo as I,
For here shal I sle my frende.   239

þe hye lord bad me to do þis dede,
But my hert gruccheþ, so god me spede,
My blode aborreþ to se my son blede,
For all on blode it is.   243

Alas, þat my hert is wondre sore,
For I am now riȝt old & hore ;
But god haþ chose þe for his owne store
In counfer of al my mys,   247

& to be offerd to hym þat is lord on hye.
& þerfore, son, take it pacientlye.
Perauenture in batayle or oþer myschef þou myȝtest dye,
Or ellis in anoþer vngoodely veniaunce.   251

Isaac. Now, fader, þen siþe it is so,
With al my hert I assent þerto.
Strecche out my nek, anon, have do,
& put me out of penaunce.   255

Habraham. Now kisse me furst, hert rote ;
Now ly doune, strecche out þi þrote !
This takeþ me ful nye, god wote,
Goode lord, to do þi plesaunce !   259

My heart refuses. God speed me.

Son, take it patiently ; thou might-est else have died in battle.

Stretch out my neck and put me out of suffering.

Now lie down.

It is very hard to do God's will.

Et extendit manuum ut inmolaret eum et dicit
angelus.

Angelus. Habraham, leue of & do not smyte ;
Withdrawe þyn hond, it is goddes wille !
Take vp Isaac, þi son so whyte,
For god wol not þat þou hym spille.   263
He seeþe, þat þou art redy for to fulfille
His comaundment, in wele and wo ;
& þerfore now he sent me þe tylle
& bad þat Isaac shuld not be sacrified so.   267
    & as for þi sacrifise,
Turn þe & take þat wedyr there,
& sacrifye hym on þat awtere,
& loke þat Isaac haue no dere,
I charge þe in all wise.   272

Abraham! leave off, do not smite.

God sees thou art ready to do His will.

Turn and take that wether there for thy sacrifice, and harm not Isaac, I charge thee.

Habraham. A, sufferen lord, þi wille be fulfilled
In hevyn, in erþe in watyr & clay !

Lord, Thy will be fulfilled.

I thank Thee
that Isaac is
not killed.

& lord, I thank þe þat Isaac is not killed.

Now, lord, I know wele þou dydest but asay.[1]   276

What I wold sey þerto, ouþer ye or nay.

þou knowest myne hert now, & so þou didest afore ;

Haddest not sent þyn aungil, Isaac had died þis
day.

But, goode lord, saue þi plesaunce, þis pref was riȝt
sore,   280

But ȝit I þanke þe hye

Go, son,
put on thy
clothes,

Þat I haue my sones lyve.

Gawe, son, do on þi cloþes blyve,

and let not
thy mother
know of this.

& let not þi moder wete of þis stryve,

I pray þe, son, hertly.   285

Deus. Habraham, loke up & herkyn to me.

Abraham,
since thou
wouldest
have obeyed
me I will

Siþe þou woldest haue done þat I charged þe,

& sparedist not to sle Isaac, þi son so fre,

The chef tresoure that thow haste,   289

Be myn owne self I swere certeyn,

reward thy
good will.

Þi goode wille I shal quyte ayeyn :

Þat shal be worship vnto you tweyn

While þe world shal last.   293

For þou sparedist not þi son for me.

Go & novmbre þe gravel in þe see,

Ouþer motes in þe sunne, & it wol be

By any estimacioun ;   297

Thy seed
shall multi-
ply.

& as þik as gravel in þe see doþe ly,

As þik þy sede shal multiply,

& oon shal be borne of þi progeny

þat to all shal cause saluacioun.   301

Habraham. A, lord, ithanked[2] euer be þy myght,

By tyme, by tyde, by day and nyght.

Let us hence
to our horses
and our men.

Now Isaac, son, let vs hens dight

To oure horses & oure men.   305

Gawe ! þei ben here fast by.

Hey, sirs ! bring þens oure horses in hy

& let us lepe up here lightly,

Fast þat we were hen.   309

---

[1] MS. *a say.*   [2] MS. *I thankcd.*

Lepe vp, son, and fast haue i-do.[1]

Isaac. All redy, fadre, I am here, lo ;

All ready, father.

Ye shal not be let whan euer ye go.

Mi moder I wolde fayne se. 313

& ʒit, that owre I sawe þis day !

I wend I shuld have gone my way.

Habraham. Ye, blessid be þat lord þat so can asay

Blessed be the Lord.

His servaund in euery degre ! 317

Et equitat versus Saram et dicit Sara.

Sara. A, welcom souereigne, withouten doute ; 318

Welcome, sovereign, how have ye fared ?

How haue ye fared whils ye haue ben oute ?

And, Isaac, son, in all þis rowte ?

Hertly welcome home be ye ! 321

Habraham. Gramercy, wif, fayre most you be falle.

Come þens, wif, out of youre halle,

Come, wife, and I will tell you all.

& let vs go walke & I wol telle you alle,

How god haþe sped þis day with me. 325

Wif, I went for to sacrifye ;

I went to sacrifice, what think ye ?

But how trowe you, telle me verylye ?

Sara. Forsoþe, souereigne, I wot not I,

Perauenture som quyk best ? 329

Some quick beast.

Habraham. Quyk ? ye forsoþe, quyk it was !

Quick, forsooth it was.

As wel I may tel you al þe case,

As anoþer þat was in þe same place,

For I wote wel it wol be wist. 333

Almighty god, þat sitteth on hye,

Almighty God bade me sacrifice Isaac.

Bad me take Isaac, þi son, þer bye

& smyte of his hed & bren hym veralye,

Aboue vpon yondre hille. 337

& when I had made fyre & smoke,

& drowe my knyf to yeve hym a stroke,

An aungel cam & my wille broke,

An angel came to tell me the Lord allowed my will.

& seid oure lord alowed my wylle. 341

Sara. Alas, all þen had gone to wrake ;

Alas, alas, where was your mind ?

Wold ye haue slayne my son Isaac !

Nay, þan al my ioy had me forsake !

Alas, where was your mynde ? 345

---

[1] MS. *I do.*

Upon the
Lord on high.
Habraham. My mynde ? upon þe goode lord on hy !
Nay, & he bid me truste it verayly.
þouȝ it had be þi self and I,
It shuld not haue ben left be hynde.   349

God gave him
to us, and
asked him
again.
God gave hym betwix vs tweyne,
& now he asked hym of vs ageyne :
Shuld I say nay ? nay, in certeyne,
Not for al þe world wide.   353
Now he knoweþ my hert verayly ;
Isaac haþe his blessing & also I,
& haþe blessid also all oure progeny,
For euer to abide.   357

Blessed be
that Lord.
Now blessid be þat lorde souereigne
þat so likeþ to say to you tweyne ;
& what þat euer he lust, I say not þer agayne,
But his wille be fulfilled.   361

Isaac hath
no harm.
[*Habraham.*] Isaac haþe no harme, but in maner I was
    sory ;
And ȝit I have wonne his love truly.
And euermore, goode lord, gramercy
þat my childe is not kylled.   365

Ye who have
seen this
play,

refuse not
what God
demands.
Now ye þat haue sene þis aray,
I warne you alle, boþe nyȝt & day,
What god comaundeþ say not nay,
For ye shal not lese þer by.   369

[*Abraham and Isaac.*   Brome MS.]

Father
Omnipotent,
Abraham. Fader of Heuyn Omnipotent,[1]
    With all my hart to The I call ;   [leaf 15]
Thow hast ȝoffe me both lond and rent,
And my lyvelod Thow hast me sent ;
I thank Thee
highly.
    I thanke The heyly, euer-more, of all.   5

Thou hast
made Adam
and Eve,
Fyrst off the erth þou maydst Adam,
    And Eue also to be hys wyffe ;
All other creatures of them too cam ;
and granted
it to me to
live here.
And now Thow hast grant to me, Abraham,
    Her in thys lond to lede my lyffe.   10

---

[1] MS. is inconsistent in the use of capitals.

In my age þou hast grantyd me thys,

  That thys ȝowng chyld wit*h* me shall won*e* ;

I love no-thyng so myche i-wysse,

Except þin owyn*e* selffe, der Fad*er* of blysse,

  As Ysaac her, my owyn*e* swete son*e*.　15

I haue dyu*er*se chyldryn moo,

  The wych I loue not halffe so wyll ;

Thys fayer swet chyld, he schereys me soo,

In eu*er*y place wer that I goo,

  That noo dessece her may I fell.　20

And therfor, Fadyr of Heuyn, I The prey,

  For hys helth and also for hys *grace* ;

Now, Lord, kepe hym both nyght [1] and day

That neu*er* dessese nor noo fray

  Cume to my chyld in noo place.　25

Now cu*m* on, Ysaac, my owyn*e* swete [2] chyld ;

  Goo we hom and take owr rest.

Ysaac. Abraham ! myne own*e* fad*er* so myld,

To folowe ȝow I am full prest,[3]

  Bothe erly & late.

Abraham. Cume on, swete chyld, I love the best [lf. 15, bk.]

  Of all the chyldryn that eu*er* I be-gat.　32

[*in heaven*].[4]

Deus. Myn angell, fast hey the thy wey,

  And on to medyll-erth anon þou goo ;

Abram's hart now wyll I asay,

  Wether that he be stedfast or noo.　36

Sey I co*m*maw[n]dyd [5] hym for to take

  Ysaac, hys ȝowng sonne, þat he love so wyll,

And wit*h* hys blood sacryfyce he make,

  Yffe ony off my freynchepe he [6] wyll ffell.　40

---

[1] Manly and *Commonplace Book* : *nygth.*

[2] Miss Smith : *swete.* Manly : *swet.*

[3] Manly supplies *prest* instead of MS. *glad*, for the sake of the rhyme.

[4] Supplied from Miss Smith's edition.

[5] Inserted in the *Anglia* version, but the MS. regularly omits the *n.*

[6] Both Miss Smith's editions insert *yf* before *he.* Manly, as above.

Show him
the way to
the place
where the
sacrifice
shall be.

Schow hym the wey on to the hylle
   Wer that hys sacryffyce schall be ;
I schall asay now hys good wyll,
   Whether he lovyþ [1] better hys chyld or me.
All men schall take exampyll be hym
   My commawmentes how they schall kepe. [2]   46

Father of
Heaven, I
pray to Thee,
for to-day
I must make
sacrifice,

Abraham. Now, Fader of Heuyn, þat formyd all thyng,
   My preyeres I make to The a-ȝeyn,
For thys day my tender offryng
   Here mvst I ȝeve to The, certeyn.   50
A ! Lord God, Allmyty Kyng,

what beast
will please
Thee best ?

   Wat maner best woll make þe most fayn ?
Yff I had ther-of very knoyng,
   Yt schuld be don with all my mayne   54
     Full sone anone.
To don Thy plesing on an hyll,
Verely yt ys my wyll,
   Dere Fader, God in Trinyte.   58

Abraham,
our Lord
commandeth
thee to take
and sacrifice
Isaac in the

The Angell. Abraham, Abraham, wyll þou rest !
   Owre Lord comandyth þe for to take
Ysaac, thy ȝowng sone that thow lovyst best,   [leaf 16]
   And with hys blod sacryfyce þat thow make.   62

Land of
Vision.

In to the Lond of V[i]syon [3] thow goo ;
   And offer thy chyld on-to thy Lord ;
I schall the lede and schow all-soo
   Vnto Goddes hest, Abraham, a-cord,   66

And folow me vp-on thys grene.

Welcome,
my Lord's
messenger.
I will not
disobey His
command.

Abraham. Wolle-com to me be my Lordes sond,
   And Hys hest I wyll not with-stond ;
ȝyt Ysaac, my ȝowng sonne in lond,
   A full dere chyld to me haue byn.   71

I would
rather lose all
my posses-
sions.

I had lever, yf God had be plesyd
   For to a for-bore all þe good þat I haue,
Than Ysaac my sone schuld a be desessyd,
   So God in Heuyn my sowll mot saue !   75

---

[1] Miss Smith's editions : *lovyd.* Manly : *lovyþ.*
[2] Manly gives here the stage-direction : *The angel begins to descend.*
[3] *i* is supplied by Holthausen.

I lovyd neuer thyng soo mych in erthe,[1]
And now I mvst the chyld goo kyll.

A! Lord God, my conseons ys stronly steryd,
And ჳyt my dere Lord, I am sore[2] aferd
To groche ony thyng a-ჳens ჳowre[3] wyll.   80

A! Lord God, my conscience is stirred, yet I fear to disobey Thee.

I love my chyld as my lyffe,
But ჳyt I love my God myche more,
For thow my hart woold wake ony stryffe,
ჳyt wyll I not spare for chyld nor wyffe,
But don after my Lordes lore.   85

I love my child as my life.

Thow I love my sonne neuer so wyll,
ჳyt smythe of hys hed sone I schall.
A! Fader of Heuyn, to The I knell,
An hard dethe my son schall fell
For to honor The, Lord, with-all.   90

Yet his head shall off to honour Thee, Lord.

[leaf 16, back]

The Angell. Abraham! Abraham! thys ys wyll seyd,
And all thys comamentes loke þat þou kepe;[4]
But in thy hart be no-thyng dysmayd.[5]
Abraham. Nay, nay, for-soth, I hold me wyll plesyd,[6]
To plesse my God with the best þat I haue;[7]   95

Abraham! keep all these commandments: be not dismayed.

For thow my hart be heuely sett
To see the blood of my owyn dere sone,
ჳyt for all thys I wyll not lett,
But Ysaac, my son, I wyll goo fett,
And cum asse fast as euer we can.   100

My heart will be heavy to see the blood of my own son; yet I will fetch Isaac.

Now, Ysaac, my owyne son dere,
Wer art thow, chyld? Speke to me.
Ysaac. My fader,[8] swet fader, I am here,
And make my preyrys to þe Trenyte.   104

Isaac, where art thou? Here, I make my prayers to the Trinity.

Abraham. Rysse vp, my chyld, and fast cum heder,
My gentyll barn þat art so wysse,
For we to, chyld, must goo to-geder,
And on-to my Lord make sacryffyce.   108

Rise up, and go with me to make sacrifice.

---

[1] Pronounced *erde*, Miss Smith.
[2] Miss Smith in *Anglia*: *sere*.   [3] Manly: *ჳowr*.
[4] Manly suggests instead of the MS. reading, *loke þou obay*.
[5] MS. *dysmasyd*.
[6] Manly suggests *apayd*. MS. *held* instead of *hold*.
[7] Manly suggests, *to the best þat I may*.
[8] Manly has *fayer*. Miss Smith: *fader*.

Ysaac. I am full redy, my fad*er*, loo !

3evyn at 3owr hand*es* I stand rygth here,

And wat-so-eu*er* 3e byd me doo,

Yt schall be don w*ith* glad cher,

Full wyll and fyne.

Abraham. A ! Ysaac, my owyn son soo der*e*,

God*es* blyssyng I 3yffe the, and myn.   115

Hold thys fagot vp on þi bake,

And her my selffe fyer schall bryng.

Ysaac. Fad*er*, all thys her wyll I packe ;

I am full fayn to do 3owr bedyng.

Abraham. A ! Lord of Heuyn, my hand*es* I wryng, [leaf 17]

Thys chyld*es* word*es* all to-wond my harte.   121

Now, Ysaac, on[1] goo we owr wey

On-to 3on mownte, w*ith* all owr mayn.

Ysaac. Gowe, my der*e* fad*er*, as fast as I may

To folow 3ow I am full fayn,

Allthow I be slendyr.

Abraham. A ! Lord, my hart brekyth on tweyn,[2]

Thys chyld*es* word*es*, they be so tend*er*.[3]   128

A ! Ysaac, son, anon ley yt down,

No leng*er* vpon þi backe yt hold[4] ;

> *Isaak.* Father, I am all readye   237
> to do your bydding mekelie,
> to beare this wood full bowne am I,
> as you comaunde me.

> *Abraham.* O Isaak, Isaak, my derling deere,   241
> my blessing now I geve the here.
> take up this fagot w*i*th good cheare,
> and on thy backe yt bringe,
> and fire w*i*th me I will take.
>
> .   .   .   .

> *Abraham.* O ! my hart will break in three,   253
> to heare thy word*es* I have pyttie.
> as thou wilt, lord, so must yt be :

---

[1] Manly corrects to *son*, presumably on analogy with v. 129.
Miss Smith has *on*.

[2] MS. *tewyn*, corrected by Miss Smith.

[3] After this verse Manly has the stage-direction : *They arrive
at the Mount.*

[4] MS. has *bere* ; Kettredge corrects to *hold*.   Miss Smith retains
MS. reading, but suggests in her footnote to line 132, *that I fere*
instead of *as I schuld.*

I am ready, father,

and will do whatsoever you bid me.

Ah ! Isaac, God's blessing I give thee.

I am glad to obey.

Now, Isaac, we go our way.

Go, father, I am ready to follow.

Lord, my heart break-eth in two.

Isaac, lay thy burden down.

For I mvst make redy bon
To honowr my Lord God as I schuld.   132

Ysaac. Loo, my dere fad*er*, wer yt ys !
  To cher ȝow all-wey I draw me ne*re* ;   I draw near
  But, fad*er*, I m*er*vell sore of thys,   to cheer you;
                                                               but I marvel
  Wy þat ȝe make thys heuy cher*e* ;   136   why your
                                                             countenance
                                                             is so sad.

And also, fad*er*, eu*er*-more dred I :
  W*er* ys ȝowr qweke best þat ȝe schuld kyll ?   Where is the
                                                             quick beast ?
Both fyer and wood we haue redy,
  But queke best haue we non on þis hyll.   140

A qwyke best, I wot wyll, must be ded,
  ȝowr sacryfyce for to make.[1]
Abraham. Dred the nowgth, my chyld, I the red,   Fear not,
                                                             the Lord will
  Owr Lord wyll send me on-to thys sted   144   send one.

Su*m*m ma*n*er a best for to take,
  Throw his swet sond.
Ysaac. ȝa, fad*er*, but my hart begynnyth to quake,   My heart
                                                             begins to
  To se þat scharpe swor*d* in ȝowr hond.   148   quake to see
                                                             your sword.

Wy ber*e* ȝe ȝowr sword drawyn soo ?
  Off ȝowr*e* countenaunce[2] I haue mych wond*er*.[lf. 17, bk.]

            to thee I will be bayne.
            lay downe thy fagot, my oune sonne deere !
Isaak. All ready, father, loe yt is here.   258
            but why make you so heavie cheare ?
            are you any thing adred ?

            father, if it be yo*ur* will,
            wher is the beast that we shall kill ?
            .   .   .   .
Abraham. Dread thie not, my childe, I red.   269
            our lord will send of his god-head,
            some maner beast into this stydd,
            ether tayme or wylde.
            .   .   .   .
Isaak. Father, tell me of this case,   277
            why you yo*ur* sword drawen hase,
            and beare yt naked in this place ;
            thereof I have great wonder.

---

[1] These two verses are reversed in the MS.
[2] Miss Smith gives this reading in a footnote, but her text and
the MS. have *conwnauns.*

Father of
Heaven,
this child
breaks my
heart.
Abraham. A ! Fader of Heuyn, so ¹ I am woo !
Thys chyld her brekys my harte on-sonder.²   152

Bear ye your
sword drawn
for me?
Ysaac. Tell me, my dere fad*er*, or that ȝe ses,
Ber ȝe ȝowr sword draw ³ for me ?

Peace, Isaac.
Abraham. A ! Ysaac, swet son, pes ! pes !
For i-wys thow breke my harte on thre.   156

Now mourn
ye more and
more.
Ysaac. Now trewly, su*m*-what, fad*er*, ȝe thynke,
That ȝe morne thus more and more.

Ah! my heart
was never
half so sad.
Abraham. A ! Lord of Heuyn, thy grace let synke,
For my hart was neu*er* halffe so sore.   160

Shall I have
harm or no ?
Ysaac. I pr*e*ye ȝow, fad*er*, þat ȝe wyll let me þ*a*t wyt,
Wyther schall I haue ony harme or noo ?

Alas, I may
not tell ye
yet.
Abraham. I-wys, swet son, I may not tell the ȝyt,
My hart ys now soo full of woo.   164

Hide it not
from me,
father.
Ysaac. Der*e*, fad*er*, I prey ȝow, hydygth ⁴ not fro me,
But su*m* of ȝour thowt þat ȝe tell me.
Abraham. A ! Ysaac, Ysaac ! I must kyll the.
Ysaac. Kyll me, fad*er* ? alasse ! wat haue I done ? 168

If I have
trespassed,
beat me with
a stave,
Yff I haue trespassyd a-ȝens ȝow owt,
W*ith* a ȝard ȝe may make me full myld ;

Isaak. Father, tell me, or I goe   273
        whether I shall have harme or noe.
Abraham. Ah dere God, that me is woe !   275
        thou burstes my hart in sunder.

·   ·   ·   ·   ·   ·   ·

Abraham. Isaac, sonne, peace ! I pray thee,   281
        thou breakes my harte even in three.
[*Isaak.*] I praye yow, father, leaue nothing from me, 283
        but tell me what you thinke.
Abraham. O Isaac, Isaac, I must thee kill.   285
        Isaak. Alas ! father, is that your will,
        youre owne childe here for to spill,
        upon this hilles brynke ?
        If I haue trespassed in any degree,   289
        with a yard you maye beate me ;

---

¹ MS. *os*, corrected by Miss Smith.
² MS. *on-too*. Holthausen corrects on the basis of the Chester
Play.
³ MS. *draw*. Holthausen : *drawyn*.
⁴ MS. Manly has : *hyd it*. Cf. v. 304.

And wit*h* ȝowr scharp sword kyll me nogth,

For i-wys, fad*er*, I am but a chyld.   172

and kill me not with your sword.

Abraham. I am full sory, son, thy blood for to spyll,

But truly, my chyld, I may not chese.

I am sorry to spill thy blood, but I may not choose.

Ysaac. Now I wold to God my mod*er* were her on þis[1] hyll!

Sche woold knele for me on both hyr kneys   176

To save my lyffe.

And sythyn that my mod*er* ys not her*e*,

I prey ȝow, fad*er*, schonge ȝo*w*r cher*e*,

And kyll me not wit*h* ȝowyr knyffe.   180

I would to God my mother were here.

Abraham. For-sothe, son, but ȝyf I the kyll,   [leaf 1ᴿ]

I schuld g*r*eve Gᴏd rygth sore, I drede ;

Yt ys hys co*m*mawment and also hys wyll

That I schuld do thys same dede.   184

If I do not kill thee I shall grieve God sorely.

He co*m*mawndyd me, son, for serteyn,

To make my sacryfyce wit*h* thy blood.

Ysaac. And ys yt Goddes wyll þat I schuld be slayn ?

Abraham. Ȝa,[2] truly, Ysaac, my son soo good,

And ther-for my hand*es* I wryng.   189

He commanded me to make sacrifice with thy blood. Is it God's will that I should be slain ? Yea, truly, Isaac.

Ysaac. Now, fad*er*, aȝens my Lord*es* wyll,[3]

I wyll neu*er* groche, lowd nor styll ;

He mygth a sent me a bett*er* desteny

Yf yt had a be hys plecer.   193

I will not stand against God's will.

put vp yo*u*r sword if yo*u*r will be,

for I am but a childe.

Abraham. O my sonne, I am sory   293

to doe thie this great anye :

.   .   .   .   .   .

Isaak. Wold God, my mother were here with me !   279

She wolde knele vpon her knee,

praying you, father, if it might bo.

for to save my life.

.   .   .   .   .   .

[*Abraham*] O Isaac, Sonne, to thee I saye :   305

God has comaunded me this daye

sacrifice—this is no naye—

to make of thy bodye.

Isaak. Is it Gods will I shold be slaine ?   309

.   .   .   .   .   .

---

[1] Miss Smith and MS. : *yis.*   [2] Miss Smith : *Za.*

[3] Manly conjectures *decre* and *wyll* instead of *plecer* in the last line of the same stanza.

Abraham. For-sothe, son, but yf I [1] ded þis dede,
 Grevosly dysplessyd our Lord wyll be.
Ysaac. Nay, nay, fad*er*. God for-bede,
 That eu*er* ȝe schuld g*r*eve hym for me. 197

ȝe haue other chyldryn, on or too,
 The wyche ȝe schuld love wyll, be kynd ;
I prey ȝow, fad*er*, make ȝe no woo,
For, be I onys ded and fro ȝow goo,
 I schall be sone out of ȝow*re* mynd. 202

Ther-for doo owr*e* Lord*es* byddyng,
 And wan I am ded, than p*r*ey for me ;
But, good fad*er*, tell ȝe my mod*er* no thyng,
 Sey þat I am in a-nother cu*n*tre dwellyng.[2]
Abraham. A ! Ysaac, Ysaac, blyssyd mot þow be ! 207

My hart begynnys [3] stronly to rysse,
 To see the blood off thy blyssyd body.
Ysaac. Fad*er*, syn yt may be noo other wysse,
 Let yt passe ou*er* as wyll as I. 211

But, fad*er*, or I goo onto my deth, [leaf 18, back]
 I prey ȝow blysse me wit*h* ȝowr hand.
Abraham. Now, Ysaac, wit*h* all my breth,
 My blyssyng I ȝeve þe upon thys lond,
 And God*es* also ther-to, i-wys.

  Father, at home yo*ur* sonnes you shall finde 317
  that yow must love by course of kinde.
  be I once out of yo*ur* mynde,
  Yo*ur* sorrow may sone cease,
  But you must doe God's bydding.
  father, tell my mother for nothing
  . . . .

  [*Abraham*] O Isaac, blessed mot thou be ! 325
  almost my wyt I lose for thee,
  the blood of thy bodye so free
  me think full loth to sheed.

  Isaake. Father, sith you must needs doe soe, 329
  let it passe lightlie and overgoe ;
  . . . .

Side notes:
If I do not do it, God will be displeased.
Nay, God forbid that you should grieve Him because of me.

Do our Lord's bidding, and when I am dead pray for me, and tell it not to my mother.
Isaac, blessed mayest thou be.

But, before I die, father, bless me with your hand.

My blessing I give thee.

---

[1] Manly : *Y.* [2] MS. *dewllyng*, corrected by Miss Smith.
[3] MS. *begynnyd.* Miss Smith gives the above emendation, and Manly *begynnetiu.*

Ysaac, Ysaac, sone, up thow stond,

Thy fayer swete mowthe þat I may kys.   218

    Isaac, stand up, that I may kiss thee.

Ysaac. Now, for wyll, my owyne fader so fyn,

And grete wyll my moder in erthe.[1]

    Farewell, greet my mother;

But I prey ȝow, fader, to hyd my eyne,

That I se not þe stroke of ȝowr scharpe sword,[1]

That my fleysse schall defyle.   223

    cover my eyes, so that I do not see the sword.

Abraham. Sone, thy wordes make me to weep[2] full sore;

Now, my dere son Ysaac, speke no more.

    Son, thy words make me weep.

Ysaac. A! my owyne dere fader, were-fore?

We schall speke to-gedyr her but a wylle.   227

And sythyn that I must nedysse be ded,

Ȝyt, my dere fader, to ȝow I prey,

Smythe but feve[3] strokes at my hed,

And make an end as sone as ȝe may,

And tery not to longe.

    Dear father, smite only a few strokes at my head.

    Tarry not long.

Abraham. Thy meke wordes, child, make me afray;[4]

So, welawey! may be my songe;   234

Excepe alonly Godes wyll.

A! Ysaac, my owyn swete chyld!

Ȝyt kysse me a-ȝen vpon thys hyll!

In all thys war[l]d[5] ys non soo myld.   238

    Ah! Isaac, kiss me again.

Isaac. Father, I pray you, hyde myne eyne   337
    that I se not your sword so kene;
    your stroke, father, wold I not seene,
    lest I against yt grill.

Abraham. My Deere sonne Isaac, speak no more,   341
    thy wordes make my heart full sore.

Isaac. O deere father, wherfore? wherfore?   343
    syth I must nedes be dead,
    of one thing I wold you praye: 345
    since I must die the death this daye,
    as few strokes as you maye,
    when you smyte of my heade.

Abraham. Thy mekenes, childe, makes me afray;   349
    my song may be ' well awaye! '

  · · · · · · ·

---

[1] Manly : *erde, swerd.*
[2] Manly : *wepe.* Miss Smith as above.
[3] MS. Manly : *fewe.*
[4] MS. and Miss Smith : *afrayed.*
[5] *ward* is the regular form in this MS. for *world* [Manly].

Ysaac. Now, truly, fad*er*, all thys teryng
    Yt doth my hart but harme ;

I pray you,
father, make
an ending.
Come,
I prey ȝow, fad*er*, make an enddyng.
Abraham. Cume vp, swet son, on-to my arme.   242

I must bind
thy arms.
I must bynd thy hands too
    All-thow thow be neu*er* soo myld.

Ah ! mercy,
father.
Ysaac. A ! mercy, fad*er* ! wy schuld ȝe do soo ?
Abraham. That thow schuldyst not let [me], my chyld.
                                           [leaf 19]

Nay, father, I
will not
hinder you ;
do as you
will with me.
Ysaac. Nay, i-wysse, fad*er*, I wyll not let ȝow ;
    Do on for me ȝowr*e* wyll,
And on the p*ur*pos that ȝe haue set ȝow,
    For God*es* love kepe yt for the styll.   250

I am sorry,
but I cannot
offend God.
I am full sory thys day to dey,
    But ȝyt I kepe not my God to greve ;
Do on ȝowr*e* lyst for me hardly,
    My fayer swete fad*er*, I ȝeffe ȝow leve.   254

Father, tell
my mother
nothing of
this.
But, fad*er*, I prey ȝow euermore,
    Tell ȝe my mod*er* no dell ;
Yffe sche wost yt, sche wold wepe full sore,
    For i-wysse, fad*er*, sche lovyt me full wyll ;
God*des* blyssyng mot sche haue !   259

Farewell,
sweet mother.
Now for-wyll, my mod*er* so swete,
    We too be leke no mor to mete.

Isaac, thou
makest me
grieve.
Abraham. A ! Ysaac, Ysaae ! son, þou makyst me to gret,
    And wi*th* thy word*es* thow dystempurst me.   263

I am sorry to
grieve thee,
father,
forgive me
for what I
have done.
Ysaac. I-wysse, swete fad*er*, I am sory to gr*e*ve ȝow,
    I cry ȝow m*er*cy of that I haue donne,
And of all trespasse þat eu*er* I ded meve ȝow ;

[*Isaac.*] now truly, father, this talking   357
    doth but m*a*ke long tarying.
    I praye you, come and make ending,
    and let me hence gone !
Abraham. Come hither, my Child, that art so sweete :
    thou must be bounden, hand and feete.
    .   .   .   .

    Isaac. Vpon the purpose that have set you,   365
        for sooth, father, I will not let you,
    .   .   .   .

        But, father, I crye you mercye.   373
        of that I haue trespassed to thee,

Now, dere fad*er*, for3yffe me þat I haue donne.

God of Heuyn be w*ith* me!   268
    God of Heaven be with me.

Abraham. A ! der*e* chyld, lefe of thy monys ;

    In all thy lyffe thow grevyd me neu*er* onys ;
    Thou hast never grieved

    Now blyssyd be thow, body and bonys,
    me, blessed be thou :

    That eu*er* thow wer*e* bred and born !   272

Thow hast be to me, chyld, full good :

    But i-wysse, child, thow I morne neu*er* so fast,

    3yt must I ned*es* here at the last
    yet I must needs shed

In thys place sched all thy blood.   276
    thy blood.

Therfor, my der*e* son, here schall þou lye,

    Onto my warke I must me stede,

I-wysse I had as leve myselffe to dey,

    Yff God wyll [be] plecyd wyth my dede ;   [leaf 19, back]

And myn owyn body for to offer.   281

Ysaac. A ! mer*c*y, fad*er*, morne 3e no mor*e*,
    Mercy, father,

    3owr wepyng maketh [1] my hart sor*e*,

As my owyn deth that I schall suffer.   284

3owre kerche, fad*er*, abowt my eyn 3e wynd !
    bind your kerchief over

Abraham. So I schall, my swettest chyld in erthe.[2]
    my eyes,

Ysaac. Now 3yt, good fad*er*, haue thys in mynd,

And smyth me not oftyn w*ith* 3owr scharp sword,[3]   288
    and smite me not oft with thy sharp sword.

    But hastely that yt be sped.

*Her*e Abra*h*am leyd a cloth on Ysaac*es* face, thu*s* seyyng :

Abraham. Now, fore wyll, my chyld, so full of gr*a*ce.
    Farewell, my child.

    forgeven, father, that yt may be
    vntill Domes daye.

Abraham. My deare sonne, let be thy mones ;   377
    my child, thou greaved me but ones.
    blessed be thou, bodye and bones,
    and I forgeve thee here.

    Loe, my deare sonne, here shalt thou lye ;   381
    vnto my worke now must I hye,
    I had as leefe myselfe to dye
    as thou my darling dere.

    .   .   .   .

---

[1] MS. *make* ; the above is Holthausen's emendation.

[2] So spelt but pronounced *erde* (Miss Smith).

[3] Manly : *swerd.*

Father, turn
down my
face.
Ysaac. A ! fad*er*, fad*er*, torne downgward my face,
 For of ʒowr*e* scharpe swo*r*d I am eu*er* a dred.   292

Abraham. To don thys dede I am full sory,
 But, Lord, Thyn hest I wyll not wi*th*stond.
Father of
Heaven,
receive me
into Thy
hands.
Ysaac. A ! Fad*er* of Heuyn, to The I crye,
 Lord, reseyve me into Thy hand.   296

Lo, now is
the time
come.
Abraham. Loo ! now ys the tyme cu*m* certeyn,
 That my sword in hys necke schall bite.[1]

I cannot find
it in my
heart to
smite.
A ! Lord, my hart reysyth The ageyn,[2]
 I may not fyndygth [3] in my harte to smygth ;   300

My hart wyll not now thertoo,
 ʒyt fayn I woold warke my Lord*es* wyll ;
But thys ʒowng innosent lygth so styll,
 I may not fyndygth [3] in my hart hym to kyll.
O ! Fad*er* of Heuyn ! what schall I do ?   305

Mercy,
father, why
do ye tarry ?
Ysaac. A ! m*er*cy, fad*er*, wy tery ʒe so,
 And let me ley thus longe on þis heth ?
Now I wold to God þe stroke wer*e* doo.
cut my suffer-
ing short.
Fad*er*, I prey yow hartely, schorte me of my woo,
 And let me not loke aft*er* my degth.   310

Isac. I praye you, father, turne doune my face   390
 a lyttle whyle, why|e you have space,
 for I am full sore adred.
Abraham. To doe this deede I am sory*e*.   393
Isaac. yea, lord, to thee I call and crye :
 on my soule thou haue mercye,
 hartelie I the praye.
Abraham. Lord I wold fayne worke thy will.   397
 this yonge Inocent that lyes so still
 full loth were me hym to kill
 by any manner of waye.
 . . . .
Harte, if thou wolde breake in three,   405
 thou shall never master me.
 I will no lenger let for thee,
 my God I may not greeve.
Isaac. A mercye, father ! why tary you so ?   409
 smyte of my head, and let me goe !
 I praie you, rydd me of my woe ;
 for now I take my leave.

---

[1] MS. *synke* : the above emendation is by Holth'ausen.
[2] Manly : *therageyn* ; the above is MS. version.
[3] MS. Cf. v. 165.

Abraham. Now, hart, wy wolddyst not thow breke on
   thre ?
   Ʒyt schall þou not make me to my God onmyld. [lf. 20]
   I wyll no lenger let for the,
   For that my God agrevyd wold be,
   Now hoold tha stroke, my owyn dere chyld.   315   Now receive the stroke, my child.

[*Her Abraham drew hys stroke and þe angel toke the sword
        in hys hond soddenly.*]

The Angell. I am an angell, thow mayist se blythe,   I am an angel sent from Heaven.
   That fro Heuyn to the ys senth ;   The Lord
   Our Lord thanke the an . C. sythe,   thanks thee a hundred
   For the kepyng of hys commawment.   319   times for keeping His commandment.

   He knowyt þi wyll and also thy harte,
   That thow dredyst hym above all thyng,
   And sum of thy hevynes for to departe   To dispel thy sadness I
   A fayr ram ʒynder I gan brynge ;   323   bring thee a fair ram,

   He standyth teyed, loo ! among þe breres.   which stands tied among the briars.
   Now, Abraham, amend thy mood,
   For Ysaac, thy ʒowng son þat her ys,
   Thys day schall not sched hys blood ;   327

   Goo, make thy sacryfece with ʒon rame.   Make sacrifice with the ram.
   Now, forwyll, blyssyd Abraham,
   For onto Heuyn I goo now hom ;
   The way ys full gayn.
   Take up thy son soo free.   332

Abraham. A ! Lord, I thanke The of Thy gret grace,   Ah ! Lord, I thank Thee for Thy great grace.
   Now am I yeyed[1] on dyuers wysse ;
   Arysse vp, Ysaac, my dere sunne, arysse,   Isaac, rise up.
   Arysse vp, swete chyld, and cum to me.   336

Ysaac. A ! mercy, fader, wy smygth ʒe nowt ?[2]   Ah, mercy, father, smite ye not ?
   A ! smygth on, fader, onys with ʒowr knyffe.
Abraham. Pesse, my swet sir, and take no thowt,   Peace, the Lord of Heaven has
   For owre Lord of Heuyn hath grant þi lyffe,   granted thy life.
   Be hys angell now,   341

[1] So in Miss Smith's two editions : Manly suggests *eped* for *cased.*
[2] MS. *not ʒyt* ; the above is Holthausen's emendation.
MYSTERY PLAYS.   E

That þou schalt not dey þis day, su*nn*e, truly.

How glad
were I if this
tale were true.
Ysaac. A ! fad*er*, full glad than wer I,   [leaf 20, back]
    I-wys, fad*er*, I sey, iwys !
    Yf thys tale wer trew.

I could kiss
thee a hun-
dred times
for joy.
Abraham. An hundred tymys, my son fayer of hew,
    For joy þi mowt now wyll I kys.   347

Ysaac. A ! my dere fad*er*, Abra*h*am,

Will not God
be angry ?
    Wyll not God be wroth þat we do thus ?
No, He hath
sent us that
ram,
*Abra*h*am.* Noo, noo! harly, my swyt son,
    For ʒyn same rame he hath vs sent
    Hether down to vs.[1]   352

which shall
die in your
stead.
ʒyn best schall dey here in þi sted,
    In the worþschup of our Lord alon ;
    Goo, fet hym hethyr, my chyld, inded.
Father, I will
go catch him.
Ysaac. Fad*er*, I wyll goo hent hym be the hed,
    And bryng ʒon best w*ith* me anon.   357

    A ! scheppe, scheppe ! blyssyd mot þou be,
    That eu*er* thow wer*e* sent down hed*er*,
    Thow schall thys day dey for me,
    In the worchup of the Holy Trynyte,
    Now cu*m* fast and goo we togede*r*   362

    To my Fad*er* of Heuyn ;
    Thow þou be neu*er* so jentyll and good,
I had rather
that thou
sheddest thy
blood than I.
    ʒyt had I leu*er* thow schedyst þi blood,
    Iwysse, scheppe, than I.   366

Lo, father,
I have
brought this
sheep.
Loo ! fad*er*, I haue browt her*e* full smerte,
    Thys jentyll scheppe, and hym to ʒow I ʒyffe :
    But, Lord God, I thank þe with all my hart,
    For I am glad that I schall leve,   370

    And kys onys my dere mod*er*.
Now be right
merry, my
child.
*Abra*h*am.* Now be rygth myry, my swete chylld,
    For thys qwyke best that ys so myld,
    Here I schall p*r*esent befor*e* all other.   [leaf 21] 374

---

[1] Holthausen substitutes for verses 350, 351 and 352 the following :—

    Noo, noo, suyt son for ʒyn same rame
    He hath sent hether doun to us.

Ysaac. And I wyll fast begynne to blowe,
　　Thys fyere schall brene a full good spyd.
But fad*er*, wyll I stowppe down*e* lowe,
　　ʒe wyll not kyll me w*ith* ʒour sword, I trowe ?　378

Abraham. Noo, harly, swet son, haue no dred,
　　My mornyng ys past.
Ysaac. ʒa ! but I woold þat sword wer in a gled,[1]
　　For, iwys, fad*er*, yt make me full yll agast.　382

[*Here Abraham mad hys offryng, knelyng and seyyng
thus :—*]

Abraham. Now, Lord God of Heuyn, in Trynyte,
　　Allmyty God Omnipotent,
My offeryng I make in the worchope of The,
　　And w*ith* thys qweke best I The p*r*esent.
Lord, reseyve Thow myn intent,
　　As [Thow] art God and grownd of our grace. 388

Deus. Abraham, Abrah*a*m, wyll mot thow sped,
　　And Ysaac, þi ʒowng son the by !
Trvly Abrah*a*m, for thys dede
　　I schall mvltyplye ʒowr*es* bother*es* sede
As thyke as sterr*es* be in the skye,　　　　393
　　　　Bothe more and lesse ;
　　And as thyke as gravell in the see,
　　So thyke mvltyplyed ʒowre sede schall be ;
　　　　Thys grant I ʒow for ʒowr*e* gocdnesse.　397

Off ʒow schall cume frowte gret [won][2]
And eu*er* be in blysse w*ith*owt ʒynd,
For ʒe drede me as God a-lon
And kepe my commawment*es* eu*er*yschon.
　　My blyssyng I ʒeffe, w*er*soeu*er* ʒe wend.[3]　402

Abraham. Loo ! Ysaac, my son, how thynke ʒe
　　Be thys warke that we haue wrogth ?
Full glad and blythe we may be,　　[leaf 21, back]
　　Aʒens þe wyll of God þat we grocched nott,
　　　　Vpon thys fayer hetth.　　　　407

---

[1] MS. glad.　　[2] Inserted by Manly.
[3] Holthausen's emendation of MS. *goo.*

Side glosses:

I will begin to blow, this fire shall burn well. Ye will not kill me if I stoop?

No, my son, my mourning is past.

I would that sword were in its sheath.

With this beast I make my offering to Thee, O Lord.

Abraham, well may thou and Isaac speed.

I will multiply the seed of both of you.

My blessing I give ye wheresoever ye go.

Isaac, think how good this work is that we have wrought.

52   *Brome Abraham and Isaac Play.*

Ysaac. A! fad*er*, I thanke owr Lord eue*r*y dell,

That my wyt servyd me so wyll,

For to drede God more than my detth.   410

Abraham. Why! derewordy son, wer thow adred?

Hardely, chyld, tell me thy lore.

Ysaac. ʒa! be my feyth, fad*er*, now haue[1] I red,

I wos neu*er* soo afrayd before,   414

As I haue byn at ʒyn hyll.

But, be my feth, fad*er*, I swere

I wyll neu*er*more cume there

But yt be a-ʒens my wyll.   418

Abraham. ʒa! cum on wi*th* me, my owyn swet son*n*,

And hom-ward fast now let vs goon.

Ysaac. Be my feyth, fad*er*, therto I grant,

I had neu*er* so good wyll to gon hom,   422

And to speke wi*th* my dere moder.

Abraham. A! Lord of Heuyn, I thanke The,

For now may I led hom wi*th* me

Ysaac, my ʒownge son*n* soo fre,

The gentyllest chyld above all other,[2]

Thys may I wyll avoee.   428

Now goo we forthe, my blyssyd son*n*.

Ysaac. I grant, fad*er*, and let vs gon,

For be my trowthe wer I at home,

I wold neu*er* gon owt vnd*er* that forme.

I pray god ʒeffe vs grace eue*r*mo,

And all thow that we be holdyng to.   434

Doctor. Lo! sove*r*eyns and sorys, now haue we schowyd,

Thys solom story[3] to grete and smale;

It ys good lernyng to lernd and lewyd,

And þe wysest of vs all,   438

Wythowtyn ony berryng.   [leaf 22]

For thys story schoyt ʒowe [her][4]

How we schuld kepe to owr po[we]re [4]

Goddes com*m*awmentes wit*h*owt grochyng. 44

---

[1] Manly's correction of MS. *hath.*
[2] Miss Smith's emendation of MS. *erthe.*
[3] Miss Smith has after "story" *hath schowyd.*
[4] Inserted by Manly.

Trowe ȝe sores, and God sent an angell,

And commawndyd ȝow to smygth of ȝowr chyldes hed,[1]

Be ȝowre trowthe ys ther ony of ȝow

That eyther wold groche or stryve ther ageyn? 446

Are there any of you who would sacrifice your child if God so commanded ?

How thyngke ȝe now, sorys, ther-by?

I trow ther be iij or iiij or moo;

And thys women that wepe so sorowfully

Whan that hyr chyldryn dey them froo, 450

As nater woll,[2] and kynd;

It ys but folly, I may well awooe,

To groche a-ȝens God or to greve ȝow,

For ȝe schall neuer se hym myschevyd, wyll I knowe,

Be lond nor watyr, haue thys in mynd. 455

Ye women who weep when your children die :

it is but folly to grudge them to God.

And groche not aȝens owr Lord God,

In welthe or woo, wether that He ȝow send,

Thow ȝe be neuer so hard bestad,

For when He wyll, He may yt a-mend. 459

Hys commawmentes treuly yf ȝe kepe with goo[d] hart,

As thys story hath now schowyd ȝow befor[n]e,[3]

And feythefully serve Hym qwyll ȝe be qvart,

That ȝe may plece God bothe euyn and morne.

Now Jesu, that weryt the crown of thorne,

Bryng vs all to Heuyn blysse! 465

Finis.

Keep His commandments

and faithfully serve Him.

May Jesus bring us all to the joy of Heaven.

[1] MS. : Holthausen corrects to ȝour chyld to slayn.
[2] *Woll* appears twice in the MS.
[3] Holthausen's emendation of MS. *before.*

[THE PLAY OF THE SACRAMENT.]

God bring

*Primus Vexillato*r. Now þe Father & þe Sune & þe Holy
Goste,
That all þis wyde worlde hat[h]¹ wrowg[h]¹t,
Save all thes semely, bothe leste & moste,

you all to
Heavenly
bliss.

And bry*n*[g]e¹ yow to þe blysse þat he hath yow to
bowght!   4

It is our pur-
pose to tell of

We be ful purposed wit*h* hart & wit*h* thowght
Off our*e* mater to tell þe entent,

marvels
wrought by
the Holy
Sacrament.

Off þe marvell*is* þat wer wondurfely wrowght
Off þe holi & bleyssed Sacrament.   8

It is a story

Secundus [*Vexillator.*] Sideyns,² & yt lyke yow to here
þe purpoos of þis play,
That [ys]¹ representyd now in yower syght

of Sir Aris-
torius of
Eraclea in
Aragon,

Whych in Aragon was doon, þe sothe to saye,
In Eraclea, that famous cyte, aryght,—   12

Therin wonneth a m*e*rchante off mekyl myght,
Syr Arystorye was called hys name,
Kend full fere wit*h* mani a wyght,
Full fer in þe worlde sprong hys fame.   16

to whom
there came
a Jew out of
Syria,

Primus. Anon to hym³ ther ca*m* a Jewe,
Wit*h* grete rychesse for the nonys,
And wo*n*neth i*n* þe cyte of Surrey,—þis [is] full
trewe,—
þe wyche⁴ had gret ple*n*te off p*r*ecyous stonys.   20

---

¹ Corrected by Stokes.
² MS. is a little difficult to decipher. Manly has *Sidseyns*,
souereyns is possible. For a similar use of this form of address *vide*
Brome Play, 435.
³ MS. *hyn* : corrected by Stokes.
⁴ Here the first four words of the next line were first written in
mistake and then crossed out.

Off þis Cristen merchante he freyned [1] sore,
Wane he wolde haue had hys entente.
Twenti pownd [2] and merchandyse mor
He proferyd for þe Holy Sacrament.   24

who offered him twenty pounds for the Holy Sacrament.

Secundus. But þe Christen merchante theroff sed nay,
Because hys profer was of so lityll valewe;
An hundder pownd [3] but he wolde pay,
No lenger theron he shuld pursewe.   28

The Christian merchant refused for so small a sum,

But mor off ther purpos they gune speke,
The Holi Sacramente for to bye;
And all for [that] [4] þe[i] [4] wolde [5] be wreke,
A gret sume off gold begune down ley.   32

but agreed for a larger,

Primus. Thys Crysten merchante consentyd, þe sothe to
     sey,
And in þe nyght affter made hym delyuerance.
Thes Jewes all grete joye made they;
But off thys betyde a stranger chance;   36

and the following night deliverd the Host to the Jew.

Thereat the Jew rejoiced,

They grevid our Lord gretly on grownd,
And put hym to cruell [6] passyon;
With daggers gouen hym many a grieuyos wound;
Nayled hym to a pyller, with pynsons plukked hym
     doune.   40

and put Christ to a great passion,

wounding Him with daggers and nails.

Secundus. And sythe thay toke þat blysed brede so sownde
And in a cawdron they ded hym boyle! [7]
In a clothe full just they yt wounde,
And so they ded hym sethe in oyle;   44

He boiled the Holy Wafer in a cauldron,

And than thay putt hym to a new tormentry,
In an hoote [8] ouyn speryd hym fast.
Ther be appyred with woundis blody;
The ovyn rofe asondre & all tobrast.   48

and outraged it in many ways.

Primus. Thus in ouer lawe they wer made stedfast;
The Holy Sacrament shewyd them grette faueur;
In contrycyon thyr hertis wer cast
And went & shewyd ther lyues to a confesour.   52

Thus he and his accomplices were converted to our faith,

and went to a confessor.

---

[1] MS. *freynend.*   [2] MS. *xxti li.*   [3] *C, li.*
[4] Holthausen.   [5] MS. *woldr.*   [6] MS. *cruell.* Manly *newe.*
[7] MS. *boylde*: corrected by Stokes.
[8] MS. has *hoote ob ouun*: corrected by Stokes.

By this
miracle
eleven were
converted.

Thus be maracle off þe Kyng of Hevyn,
And by myght and power govyn to þe prestis
          mowthe,
In an howshold wer convertyd i-wys elevyn.[1]
At Rome þis myracle ys knowen well kowthe.   56

This miracle
was presented
at Rome in
1461.

Secundus. Thys marycle at Rome was presented, for
          sothe,
Yn the yere of your [2] Lord, a M¹ cccc lxi.[3]
That þe Jewes þat Holy Sacrament dyd with,[4]
In the forest seyd of Aragon.   60

Below thus God at a tyme showyd hym there,
Thorwhe hys mercy & hys mekyll myght ;
Unto the Jewes he gan [5] appere
That þei shuld nat lesse hys hevenly lyght.   64

Therefore,
friends, con-
fess to your
holy father,
and be not in
despair.

Primus. So therfor, frendis, with all your myght
Vnto youer gostly father shewe your synne ;
Beth in no wanhope daye nor nyght.
No maner off dowghtis þat Lord put in :   68

For þat þe dowghtis þe Jewys than in stode,—
As ye shall se pleyd, both more and lesse,—
Was yff þe Sacrament wer flesshe & blode ;
Therfor they put yt to suche dystresse.   72

If it please
you to see this
play,
you shall do
so at Croxston
on Monday.

Secundus. And yt place yow, thys gaderyng þat here ys,
At Croxston on Monday yt shall be sen ;
To sen the conclusyon of þis lytell processe
Hertely welcum shall yow bene.   76

May Christ
save you
and bring you
to Heavenly
bliss.

Now Ihesu yow sawe from treyn [6] & tene,
To send vs hys hyhe ioyes of hevyne,
There myght ys withouton mynd to mene !

Blow up,
minstrel!

Now, mynstrell, blow vp with a mery stevyn !   80

          Explicit.[7]

---

[1] MS. I wyll wys XI ; but *wyll* is crossed out.
[2] Manly corrects to *ouer.*
[3] MS. has M¹ cccc .c. lxi.   But the dots before and after the 5th
c mean that it is a mistake.
[4] Cf. v. 627 ; where *with* is also apparently allowed to "jingle"
with *soth.*
[5] MS. *gayn.* Manly, as above.   [6] Holthausen *trey.*
[7] Written to the right.

Here after foloweth þe Play of þe Conuersyon
of Ser Jonathas þe Jewe by Myracle of
þe Blyssed Sacrament.

Aristorius Mercator. Now Cryst, þat ys ouer Creatour,
    from shame he cure us;
    He maynteyn vs with myrth þat meve vpon þe
      mold;
    Vnto hys endlesse joye myghtly he restore vs,
      All tho þat in hys name in peas well them hold; 4

Christ restore us to eternal joy.

For of a merchante most myght therof my tale ys told,
    In Eraclea ys non suche, woso wyll vnderstond,
For off all Aragon I am most myghty of syluer & of
      gold,—
    For, & yt were a countre to by, now wold I nat
      wond. 8

I am a merchant of Eraclea in Aragon.

Syr Arystory is my name,
    A merchante myghty of a royall araye;
Ful wyde in þis worlde spryngyth my fame,
    Fere kend and knowen, þe sothe for to saye. 12

Sir Aristorius is my name.

In all maner of londis, without ony naye,
    My merchandyse renneth, þe sothe for to tell;
In Gene and in Jenyse and in Genewaye,
    In Surrey [1] and in Saby and in Salern I sell; 16

I am known in all lands for my merchandise.

In Antyoche & in Almayn moch ys my myght,
    In Braban & in Brytayn I am full bold,
In Calabre and in Coleyn þer rynge I full ryght,
    In Dordrede & in Denmark be þe chyffe told; 20

---

[1] MS. *Seycryc*. Manly as above.

In Alysander I haue abundaunse in the wyde world.
In France & in Farre fresshe be my flower[*is*],
In Gyldre and in Galys haue I bowght & sold,
  In Hamborowh*e* & in Holond moche m*er*chantdyse
    is owr*is*;   24

In Jerusalem and in Jherico amo*n*g the Jewes jentle,
  Amo*n*g the Caldeys and Cattlyng*is* kend ys my
    komyng;
In R*a*ynes & in Rome to Seynt Petyrs temple,
  I am knowen certenly for bying and sellyng;   28

In Mayn*e* and in Melan full mery haue I be;
  Owt of Navern to Naples moch good ys þ*a*t I
    bryng;
In Pondere and in Portyngale moche ys my gle;
  In Spayne & in Spruce moche ys my spedyng;   32

In Lombardy & in Lachborun there ledde ys my
  lykyng;

In Taryfe & in Turkey, there told ys my tale;
And in þe dukedo*m* of Oryon moche have I in weldyng:
And thus thorowght all þis world sett ys my sale. 36

No ma*n* in thys world may weld more rychesse;
  All I thank God of hys grace, for he yt me sent;
And as a lord*is* pere thus lyve I in worthynesse.
  My curat way*te*th[1] vpon me to know myn entent; 40

And me*n* at my weldyng, & all ys me lent
  My well for to worke in thys worlde so wyde.
Me dare they not dysplese by no condescent.
  And who so doth, he ys not able to abyde.   44

Presbyter. No ma*n* shall you tary ne toroble thys tyde,
  But ev*er*y ma*n* delygently shall do yow plesance;
And I vnto my connyng[2] to þe best shall hem guyde
  Vnto God*is* plesyng to s*er*ue to attrue*n*ance.   48

For ye be worthy and notable in substance of good,
  Of m*er*chant*es* of Aragon ye have no pere,—
And therof thank God þat dyed on þe roode,
  That was your maker*e* and hath yow dere.   52

Margin notes:
Throughout all the world the sails of my ships are set.

I am rich,

and a lord's equal.

Men dare not displease me.

Every man shall do your pleasure,

for you are a most worthy merchant.

Therefore thank God.

---

[1] MS. *waytheth*.   [2] MS. *comnyng*: obviously a slip.

Aristorius. For soth, syr pryst, yower talkyng ys good ;

    And therfor affter your talkyng I wyll atteyn

    To wourshyppe my God that dyed on þe roode,

    Neuer whyll þat I lyve ageyn þat wyll I seyn.   56

    But, Peter Powle, my clark, I praye the goo wele pleyn

    Thorowght all Eraclea, that thow ne wonde,

    And wytte yff ony merchante be come to þis reyn

    Of Surrey or of Sabe or of Shelysdown.   60

Clericus. At youer wyll for to walke I wyl not say nay,

    Smertly to go serche at þe wateris syde ;

    Yff ony pleasant bargyn be to your paye,

    As swyftly as I can I shall hym to yow guyde.   64

    Now wyll I walke by thes pathes wyde,

    And seke the haven both vp and down,

    To wette yf ony on knowþ shyppes therin do ryde

    Of Surrey or of Saby [or] of Shelysdown.   68

Now shall þe merchantis man withdrawe hym and the
Jewe Jonathas shall make hys bost.

Jonathas. Now, almyghty Machomet, marke in þi mageste,

    Whose laws tendrely I have to fulfyll,

    After my dethe bryng me to thy hyhe see,

    My sowle for to save yff yt be thy wyll :   72

    For myn entent ys for to fulfyll,

    As my gloryus God the to honer,

    To do agen thy entent, yt should gr[e]ue me yll,

    Or agen thyn lawe for to reporte.   76

    For I thanke the hayly þat hast me sent

    Gold, syluer & presyous stonys,

    & abu[n]ddance of spycis þou hast me lent,

    As I shall reherse before yow onys :   80

    I have amatystis, ryche for þe nonys,

    And baryllis that be bryght of ble ;

    And saphyre semely, I may show yow attonys,

    And crystalys clere for to se ;   84

    I have dyamantis derewourthy so to dresse,

    And emerawdis, ryche I trow they be,

Marginal glosses:

Your advice is good.

Peter Paul,

go see if any merchant of Syria is arrived.

I go.

I will see if there be any bargain to your profit.

Almighty Mahomet,

I will fulfil thy laws.

I thank thee that thou hast sent silver, and gold, and precious stones.

Onyx and acha*tis* [1] both more & lesse,
    Topazyons, smaragd*is* of grete degre,   88

Perlys precyous grete plente ;
    Of rubes ryche I have grete renown ;
Crepawd*is* & calcedonyes semely to se,
    And curyous carbu*n*clys here ye fynd moren ; 92

Spyc*is* I hawe both grete and smale
    In my shyppes, the sothe for to saye,
Gyngere, lycoresse and cannyngalle,
    And fyg*is* fatte to plese yow to paye ;   96

I have spices,
too, in my
ships.

Peper and saffyro*n* & spyc*is* smale,
    And dat*is* wole dulcett for to dresse,
Almu*n*dis and reys, full euery male,
    And reysones both more & lesse :   100

Cloueys, grenynis & gynger grene,
    Mace, mastyk that myght ys,
Synymone, suger, as yow may sene,
    Long peper and Indas lycorys ;   104

Orengis and apples of grete apryce,
    Pungarnet*is* & many other spyc*is*,—
To tell yow all I haue now, i wys,
    And moche other m*er*chandyse of sundry spycis. 108

My name is
Jew Jona-
than;
Jason, Jas-
don, Masphat
and Malchus
wait upon
me.

Jew Jonathas ys my name,[2]
    Jazun & Jazdun þei waytyn on my wyH,
Masfat & Malchus they do the same,
    As ye may knowe yt ys bothe rycht & skyH. 112

I tell yow aH, bi dal and by hylle,
    In Eraclea ys noon so moche of myght.
Werfor ye owe tenderli to tende me tyH,

I am the chief
merchant of
the Jews.

    For I a*m* chefe merchante of Jewes, I tell yow be
        ryght.   116

But Jazun & Jazdun, a mater wollde I mene,—
    Mervelously yt ys ment in mynde,—

---

[1] MS. *ajachatis.*
[2] MS. has : *Jew Jonathas ys my ys name ;* but the second *ys* is
crossed out.

þe beleve of thes *Crys*ten me*n* ys false, as I wene ;

For þe beleve in a cake,—me þynk yt ys onkynde.

The belief of these Christians is false. They believe in a cake,

And a*ll* they seye how þe prest dothe yt bynd,[1]—

And be þe myght of hys word make yt flesshe and blode,—

and say the priest can make of it flesh and blood.

And thus be a conceyte þe wolde make vs blynd,—

And how þ*at* yt shuld be he þ*at* deyed upon þe rode. 124

Jasun. Yea, yea, master, a strawe for talis !

That ma not fale in my beleve ;

A straw for tales !

But myt we yt gete onys wit*h*in our pales,

I trowe we shuld sone afft*er* putt yt in a preve.[2] 128

Could we but get posses- sion of it.

Jazdun. Now, be Machomete so myghty, þat ye doon of meue,

I wold I wyste how þat we myght yt gete ;

I swer be my grete God, & ellys mote I nat cheue

But wyghtly theron wold I be wreke. 132

Masphat. Yea, I dare sey feythfulli þat ther feyth [ys fals :] [3]

That was neu*er* he that on Caluery was kyld,

Or i*n* bred for to be blode yt ys ontrewe als ;

But yet wit*h* ther wyles þei wold we were wyld. 136

Malchus. Yea, I am myghty Malchus, þ*at* boldly am byld ;

That brede for to bete byggly am I bent.

Onys out of ther hand*is* & yt myght be exyled,

To help castyn yt in care wold I consent. 140

Jonat[h]*as.* Well, syrse, than kype cunsel, I cummande yow all,

& no word of all thys be wyst.

But let us walke to see Arystories ha*ll*,

& affterward more conse*ll* amo*ng* vs shall caste. 144

Well, sirs, take counsel.

Let us see Aristorius' hall, and anon speak more of this.

---

[1] The first part of this verse is written at the bottom of the preceding page, and then repeated at the top of this.

[2] MS. had at first *in a pye* : this was then crossed out, and the above substituted.

[3] Manly's suggestion : MS. is incomplete.

With hym to bey & to sel I am of powere prest :

I must strike a bargain.

 A bargyn with hym to make I wyll assaye ;

For gold & syluer I am nothyng agast

 But þat we shall get þat cake to ower paye.   148

Her shall ser Ysodyr, þe prest speke ont[o] ser Arystori, seyng on thys wyse to hym; & Jonat[h]as goo don of his stage.

Presbiter. Syr, be yowr leue, I may [nat] lengere dwell ;

I must go say my evensong.

 Yt ys fer paste none, yt ys tyme to go to cherche,

Ther to saye myn evynsong, forsothe as I yow tell,

 And syth come home ageyne, as I am wont to werche.

Sir, go as you please,

Aristorius. Sir Isydor, I praye yow walke at your wylle

 For to serfe God yt ys well done,

but come again to sup with me.

And Syr com agene, ye shall suppe your fylle,

 And walke then to yo[u]r chamber as ye are wont

  to doon.   156

Her shall the marchant men mete with þe Jewes.

Good-day, Peter Paul! where is thy master ?

Jonathas. A ! Petre Powle, good daye and wele i-mett !

 Wer ys thy [1] master, as I the pray ?

Clericus. Lon[g] from hym haue I not lett

 Syt I cam from hym, þe sothe for to saye.   160

Wat tidyng with yow, ser, I yow praye,

 Affter my master þat ye doo frayen ?

Have you any bargain to make with him ?

Haue ye ony bargen þat wer to hys paye ?   163

 Let me haue knowlech ; I shall wete hym to seyn.

I have bargains royal and rich.

Jhonathas. I haue bargenes royalle and ry[c]h

 For a marchante with to bye and sell ;

In all thys lond is ther non lyke

 Off abondance of good, as I will tell.   168

Her shall þe clerk goon to ser Aristori, saluting him thus :

All hail, master.

Clericus. All hayll, master, & wel mot yow be !

 Now tydyngis can I yow tell :

The greatest merchant in Syria is come.

þe grettest marchante in all Surre

 Ys come with yow to bey & sell :   172

[1] MS. *they.*

Syr Jonathas ys hys nam,

 A marchant of ryght gret fame ;

 This tale ryght well he me told.

 He wollde sell yow, wit*h*out blame,

  Plente of clothe of golde.¹   177

Sir Jonathan is his name.

*Aristori*us. Petre Powle, I can þe thanke !

 I prey þe rychely araye myn ha*ll*

 As owyth for a marchant of the banke ;

  Lete non defawte be fownd at a*ll*.   181

I thank thee, Peter Paul, richly array my hall.

*Cleric*us. Sekyrly, mast*er*, no more ther sh*a*ll !

 Styffly about I thynke to stere,

 Hasterli to hang*e* yo*ur* pa*r*lowr wit*h* pall,

  As longeth for a lordis pere.   185

Certainly, master.

*Here sh*a*ll þe Jewe merch*a*nte & his men come to þe Cris*ten merch*a*nte.*

Jonathas. A*ll* haylle, syr Aristorye, semele to se,

 The myghtyest me*r*chante off Arigon !

 Off yower welfare fayn w*c*t wold we,

  And to bargeyn wit*h* you þis day am I bou*n*.   189

All hail, Sir Aristorius.

*Aristori*us. Sir Jonathas, ye be wellecu*m* vnto my*n* ha*ll* !

 I pray yow come vp & sit bi me,

 And te*ll* me wat good ye haue to se*ll*,

  And yf ony bargeyn² mad may be.   193

Sir Jonathan, ye are welcome to my hall: what have ye to sell?

Jonathas. I haue clothe of gold, p*r*ecyous stons & spyc*is*

  plente.

 Wyth yow a bargen wold I make ;—

 I wold bartre wyth yow in pryvyte

  On lyte*ll* thyng, ye wylle me yt take.   197

Cloth of gold, stones and spices.

I would barter for one little thing, privately with you, if you will.

 Prevely on þis stownd

  And I wolle sure yow be thys lyght,

  Neu*er* dystrie yow daye nor nyght,

  But be sworne to yow full ryght

 & geve yow twenti pownde.³   202

---

¹ Verses 173 and 177 are written to the right of the others.
  ² MS. *bargeny.*   ³ MS. xxᵗⁱ li.

What thing
is that, Sir
Jonathan?
Aristorius. Ser Jonathas, sey me for my sake,
    What maner of marchandis ys þat ye mene?

Your God
in a cake.
Jonathas. Yowr God, þat ys full mytheti, in a cake,
    And thys good anoon shall yow seen.   206

Nay, that
shall not be,
not for a hun-
dred pounds.
[*Aristorius.*] Nay, in feyth, þat shall not bene.
    I wollnot for an hundder pownd
    To stond in fere my Lord to tene;
    & for so lyteH a walew in conscyen[c]e to stond
        bownd.   210

I would like
to prove God
Almighty,
Jonathas. Ser, þe entent ys if I myght knowe or vnder-
        take,

and then
amend my
life.
    Yf þat he were God aH-myght;
    Off all my mys I woll amende make
    & doone hym wourshepe bothe day & nyght.   214

Aristorius. Jonathas, trowth I shall þe tell:
I dare not do
that deed, |
    I stond in gret dowght to do þat dede,
    To yow þat bere all for to sell
    I fere me þat I shuld stond in drede;   218

    For & I vnto þe chyrche yede,
for the priest
would tell the
bishop, and
impeach me
of heresy.
    & preste or clerke myght me aspye,
    To þe bysshope þei wolde go teH þat dede
    & apeche me of eresye.   222

Jonathas. Sir, as for þat, good shyffte may ye make,
You can do it
in the night. |
    &, for a vaylle, to walkyne on a nyght
    Wan prest & clerk to rest ben take;
    Than shall ye be spyde of no wyght.   226

Tell me, Sir
Jonathan,
what pay-
ment will you
make?
Forty pounds.
Aristorius. Now sey me, Jonathas, be this lyght!
    Wat payment þerfor wollde yow me make?
Jonathas. Forty pownd,[1] & pay yt fulryght,
    Evyn for þat Lorde sake.   230

No, not for a
hundred.
Aristorius. Nay, nay, Jonathas, there-agen;
    I wold not for an hundder[2] pownd.
Sir, here is
your asking.
Jonathas. Ser, hir ys yower askyng toolde pleyn,
    I shall yt tell in this stownd.   234

[1] MS. xl. li.   [2] MS. C.

Here is a hundder pownd,[1] neyther mor nor lesse,
   Of dokett*is* good, I dar well saye ;
Tell yt er yow from me passe ;
   Me thynketh yt a royall*e* araye.   238

Here is a hundred pounds.

But fyrst, I pray yow, tell me thys :
   Off thys thyng whan shaH I hafe delyu*er*ance?
Aristori[*us*]. To morowe betymes ; I shall not myse ;
   This nyght therfor I shaH make p*ur*veance.   242

But first tell me when will you deliver it to me.
To-morrow betimes.

Syr Isodyr he ys now at chyrch,
   There seyng hys evensong,
As yt ys worshepe for to werche ;
   He shall sone cu*m* home, he wyll nat be long,   246

Sir Isidorus is now at church;
he will soon come home,

Hys soper for to eate ;
   And when he ys buskyd to hys bedde,
   Ryght sone there after he shalbe spedd.—
No speche among ʒow ther be spredd ;
   To kepe y*our* toung*is* ye nott lett.[2]   251

and go to bed then.

Jonathas. Syr, almyghty Machomyght be w*ith* yow !
   And I shalle cume agayn ryght sone.
*Aryst*orius. Jonathas, ye wott what I haue sayd, & how
   I shall walke for that we haue to donn.   255

Mahomet be with you.
You know what I have said.

Here goeth þe *Iewys away &* þe *preste* comm*yth home.*

Presbiter. Syr, Almyghty God mott be yow*er* gyde
   And glad yow where-soo ye rest !
*Arist*orius. Syr, ye be welcom home thys tyde.
   Now, Peter, gett vs wyne of the best.   259

Almighty God be with you, and bless you.
Sir, ye are welcome.

Clericus. Syr, here ys a drawte of Romney Red,
   Ther ys no better in Aragon,
And a lofe of lyght bred,—
   Yt ys holesam*e* as sayeth þe fesycyoun.   263

Peter, get us wine.

*Aryst*or*ius.* Drynke of, S*er* Isoder, and be of good chere !
   Thys Romney ys good to goo w*ith* to reste ;
Ther ys no precyouser fer nor nere,
   For alle wykkyd metys yt wyll*e* degest.   267

Drink off, Sir Isidorus, and be of good cheer.

[1] MS. C. li.
[2] Verses 247 and 251 are written in the margin to the right.

*Pres*b*iter.* Syr, thys wyne ys good at a taste,
          And ther-of haue I drunke ryght well*e.*

To bed to gone thus haue I cast,
          Euyn strayt after thys mery mele.   271

Now, S*er,* I pray to God send yow good nyght.[1]
          For to my chamber now wyⱶ I gonne.
*Aristori*us. S*er,* wit*h* yow be God almyght,
          And sheld yow euer from yowr fone.   275

          [*Exit the priest.*]   *Here shall Aristori*us *call hys clarke to
                              hys presens.*

          Howe, Peter ! In the ys all my trust,
            In especyaⱶ to kepe my conseⱶ :
For a lytyⱶ waye walkyne I must.
            I wyⱶ not be long*e* ; trust as I the teⱶ.   279

                    [*He goes toward the church.*]

Now preuely wyⱶ I preue my pace,
            My bargayn thys nyght for to fulfyⱶ.
S*er* Isode*r*¹ shaⱶ nott know of thys case,
            For he hath oftyn sacred as þat ys skyⱶ.   283

          The chyrche key ys at my wyⱶ ;
            Ther ys no thyng*e* þat we shaⱶ tary,
I will not
stop until it
is done.   I wyⱶ nott abyde by dale nor hyⱶ
            Tyⱶ yt be wrowght, by Saynt Mary !   287

          Here shal he enter þe chyrche & take þe Hoost.

Now I have
it, I will go to
Sir Jonathan
to fulfil my
promise. Ah ! now haue I aⱶ my*n* entent ;
            Vnto Jonathas now wyⱶ I fare ;
          To fuⱶfyⱶ my bargayn haue I ment,
            For þat mony wyⱶ amend my fare,
              As thynkyth me.[2]   292

                    [*Exit from the church.*]

          But nowe wyⱶ I passe by thes pathes playn*e* ;
            To mete wit*h* Jonathas I wold fayne.
Ah ! yonder he commyth in certayne ;
            Me thynkyth I hym see.[2]   296

          ¹ MS. has *rest.*   ² Written in the margin to the right.

Welcom, Jonathas, gentyłł and trew,
  For wełł and trewly þou kepyst thyn howre ;
Here ys þe Host, sacred, newe,
  Now wyłł I home to halle & bowre.   300

Jonathas. And I shałł kepe thys trusty treasure
  As I wold doo my gold and fee.
Now in thys clothe I shałł the couer,
  That no wyght shałł the see.   304

*Here shall Arystory goo hys waye & Jonathas and hys
  seruantis shałł goo to þe tabylle þus sayng :*

Jonathas. Now, Jason & Jasdon, ye be Jewys jentyłł,
  Masfatt & Malchus, that myghty arn in mynd,
Thys merchant from the Crysten temple   307
  Hathe gett vs thys bred that make us thus blynd.

Now, Jason, as jentyłł as euer was the lynde,
  Into the forsayd parlowr preuely take thy pase ;
Sprede a clothe on the tabyłł þat ye shałł þere fynd,
  & we shałł folow after to carpe of thys case.   312

Now þe Jewys goon & lay the Ost on þe tabyłł, sayng :

Jonathas. Syris, I praye yow ałł, harkyn to my sawe !
  Thes Crysten men carpyn of a mervelows case ;
They say þat þis ys Ihesu þat was attaynted in ower lawe
  & þat thys ys he þat crwcyfyed was.   316

On thes wordys there lawe growndyd hath he
  That he sayd on Sherethursday at hys soper :
He brak the brede & sayd *Accipite*,
  And gave hys dyscyplys them for to chere :   320

And more he sayd to them there,
  Whyle they were ałł together & sum,
Syttyng at the table soo clere,
  Comedite, Corpus meum.   324

And thys powre he gaue Peter to proclame,
  And how the same shuld be suffycyent to ałł
    prechors ;
The bysshoppys and curatis saye the same,   327
  And soo, as I vnderstond, do ałł hys progenytors.

[marginal notes:]
Welcome, Jonathan,

here is the Host : now I will go home.

I will keep this treasure.

Jason and Jasdon, Masphat and Malchus, the Christian merchant hath got us that bread.

Jason, spread a cloth in the parlour.

Sirs, the Christians say this is Jesus that was condemned in our law.

On these words is grounded their law of the Sacrament.

Some men say
another law :
that He was
born of a
virgin.

Jason. Yea, su*m* men in þat law reherse another :
     They say of a maydyn borne was hee,
     & how Joachyms dowgʜter shuld be hys mother,
     & how Gabreʜ apperyd & sayd Aue ;   332

     & wit*h* þat worde she shuld conceyuyd be,
     & þat in hyr shuld lyght the Holy Gost,—
Ageyns ow*er* law thys ys false heresy,—
     And yett they saye he ys of myght*is* most.   336

They say He
is our King,

Jasdon. They saye þat Ihe*su* to be ow*er* kyng*e*,
     But I wene he bowght þat fuʜ dere.
But they make a royaʜ aray of hys vprysyng ;
     & that in eu*er*y place ys pr*e*chyd farre & nere.   340

and that He
appeared to
Thomas and
Mary Magde-
lene.

     & how he to hys dyscyples ag*a*yn dyd appere,
     To Thomas and to Mary Mawdelen,
     & syth how he styed by hys own powr*e* ;

This ye know
is heresy.

     And thys, ye know weʜ, ys heresy fuʜ playn.   344

He sent them
wit to under-
stand all
languages,

Masphat. Yea & also they say he sent them wytt &
     wysdom
For to vnderstond eu*er*y langwage ;
     When þe Holy Gost to them came,   347
     They faryd as dronk men of pyment*e* or v*er*nage ;

and He lik-
ened Himself
to a lord.

     & sythen how þat he lykenyd hymself a lord of p*er*age,
     On hys fatherys ryght hond he hym sett.

They believe
Him wiser
than the
Sybil, and
stronger than
Alexander.

They hold hym wyser þan eu*er* was Syble sage,
     & strenger than Alexander, þat aʜ þe wor[l]de ded
     gett.   352

Malchus. Yea, yet they saye as fols, I dare laye my
     hedde,

This same
bread shall
be our judge
at the Judg-
ment.

     How they that be ded shaʜ com agayn to Judge-
     ment,
And ow*er* dredfuʜ Judge shalbe thys same brede,
     And how lyfe eu*er*lastyng them shuld be lent.   356

     & thus they hold, all at on consent,

Because Phi-
lip said for a
joke: "jude-
care vivos et
mortuos."

     Because that Phylyppe sayd for a lytyʜ glosse—
To turn vs from owr beleve ys ther entent,—
     For that he sayd, "*judecare viuos* et *mortuos.*"   360

Jonathas. Now, ser*i*s, ye haue rehersyd the substance of
    their lawe,[1] Now, sirs,

But thys bred I wold myght be put in a p*r*efe I will put this
Whether þis be he that in Bosra of vs had awe.   363 bread to
proof.
Ther staynyd were hys clothys, þis may we belefe ;

Thys may we know, ther had he grefe,
    For ow*er* old bookys veryfy thus,—
Theron he was jugett to be hangyd as a thefe,—
    " *Tinctis Bosra vestibus.*"   368

Jason. Yff þat thys be he that on Caluery was mad If this is He,
    red,
Onto my mynd, I sha‡ kenne yow a conceyt good :
Surely w*i*t*h* ow*er* daggars we sha‡ ses on thys bredde, let us stick
    & so w*i*t*h* clowt*i*s we sha‡ know yf he haue eny our daggers
into Him and
see if there
    blood.   372 be blood.

Jasdon. Now, by Machomyth so myghty, þat meuyth in Now, by Ma-
    my mode ! homet, that
is a masterly
idea.
Thys ys maste*r*ly ment, thys matter thus to meue :
& w*i*t*h* ow*er* strokys we sha‡ fray hym as he was on
    the rode,
That he was on don w*i*t*h* grett repreue.   376

Masphat. Yea, I pray yow, smyte ye in the myddys of Yea, smite in
    þe cake, the middle
of the cake.
& so sha‡ we smyte þe*r*on woundys fyve :
We wy‡ not spare to wyrke yt wrake,
To prove in thys brede yf þer be eny lyfe.   380

*Malch*us. Yea, goo we to, than, and take ower [2] space,
    & looke ow*er* daggar*i*s be sharpe & kene :
& when eche man a stroke smytte hase,   383 When each
has struck,
In þe mydy‡ p*ar*t there-of ow*er* master sha‡ bene. the Master
shall be in
the middle.

Jonathas. When ye haue a‡ smytyn, my stroke shalbe When ye have
    sene ; all struck,
W*i*t*h* þis same dagger that ys so styf & strong,
In þe myddys of thys prynt I thynke for to prene ; I shall strike
On lashe I sha‡ hym*e* lend*e* or yt be long.   388 right in the
middle.

---

[1] MS. has ou*r* *lawe.*   [2] MS. *yower.*

*Here shall þe iiij Jewys pryk þer dagger*is *in iiij* quarter*s,*
                þus sayng :

Have at it!   *Jason.* Haue at yt ! Haue at yt, w*ith* a*ll* my myght !
                Thys syde I hope for to sese !
This side I   *Jasdon.* & I shall w*ith* thys blade so bryght
will attack.
                Thys other syde freshely afeze !   392

                Masphat. & I yow plyght I sha*ll* hym not please,
With this I   For w*ith* thys punche I sha*ll* hym pryke.
prick Him.
With this   *Malchus.* & w*ith* thys augur ¹ I sha*ll* hym not ease,
auger I buffet
Him;   Another buffett sha*ll* he lykke.   396

                Jonathas. Now am I bold w*ith* batayle hym to bleyke,
                þis mydle part alle for to prene ;
a stout stroke   A stowte stroke also for to stryke,—
in the middle.
                In þe myddys yt shalbe sene !   400

                    *Here þe Ost must blede.*²

Out! harrow!   Ah ! owt ! owt ! harrow ! what deuy*ll* ys thys ?
what devil is
this?   Of thys wyrk I am on were ;
It bleeds.   Yt bledyth as yt were woode, I wys ;
                But yf ye helpe, I sha*ll* dyspayre.   404

A fire and a   *Jason.* A fyre ! a fyre ! & that in hast !
cauldron!
                Anoon a cawdron fu*ll* of oyle !
I will help to   *Jasdon.* And I shalle helpe yt wer in cast,
cast it in.
                All þe iij howr*is* for to boyle !   408

                    [*Malchus goes to get the oil.*]³

Here is a   *Masphat.* Yea, here is a furneys stowte & strong,
furnace and
cauldron.   And a cawdron therin dothe hong !
Where art   Malcus, wher art thow so long,
thou, Mal-
chus?   To helpe thys dede were dyght ?   412

Here are four   *Malc*[*h*]*us.* Loo, here ys iiij galons off oyle clere !
gallons of oil;
blow up the   Haue doon fast ! blowe up þe fere !
fire:
bring that   Sỵr, bryng that ylke cake nere,
cake here.
                Ma*n*ly, w*ith* all yowre myghthe.²   416

                ¹ MS. *angus.* Perhaps a mis-copying of *augur.*
                ² Written to the right in the margin.   ³ Manly.

Jonathas. And I shall bryng þat ylke cak
And throw yt in, I undertake.
Out! Out! yt werketh me wrake!
I may not awoyd yt owt of my hond.
I wylle goo drenche me in a lake.
And in woodnesse I gynne to wake!
I rene, I lepe ouer þis land.   423

I cannot cast it from my hand.

I begin to go mad.

Her he renneth wood, with the Ost in hys hond.

Jason. Renne, felawes, renne, for Cokkis peyn!
Fast we had ower mayster agene!
Hold prestly on thys pleyn
  & faste bynd hyme to a poste.
Jasdon. Here is an hamer & naylys iij, I s[e]ye;
Lyffte vp hys armys, felawe, on hey,
Whyll I dryue þes nayles, I yow praye,
  With strong¹ strokis fast.   431

Run, fellows:

bind him to a post.

Here are hammer and nails.

Masphat. Now set on, felouse, with mayne & myght,
And pluke hys armes awey in syght!
Wat! I se he twycche, felovse, a-ryght!
Alas, balys breweth ryght badde!   435

Now pluck his arms away.

Here shall thay pluke þe arme, & þe hand shalle hang stylle with þe Sacrament.

Malchus. Alas, alas, what deuyll ys thys?
Now hat[h] he but oon hand i-wyse!
For sothe, mayster, ryght woo me is
  þat ye þis harme haue hadde.   439

Alas! what devil is this! Now he has only one hand.

Jonathas. Ther ys no more; I must enduer!
Now hastely to ower chamber lete us gon;
Tyll I may get me sum recuer;
And therfor charge yow euery-choon
That yt be consell that we have doon.   444
                                      [*Exeunt.*]

I must endure it:

till I get some remedy.

Here shall þe lechys man come into þe place sayng:

Colle. Aha! here ys a fayer felawshyppe,
Thewhe I be nat sh[a]pyn, I lyst to sleppe:
I haue a master I wolld he had þe pyppe,
  I tell yow in consel.   448

Ah! here is a fair fellowship.

¹ Crossed out in the MS.

My master
is a man of
science: but
of no thrift.

He ys a ma*n* off aħ syence,
But off thryfte—I may wit*h* yow dyspe*n*ce !
He syttyth wit*h* su*m* tapstere in þe spence :
    Hys hoode there wyħ he seħ.   452

Master Brun-
dyche of
Brabant is
his name.

Mayster Brendyche of Braban,
I telle yow he ys þat same ma*n*,
Called þe most famous phesy[cy]an
    þat eue*r* sawe uryne.   456

He sees as
well at noon
as at night.

He seeth as wele at noone as at nyght,
And su*m*tyme by a candelleyt
Can gyff a judgyment aryght—
    As he þ*at* hathe noo eyn.   460

He is a bone-
setter,

and in every
tavern
debtor:
which is a
good sign.

He ys allso a boone-setter ;
I knowe no man go þe better ;
In euery tau*er*ne he ys detter ;
    þat ys a good tokenyng.   464
But eue*r* I wonder he ys so long ;
I fere ther gooth sum-thyng awrong,
For he hath dysa[rv]yde to be hong,—
    God se*n*d neue*r* worse tydyng !   468

He had a lady late in cure ;
I wot by þis she ys full sure ;
There shall neue*r* *Crys*ten creature
    Here hyr tell no tale.   472

If I stood
here till mid-
night, I could
not tell my
master's cun-
ning insight
in good ale.

And I stode here tyħ mydnyght,
I cowde not declare aryght
My masteris cu*n*yng insyght—
    þat he hat[h] in good ale.   476

What devil
delayeth him!

But what deuyll delayeth hym, so long to tarye !
A seekman myght soone myscary.
Now alle þe deuyllys of hell hym wari ;
    God giue me my boon !   480

We will make
a cry.

I trowe best, we mak a crye :
Yf any ma*n* can hym aspye[1]
Led hym to þe pyllere[ye] :
    In fayth, yt shall be don.   484

---

[1] MS. appears to have *cam I aspye.*

Here shalle he stond vp & make proclamacion, seyng thys :

Colle. Yff therbe eyther man or woman
    That sawe Master Brundyche of Braban,
    Or owyht of hym tel can,
      Shall wele be quit hys mede ;   488
    He hath a cut berd & a flatte noose,
    A therde-bare gowne & a rente hoose ;
    He spekyt[h] neuere good matere nor purpoose ;
      To þe pyllere ye hym led[e].   492

Has any man seen master Brundyche ?

He has a cut beard, flat nose, thread-bare gown and rent hose.

[*The master has entered during the proclamation.*]

Master Brundyche. What, thu boye, what ! janglest
    here ?
Coll[e]. A ! master, master, but to your reuerence !
    I wend neuer to a seen yowr goodly chere,
      Ye tared hens so long.   496
Master Brundyche. What hast thow sayd in my absense ?
Coll[e]. Nothyng, master, but to yowr reuerence,
    I haue told all þis audiense—
      And some lyes among.   500

What, bab-blest thou here ?

Alas, master,

ye tarried so long.

What hast thou said ?

Nothing but to your rever-ence—and some lies as well.

    But, master, I pray yow, how dothe yowr pacyent
    That ye had last vnder yowr medycamente ?
Master Brundyche. I warant she neuer fele anoyment.
    Coll[e]. Why, ys she in hyr graue ?   504
Master Brundyche. I haue gyven hyr a drynke made full
    well
    Wyth scamely and with oxennell,
    Letuce, sauge and pympernell.
Colle. Nay, than she yt full saue,   508

How doth your patient ?

I have given her a drink of scamely and oxennell, etc.

Then she is safe.

    For, now ye ar cum, I dare well saye
    Betwyn Douyr & Calyce þe ryght wey
    Dwellth non so cunnyng, be my fey,
      In my judgyment.   512
Master Brundyche. Cunnyng ? Yea, yea, & with pratise ;
    I haue sauid many a manys lyfe.
Coll[e]. On wydowes, maydese and wy[v]se
      Yowr connyng yow haue nyhe spent.   516

Between Calais and Dover there dwells no man so cun-ning as you.

*M*aster *B*rundyche. Were ys bowgtt wi*th* drynke *pro*-
fytable?

Coll[e]. Here mast*er*, mast*er*, ware how ye tugg.
The devyℍ, I trowe, wi*th*in shrugg,
For yt gooth rebyℍ rable.   520

Here is a
great congre-
gation.
*M*aster *B*rundyche. Here ys a grete congregacyon,
And aℍ be not hole, wi*th*out negacyon ;
I wold have certyfycacyon :

Stand up and
make pro-
clamation.
Stond vp & make a p*r*oclamacion.   524
Haue do faste, and make no pausa[c]yon,
But wyghtly make a declaracion
To aℍ people þat helpe w[o]lde haue.   527
Hic int*er*im *proclamatio*nem *faciet.*

All manner
of men who
have sickness
turn to
master Brun-
dyche:
Coll[e]. All manar off me*n* þat haue any syknes,
To Mast*er* Brentberecly loke þat yow redresse.
What dysease or syknesse þat eu*er* ye haue,
He wyll neu*er* leue yow tyℍ ye be i*n* yow[r] graue.
Who hat[h] þe canker, þe colyke, or þe laxe,
The tercyan, þe quartan, or þe brynny[n]g axs,—
For wormys, for gnawy*n*g, grindy*n*g in þe wombe or
in þe boldyro—   534
Alle maner red eyn, bleryd eyn, and the myregrym
also,
For hedache, bonache, & therto þe tothache,—
The colt-euyll, and the brostyn men he wyll undertak,
All tho þat [haue] þe poose, þe sneke, or þe teseke,—
Thowh a ma*n* w[e]re ryght heyle, he cowd soone make
hym seke.

inquire for
him at the
Tolkote, his
lodging,
beside Bab-
well Mill.
Inquyre to þe Tolkote, for ther ys hys loggyng,
A lytyℍ besyde Babweℍ Myℍ, yf ye wyll haue under-
stondyng.   541

*M*aster *B*rundyche. Now, yff therbe ether ma*n* or
woma*n*
That nedethe helpe of a phesyscion—
Coll[e]. Mary, mast*er*, þat I tell can,
& ye wyll vnderstond.[1]   545

---

[1] Written to the right in the margin.

Master Brundyche. Knoest any abut þis plase?

Coll[e]. Ye, þat I do, master, so haue grase;

Here ys a Jewe, hyght Jonathas,

Hath lost hys ryght hond. 549

Master Brundyche. Fast to hym I wold inquere.

Coll[e]. For God, mas*ter*, þe gate ys hyre.

Master Brundyche. Than to hym I wyll go nere. 552

My master, wele mot yow be!

Jonathas. What doost here, felawe? what woldest thu hanne?

Master Brundyche. Syr, yf yow nede ony surgeon or physycyan,

Off yow[r] dysese help yow welle I cane,

What hurt*is* or hermes so-eu*er* they be. 557

Jonathas. Syr, thu art ontawght to come in thus henly,

Or to pere in my presence thus malap*er*tly.

Voydeth from my syght, & þat wyghtly,

For ye be mysse-a-vysed. 561

Coll. Syr, þe hurt of yowr hand ys knowen full ryfe,

And my mast*er* have sauyd many a manes lyfe.

Jonathas. I trowe ye be cum to make sum stryfe.

Hens fast, lest þat ye be chastysed. 565

Coll[e]. Syr, ye know well yt can nott mysse;

Men that be masters of scyens be p*ro*fytable.

In a pott yf yt please yow to pysse,

He can tell yf yow be curable. 569

[*Jonathas.*] Avoyde, fealows, I love not yow*er* bable!

Brushe them hens bothe & that anon!

Gyff them ther reward þat they were gone! 572

Here shall þe iiij Jewys bett away þe leche & hys man.

Jonathas. Now haue don, felawys, & that anon,

For dowte of drede what after befall!

I am nere masyd, my wytte ys gon;

Therfor of helpe I pray yow all. 576

And take yowr pynsonys þat ar so sure,

&ˌpluck owt the naylys won & won;

Also in a cloke ye yt cure

& throw yt in þe cawdron, & þat anon. 580

Sidenotes: Knowest thou any about this place? Yea, here is a Jew called Jonathan, who hath lost his right hand. What doest thou here? Sir, if you need any surgeon or physician, I am here to help. Sir, thou art untaught to come in thus. Out of my sight. Sir, the hurt to your hand is well known. You come to make some strife. Men that are masters in science are profitable. Out, fellows, I love not your babble. Now have done. I am nearly mad. Take out the nails and cast it in a cauldron.

Here shaH Jason pluck owt the naylys & shake þe
hand into þe cawdron.

Jason. And I shaH rape me redely anon
    To plucke owt the naylys that stond so fast,
    & bear thys bred & also thys bone
    & into the cawdron I wyH yt cast.   584

Jasdon. And I shaH with thys dagger so stowte
    Putt yt down that yt myght plawe,
    & steare the clothe rounde abowte
    That nothyng ther-of shalbe rawe.   588

Masphat. And I shaH manly, with aH my myght ;
    Make the fyre to blase & brenne,
    & sett thervnder suche a lyght
    That yt shaH make yt ryght thynne.   592

Here shaH þe cawdron byle, apperyng to be as blood.

Malchas. Owt & harow ! what deuyH ys here-in ?
    Alle thys oyle waxyth redde as blood,
    & owt of the cawdron yt begynnyth to rinn.
    I am so aferd I am nere woode.   596

Here shaH Jason & hys compeny goo to ser Jonathas
sayng :

Jason. Ah ! master, master, what there ys with yow,
    I can not see owr werke wyll avayle ;
    I beseche yow avance yow now
    Sumwhatt with yowr counsayle.   600

Jonathas. The best counsayle that I now wott,
    That I can deme, farre & nere,
    Ys[1] to make an ovyn as redd hott
    As euer yt can be made with fere ;   604

And when ye see yt soo hott appere,
    Then throw yt into the ovyn fast,—
    Sone shaH he stanche hys bledyng chere,—
    When ye haue done, stoppe yt,— be not agast ! 608

Marginal notes:
- I will pluck out the nails
- and cast it into the cauldron.
- I will stir it round with this dagger.
- I will make the fire burn.
- Out, what devil is this? The oil is become blood.
- Master, give us your counsel.
- Make an oven red hot,
- and throw it into the oven to stop the bleeding.

---

[1] Was written by the scribe in the preceding verse, but its proper place is evidently here.

Jasdon. Be my fayth, yt shalbe wrowgh[t],
    & that anon, in gret hast.
Bryng on fyryng, ser*is*, here ye nowght ?
    To hete thys ovyn be nott agast.   612

It shall be done.

Bring firing.

Masphat. Here is straw & thornys kene :
    Come on, Malchas, & bryng on fyre,
For that shall hete yt well, I wene ;
          Here þei kyndyll þe fyre.
Blow on fast, that done yt were !   616

Here is fire.

Malchas. Ah, how ! thys fyre gynnyth to brenne clere !
    Thys ovyn ryght hotte I thynk to make.
Now, Jason, to the cawdron þat ye stere
And fast fetche hether that ylke cake.   620

Now, Jason, stir the cauldron and fetch the cake.

Here shall Jason goo to þe cawdron and take owt the Ost with hys pynsonys and cast yt in-to the ovyn.

Jason. I shall with thes pynsonys without dowt,
    Shake thys cake owt of thys clothe,
& to the ovyn I shall yt rowte
    And stoppe hym there, thow he be loth.   624

I bring it with these pincers.

Thys cake I haue caught here in good sothe,—
    The hand ys soden, the fleshe from þe bonys,—
Now into the ovyn I wyll therwith.
    Stoppe yt, Jasdon, for the nonys !   628

Stop it, Jasdon, for the present.

Jasdon. I stoppe thys ovyn, wythowtyn dowte,
    With clay I clome yt vppe ryght fast,
That non heat shall cum owte.
    I trow there shall he hete & drye in hast !   632

I stop it and seal it with clay.

Here the ovyn must ryve asunder & blede owt at þe cranys, & an image appere owt with woundis bledyng.

Masphat. Owt ! owt ! here is a grete wonder !
    Thys ovyn bledyth owt on euery syde !
Malchas. Yea, þe ovyn on peacys gynnyth to ryve asundere ;
    Thys ys a mervelows case thys tyde.   636

Out! the oven bleedeth on every side.

Here shall þe image speke to the Juys sayng thus :
Jhesus. O mirabiles Judei, attendite et videte
     Si est dolor sicut[1] dolor meus.   638

Oh Jews, why
are ye unkind
to your King?
Oh ye merveylows Jewys,
    Why ar ye to yower kyng onkynd,
    & [I] so bytterly bowt yow to my blysse ?
    Why fare ye thus fule with yowr frende ?   642

Why do ye
torture Me?
Why peyne yow me and straytly me pynde,
    And I yower loue so derely haue bowght ?
    Why are ye so vnstedfast in your mynde ?
    Why wrath ye me ? I greve yow nowght.   646

Why will ye
not believe?
Why wyll ye nott beleve that I haue tawght,
    And forsake your fowle neclygence,
    And kepe my commandementis in yower thowght,
    And vnto my godhed to take credence ?   650

Why do ye
blaspheme
and torment
Me?
Why blaspheme yow me ? Why do ye thus ?
    Why put yow me to a new tormentry,
    And I dyed for yow on the crosse ?
    Why consyder not yow what I dyd crye ?   654

While I was
with you,
ye did me
injury.
Whyle that I was with yow, ye ded me velanye.
    Why remember ye nott my bitter chaunce,
    How yower kynne dyd me awance
    For claymyng of myn enherytaunce ?
    I shew yow the streytnesse of my greuaunce,
    And all to meue yow to my mercy.   660

Jonathas. Tu es protector vite mei ;[2] a quo trepidabo ?
Thou art my
protector, of
whom shall I
be afraid?
O thu, Lord, whyche art my defendowr,
    For dred of the I trymble & quake.
    Of thy gret mercy lett vs receyue þe showre ;
    & mekely I aske mercy, amendys to make.   665

Here shall they knele doun all on ther kneys, saying :—
Let us bap-
tize our
hearts with
our tears.
Jason. Ah ! Lord, with sorow & care & grete wepyng
    All we felawys lett vs saye thus,
    With condolent harte & grete sorowyng :   668
    Lacrimis nostris conscienciam nostram baptizemus !

       [1] MS. has *similis.*   [2] MS. has *mee.*

Jasdon. Oh thow blyssyd Lord of mykyłł myght,
Of thy gret mercy, thou hast shewyd vs þe path,
Lord, owt of grevous slepe & owt of dyrknes to lyght,
Ne grauis sompnus irruat. 673

O, Thou, Blessed Lord, hast showed us the path from darkness to light.

Masphat. Oh Lord, I was very cursyd, for I wold know
þi crede.
I can no men[d]ys make, but crye to the thus :
O gracyows Lorde, forgyfe me my mysdede !
With lamentable hart : *miserere mei, Deus !* 677

Have mercy on me, O God!

Malchas. Lord, I haue offendyd the in many a sundry
vyse,
That styckyth at my hart as hard as a core.
Lord, by þe water of contryc[i]on lett me aryse :
Asparges me, Domine, ysopo, et mundabor. 681

Cleanse me with hyssop, O Lord.

Jhesus. All ye that desyryn my seruauntis for to be
And to fulfyłł þe preceptis of my lawys,
The intent of my commandement knowe ye :
Ite et ostendite vos sacerdotibus meis. 685

Go show yourselves to my priests.

To all yow þat desyre in eny wyse
To aske mercy, to graunt yt redy I am.
Remember & lett yower wyttis suffyce,
Et tunc non auertam a vobis faciem meam. 689

I will not turn away my face from you.

Ser Jonathas, on thyn hand thow art but lame,
And þis thorow thyn own cruelnesse.
For thyn hurt þow mayest þi-selfe blame,
Thow woldyst preve thy power me to oppresse ; 693

Sir Jonathan,

But now I consydre thy necesse ;
Thow wasshest thyn hart with grete contryc[i]on ;
Go to the cawdron,—þi care shalbe the lesse,—
And towche thyn hand to thy saluac[i]on. 697

go to the cauldron and touch thy hand to thy salvation.

*Here shall ser Jonathas put hys hand in-to þe cawdron,
and it shalbe hole agayn ; & then say as fo[lo]wyth :*

Jonathas. Oh thow my Lord God and Sauyouer, osanna !
Thow Kyng of Jews & of Jerusalem !
O thow myghty, strong Lyon of Juda,
Blyssyd be the tyme þat þow were in Bedlem ! 701

O Lord God, blessed be the time when Thou wast born in Bethlehem.

Oh þou myghty, strong, gloryows and *gra*cyows oyle
    streame,

O, Almighty
Conqueror,

Thow myghty conquerrowr of infernaꝶ tene,
I am quyt of moche combrance thorowgh thy meane,
That euyr blyssyd mott þow bene!   705

alas, that I
acted against
Thy will.

Alas, þat eu*er* I dyd agaynst thy wyꝶ,
    In my wytt to be soo wood;
That I w*it*h ongoodly wyrk shuld soo gryꝶ!
    A3ens my mys-gou*er*nau*n*ce thow gladdyst me w*it*h
      good :   709

I was soo prowde to prove the on þe Roode,
    & þou haste sent me lyghtyng þat late was lame;
To bete the & boyꝶ the I was myghty in moode,
    & now þou hast put me from duresse and dysfame.

But, Lord, I take my leve at thy high presens,   714
    & put me in thy myghty mercy;

I will go
fetch the
bishop, and
show him our
offence.

The bysshoppe wyꝶ I goo fetche to se ower offens,
    & onto hym shew ower lyfe, how þat we be gylty.

*Here shall þe ma*st*er Jew goo to þe byshopp & hys men
    knele styll.*

Hail, father
of grace,

Jonathas. Hayle, father of grace! I knele vpon my knee,
    Hertely besechyng yow & i*n*terely,
A swemfuꝶ syght aꝶ for to see
    In my howse apperyng verely :   721

The holy Sacrament, þe whyche we haue done tor-
    me*n*try,

we have put
Him to a new
passion.

And ther we haue putt hym to a newe passyon,
A chyld apperyng w*it*h wondys bloody :
A swemfuꝶ syght yt ys to looke vpon.   725

*Ep*iscopus. Oh Jhe*s*u, Lord, fuꝶ of goodnesse!
    W*it*h the wyꝶ I walke w*it*h aꝶ my myght.
Now, aꝶ my pepuꝶ, w*it*h me ye dresse
    For to goo see that swymfuꝶ syght.   729

Now, aꝶ ye peple that here are,
    I co*m*mande yow, euery man,
On yow*er* feet for to goo, bare,
    In the devoutest wyse that ye can.   733

Here shall þe bysshope enter into þe Jewys howse
               & say :

O Jhesu fili Dei   O Jesu, Son
                                                           of God,
  How thys paynfull passyon rancheth my*n* hart !
Lord, I crye to the, *miserere mei,*   have mercy
                                                           on me.
  From thys rufull syght þou wylt reue*r*te. 737

Lord, we all wi*th* sorowys smert,
  For thys vnlefull work we lyue in langowe*r* ;
Now, good Lord, in thy grace let vs be grett,   Send us help
                                                           of Thy mercy.
  & of thy soue*r*eyn marcy send vs thy socower; 741

& for thy holy grace forgyfe vs ower errowr.
  Now lett thy pece [1] spryng and sprede ;
Thowgh we haue be vnrygh[t]full, forgyf vs o*ur*   Forgive us
                                                           our error.
    rygore,   744
  & of owe*r* lamentable hart*is*, good Lord, take hed[e].

Here shall þe im[a]ge change agayn onto brede.

Oh th[o]u largyfluent Lord, most of lyghtnesse,
  Onto owr prayers thow hast applyed :
Th[o]u hast receyuyd them wi*th* grett swettnesse,
  For all ower dredfull dedys þou hast not so denyed.

Full mykyll owte thy name for to be magnyfyed
  Wi*th* mansuete myrth and gret swettnes,
& as o*ur* gracyows God for to be gloryfyed,
  For th[o]u shewyst vs gret gladnes.   753

Now wyll I take thys Holy Sacrament   Now I take
                                                           this Holy
  Wi*th* humble hart & gret devoc[i]on,   Sacrament
And all we wyll gon wi*th* on consent
  And bear yt to chyrche wi*th* sole[m]pne pro-   and bear it
                                                           again to
    cessyon ;   757   church.

Now folow me, all & sume !   All follow me,
                                                           singing,
  And all tho that bene here, both more & lesse,
Thys holy song, *O sacru*m *Dominum,*   O Holy Lord.
  Lett us syng all wi*th* grett swetnesse.   761

        [1] MS. has *petc.*

Here shall þe pryst, ser Isoder, aske hys master what þis menyth.

Sir Aristo-
rius, what
meaneth
this ?
Presbiter. Ser Arystory, I pray yow, what menyth all
thys ?

Sum myracle, I hope, ys wrowght be Godd*is* myght ;
The bysshope co*m*myth [in] processyon w*ith* a gret
meny of Jewys ;
I hope sum myracle ys shewyd to hys syght.   765

To chyrche in hast wyll I runn*e* full ryght,
For thether, me thyn̄k, he begynnyth to take hys
pace.
The Sacrame*n*t so semly is borne in syght,
I hope that God hath shewyd of his grace.   769

I will tell you
the truth:
*Arystor*ius. To tell yow the trowth I wylle not lett :
Alas þ*at* eu*er* thys dede was dyght !
An onlefull bargayn I began for to beát ;
I sold our
Lord to those
same Jews.
I sold yon same Jewys ow*er* Lord full ryght   773
For couytyse of gold,[1] as a cursyd wyght.
Woo the whyle that bargayn I dyd eu*er* make !
But yow be my defensour in owr dyocesans syght ;
For an heretyke I feare he wyll me take.   777

Your wit was
not well ad-
vised,
Presbiter. For sothe, nothyng well-avysed was your wytt ;
Wondrely was yt wrowght of a man of dyscresc[i]on
to put your
soul into such
peril.
In suche p*er*ayle yo*ur* solle for to putt ;
But I wyll labor for yo*ur* absolucyon.   781

Let us hasten
thither
to make
amends.
Lett vs hye vs fast that we were hens,
And beseche hym of hys benygne g*r*ace,
That he wyll shew vs his benyvolens
.To make amendys [2] for yow*er* trespas.   785

*Here shall þe merchant and hys prest go to þe chyrche & þe
bysshop shall entre þe chyrche and lay þe Os[t] v[p]on
þe auter, sayng thus :*

[*Episcopus.*] *Estote fortes in bello et pugnate cum antico
serpente,
Et accipite regnum eternum, et cetera.*   787

---

[1] MS. has certainly *good*, but the sense seems to require *gold*.
[2] MS. *menyn.*

My chyldern, be ye [1] strong in batayℋ gostly

    For to fyght agayn the fell serpent,

That nyght and day ys eu*er* besy ;

    To dystroy owr sollys ys hys intent.   791

Be strong in battle, and fight the old serpent.

Look ye [2] be not slow nor neclygent

    To arme you in the ve*r*tues seuyn ;

Of synnys fo*r*getyn take good avysement,

    And knowledge them to yow*er* confessor fuℋ euyn ;   795

Arm you in the seven virtues.

For that se*r*pent, the deuyℋ, ys fuℋ strong

    Meruelows myscheues for man to mene ;

But that the Passyon of Cryst ys meynt vs among,

    And that ys in dyspyte of hys infernaℋ tene.   799

Beseche ow*er* Lord & Sauyow*er* so kene

    To put doun that se*r*pent, cu*m*berer of man,

To wi*th*draw hys furyous froward doctryn bydene,

    Fulfyllyd of þe fend callyd Leuyathan.   803

Beseech your Lord to put down the serpent.

Gyff lawreℋ to that Lord of myght

    That he may bryng vs to the joyous fruycion,

From vs to put the fend to flyght,

    That neu*er* he dystroy vs by hys temptac[i]on. 807

Give laurel to that Lord of might.

*Pr*es*bit*er. My father vnder God, I knele vnto yow*er* kne,

    In yowr myhty mys*er*icord to tak vs in reme*m*brance ;

As ye be materyaℋ to ow*er* degre,

    We put vs in yow*er* moderat ordynance,   811

Yff yt lyke yow*er* hyghnes to here ow*er* greuau*n*ce ;

    We haue offenddyd sorowfully in a syn mortaℋ,

Wherfor we fere vs owr Lord wyℋ take vengaunce

    For owr synnes both grete and smaℋ.   815

We have offended direly.

*Ep*iscop*us.* And in fatherhed, that longyth to my dygnyte,

    Vnto yow*er* grefe I wyℋ gyf credens.

Say what ye wyℋ, in þe name of the Trynyte,

    Agayn[s]t God yf ye haue wroght eny inco*n*ueny-ence.   819

Say on.

[1] MS. has *ye be.*   [2] MS. *be ye.*

Aristorius. Holy Father, I knele to yow vnder bene-
   dycite.

I have
offended in
the sin of
covetous-
ness,

I haue offendyd in the syn of couytys :
 I sold *our* Lordys body for lucre of mony
  & delyu*er*yd to the wyckyd *with* cursyd advyce. 823

and presumed
to go to the
altar.

And for that p*re*sumpc[i]on gretly I agryse
 That I p*re*sumed to go to the auter
  There to handylle þe holy sacryfyce,—
   I were worthy to be putt in breny*n*g fyre. 827

But, gracyous lord, I can no mo*re*,
 But put me to Goddys m*er*cy & to yow*er* grace :
  My cursyd werkys for to restore,
   I aske penaunce now in thys place. 831

For this
offence do
good deeds,

*Ep*iscop*us.* Now for thys offence that þou hast donne
 A3ens the Kyng of Hevyn & Emper*our* of Hełł,
  Eu*er* whyłł þou lyuest good dedys for to done

and renounce
buying and
selling.
Chastise thy
body,
fast and pray.

   And neu*er*more for to bye nor sełł : 835
Chastys thy body as I shall the tełł,
 With fastyng & prayng & other good wyrk,
  To *with*stond the temtacyon of fend*is* of hell ;
   & to całł to God for grace looke þou neu*er* be
    irke. 839

Thou, priest,
for thy negli-
gence
deservest
imprison-
ment.

Also, þou preste, for thy neclygens,
 That thou were no wyser on thyn office,
  Thou art worthy inp*re*su[n]ment for thyn offence ;
   But beware eu*er* herafter ånd be mor wyse. 843

And ałł yow creaturys & curatys that here be,
 Off thys dede yow may take example
  How that you*r* lockys pyxyd ye shuld see,[1]

Beware of the
key of God's
temple.
I ask for us
all a general
absolution.

   And beware of the key of Goddys temple. 847

Jonathas. And I aske crystendom *with* great devoc[i]on,
 With repentant hart in all degrees,
  I aske for vs all a gen*er*ałł absoluc[i]on.

   Here þe Jays must knele al down.

  For that we knele ałł vpon ow*er* knees ; 851

    MS. has *pyxys lockyd.*

For we haue greuyd ow*er* Lord on grovnd

     & put hym to a new paynfuħ passion :

     W*ith* daggars styckyd hym w*ith* greuos wo[u]nde,

     New naylyd hym to a post & w*ith* pynsonys pluckyd

        hym down.   855

We have grieved our Lord and put Him to a new passion.

Jason. And syth we toke that blyssyd bred so sownd

     And in a cawdron we dyd hym boyle,

     In a clothe fuħ just we hym wou*n*de

     And so dyd we seth hym in oyle.   859

We boiled Him in a cauldron,

Jasdon. And for that we myght not oue*r*com hym w*ith*

       tormentry,

     In an hott ovyn we speryd hym fast,

     Ther he apperyd with wo[u]nd*is* all bloody :

     The ovyn rave asund*er* & aħ to-brast.   863

and shut Him in an oven.

Masphat. In hys law to make vs stedfast,

     There spak he to vs woord*is* of grete favor ;

     In contrycyon owr hart*is* he cast

     And bad take vs to a confessor.   867

He bade us take a confessor.

Malchus. And, therfor, all we w*ith* on consent

     Knele onto yow*er* hygh soue*r*eynte,

     For to be crystenyd ys ow*er* intent ;

     Now all ow*er* dedys to yow shewyd haue we.   871

Therefore we all kneel to your high sovereignty.

Here shall þe *bysshope crysten* þe *Jewys w*ith* gret*

solempnyte.

*Ep*iscop*us.* Now the Holy Gost at thys tyme mot yow

     blysse

     As ye knele aħ now in hys name,

     And w*ith* the water of baptyme I shaħ yow blysse

     To saue yow aħ from the fendis blame.   875

The Holy Ghost bless you.

     Now, that fendys powr*e* for *to* make lame,

     In þe name of þe Fath*er*, þe Son & þe Holy Gost,

     To saue yow from the deuyllys flame,

     I crysten yow aħ, both lest and most.   879

I baptize you in the name of the Father, Son and Holy Ghost.

Ser Jonathas. Now owr father and byshoppe þat we weħ

     know,

     We thank yow interly, both lest and most.

We thank you, both least and greatest.

Now ar we bownd to kepe Crystis lawe
& to *ser*ue þe Father, þe Son & þe Holy Gost.   883

Now wyH we walke by contre & cost,
Our wyckyd lyuyng for to restore :

We will trust
in God, and
never more
offend.

And trust in God, of myght*is* most,
Neuer to offend as we have don before.   887

Now we take ower lea[v]e at lesse & more—
Forward on ow*er* vyage we wyH vs dresse ;
God send yow aH as good welfare
As hart can thynke or towng expresse.   891

Into my
country I will
go, and
amend my
life.

Arystorius. Into my contre now wyH I fare
For to amende myn wyckyd lyfe,
& to kep[e] þe people owt of care
I wyll teache thys lesson to man & wyfe.   895

Now take I my leave in thys place,

I will go do
my penance.

I wyH go walke, my penaunce to fullfyH ;
Now, God, aȝeyns whom I haue done thys trespas,
Graunt me forgyfnesse yf yt be thy wylle !   899

I almost
weep for joy
at this.

Presbiter. For joy of thys me thynke my hart do wepe,
That yow haue gyuyn yow aH Cryst*is* s*er*uaunt*is*
    to be,
Hym for to s*er*ue w*ith* hart fuH meke—
God, fuH of pacyens & humylyte—   903

And the conuersion[1] of aH thes fayre men,
W*ith* hart*is* stedfastly knett in on,
Godd*is* lawys to kepe & hym to serue bydene,
As faythfuH Crystanys eu*er*more for to gon*n*e.   907

Evermore
serve God
Omnipotent.

*E*p*iscopus.* God Omnypotent, euermore looke ye s*er*ue
W*ith* deuoc[i]on & prayre whyH þat ye may ;
Dowt yt not he wyH yow p*r*eserue
For eche good prayer þat ye sey to hys pay ;   911

Serve the
Holy Trinity

& therfor in eu*er*y dew tyme loke ye not delay
For to s*er*ue the Holy Trynyte,

and the
Virgin.

And also Mary, that swete may,
And kepe yow in p*er*fyte loue & charyte.   915

---

[1] MS. *conuersacons.*

Crystis commandementis *ten*[1] there bee ;
Kepe welle them ; doo as I yow teH.
Almyght God shaH yow please in eu*er*y degre,
And so shaH ye saue yow*er* sollys from heH. 919

For there ys payn & sorow crueH,
& in heuyn ther ys both joy & blysse,
More then eny towng can tell,
There angellys syng w*ith* grett swetnesse ; 923

To the whyche he bryng vs
Whoys name ys callyd Jhe*s*us,
And in wyrshyppe of thys name gloryows
To syng to hys honor *Te Deum Laudamus.* 927

Finis.

Keep Christ's ten commandments,

and save your souls from Hell,

where is torment.

Te Deum Laudamus.

Thus endyth the Play of the Blyssyd Sacrament, whyche myracle was don in the forest of Aragon, in the famous cite Eraclea, the yere of ow*er* Lord God M[1] cccc. lxi., to whom be honow*er*, Amen !

The namys & number of the players :

Jh[es]us	Jason, Jude*us* ij^us
Episcopus	Jasdon, Jude*us* iij^us
Aristorius, *Christianus* mercator	Masphat, Jude*us* iiij^us
[Isoder, presbiter]	Malchas, Jude*us* v^tus
Clericus	M[agister] phisicus
Jonathas, Jude*us* I^mus	Colle, seru*us*

IX. may play yt at ease.
R. C.

¹ MS. x.

[THE PRIDE OF LIFE.]

[A MORALITY.]

[PROLOCUTOR.]

Listen, one
and all.

Pees, & horkynt hal ifer,
　[Ric]¹ & por, yong & hold,
Me*n* & weme*n* þat² bet her,
　Bot lerit & leut, stout & bold.　　　　　4

Lordi*n*ge & ladiis þat beth hende,
　Herkenith al w*ith* mylde mode ;
[Swillke]³ ga*m* schal gyn & ende :
　Lorde us wel spede þat sched his blode !　　8

Now stond*i*t stil & beth hende,

Pray for the
weather.

　And prayith⁴ al for þe wed*er*,
[&]¹ ʒe schal or ʒe he*n*nis we*n*de
　Be glad þat ʒe come hidir.　　　　　12

Ye shall hear
of mirth and
care,

Here ʒe schulli*n* here spelle
　Of mirth & eke of kar*e* ;
H*er*kenith & i wol ʒou telle
　[How þe proud]⁵ schal fare.　　　　　16

and of the
King of Life.

[Of þe Kyng of]⁶ Lif, i wol you telle,
　[Qwho stond*i*t] first biffore
[All men þat bet]⁷ of fflessch & ffel
　[& of women i-]bore.　　　　　20

He is of a
kingly race,

[He is, forsot, ful]⁷ stronge to stond,
　[And is]⁸ by comin of kinge,

---

¹ Inserted by Mill : the MS. is unreadable.
² MS. has *y* for þ.　　³ Brandl : *menske gam.*
⁴ The MS. is very faded here, but I believe this to be the true
reading.　Brandl has *and teryith*, and translates *for* as *in spite of.*
⁵ Holthausen [*How þis oure game*].
⁶ Brandl and Holthausen [*Of þe King of*].
⁷ Holthausen.　　⁸ Both Brandl and Holthausen.

[Givet] [1] lawis in eche a londe,
　[& nis] [2] dradd of no thinge, **24** and giveth laws everywhere.

[In] pride & likinge his lif he ledith,
　Lordlich he lokit with eye ; He lives in pride,
[Prin]ce & dukes, he seith, him dredith,
　[And he] dredith no deth ffor to deye. **28** and all fear him.

[He] [3] hath a lady louelich al at likinge, He hath a lovely lady
　Ne may he of no mirth mene ne misse ;
He seit in swetnisse he wol set his likinge
　& bringe his bale boun in to blisse. **32**

Knytis [4] he [5] hat cumlic, and comely knights.
　In bred & in leint ;
Not i neuir non suc
　Of stocey ne off strynt. **36**

Wat helpit [6] to yilp mucil of his mit
　Or bost to mucil of his blys ?
For [3] sorou may sit onis sit
　[& m]yrt[h m]ay [7] he [5] not miss. **40**

& her is ek þe ladi of lond,
　[þe faire]st a lord for [8] to led ;
[& glad] may he [5] be fort to stond
　[& be]hold þat [9] blisful bled. **44**

[þa]t ladi is lettrit in lor The lady is lettered
　As cumli becomit for a quen,
& munit hir mac euirmor, and always warns her mate.
　As a dar for dred him to ten. **48**

Ho bid him bewar or þe [5] suirt, She bids him beware of death,
　[F]or in his lond Det wol alond ;
[As] ho leuit him gostlic in hert
　[Ho b]it him bewar of his hend. **52** and think of his end.

[Ho] begynit to charp of char
　þes wordis wytout lesing ;
" Det dot not spar Death spares neither kaiser nor king.
　Knytis, [10] cayser ne kyng. **56**

---

[1] Both Brandl and Holthausen. 　　[2] Holthausen.
[3] Holthausen. 　[4] MS. *kyntes.* 　[5] MS. *ʒe.*
[6] MS. *lelpit.* 　Mill's emendation.
[7] M. . . . . *mry* . . . perhaps the scribe wrote *ry* for *yr.*
[8] MS. *sort to.* 　　[9] MS. has *y* for þ. 　　[10] MS. *kyntis.*

Leave thy
pleasure.

Nou lord leu þi likynd
   Wyt bringit ȝe soul gret bal."

That is a
woman's tale.

þis[1] answer ho had of þe[2] kyng ;
   "ȝe þis[1] [is] a womanis tal."   60

The King
took it not
to heart.

þe[2] kyng hit ne toke not to hert
   For hit was a womanis spec,
[& y]et hit mad him to smert
   [wh][3]an him mit help no lec.   64

[þe][3] quen yit can hir undirstond
   Wat help þar[1] mit be

The Queen
sent for the
bishop.

& sent aftir þe[1] bi[s]cop[4] of þe[2] lond
   For ho chont mor þan[1] ȝe.   68

He came and
preached all
he knew.

He[2] cham & precit al þat[1] he[2] couþe,
   & warnit him hal of his hind ;
[H]it saurit not in þe[2] kyngis mout
   Bot hom he[2] bad him wynd.   72

Wand þe[2] biscop[4] is yam wend
   Fram þat[1] k[e]ne stryf

Then Death
sent his
messenger
to the King
of Life.

[Deth did a me]ssenger þan[1] send
   [Unto] þe[2] King of Lif.   76

[&] eny him wold do undirston
   [þat now] he[2] may del & dit,

He would
come to try
his might.

[He] wold cum into his ouin lond
   On him to kyt his mit.   80

Deth comit, he[5] dremit a dredfful dreme
   Welle aȝte al carye ;
& slow ffader & moder & þen heme
   He ne wold none sparye.   84

Death and
Life together
strive.

Sone affter hit befel þat Deth & Life
   Beth togeder i-take ;
& ginnith & striuith a sterne strife
   King of Life to wrake.   88

Death feareth
not his
knights.

With him driuith adoun to grounde,
   He dredit nothing his kniȝtis ;
& delith him depe depis wounde
   & kith on him his miȝtis.   92

---

[1] MS. has *y* for þ.   [2] MS. ȝe.   [3] Holthausen.
[4] MS. *bicop*.   [5] MS. *and*.

Qwhe*n* þe body is dou*n* i-bro3t
  þe soule sorow awakith ;
þe bodyis p*r*ide is der*e* a-bo3t,
  þe soule þe ffendis takith.   96

When the body is ill the soul's sorrow awakes.

& throgh p*r*iere of Our*e* Lady mylde
  Al godenisse scho wol qwyte ;
Scho wol p*r*ey he*r* son so mylde
  þe soule & body schul dispyte.   100

Our Lady will reward all goodness.

þe cors þ*at* ner*e* knewe of car*e*,
  No more þe*n* stone i*n* weye,
Schal be of sorow & sore care
  & þrawe be twene ha*m* tweye.   104

þe soule þer on schal be weye
  þat þe ffende*s* haue i-ka3te ;
& Our*e* Lady schal þerfor preye
  So þat wit*h* he*r* he schal be lafte.   108

Our Lady shall pray for the soul caught by the fiends.

Nou be*i*t i*n* pes & be*i*t hende,
  & distourb*i*t no3t our*e* place
ffor þ*i*s our*e* game schal gi*n* & ende
  Throgh Jhe*s*u C*r*istis swete *grace*.   112

Now peace,

our play shall begin and end.

I.

REX VIU*US* *INCIPIET* SIC DICEND*UM*.

Pes, now, 3e p*r*inces of power*e* so prowde,
  3e ki*n*ges, 3e ke*m*pes, 3e kni3te*s* i-korne,
3e barons bolde, þat be*i*t me o bowte ;
  Do schal 3u my sawe, swaynis i[s]worne.   116

Peace, kings, warriors, knights and

Sqwieris stoute, stondit now stille,
  & lesten*i*t to my heste*s* i hote 3u now he*r*,
Or [I] schal wirch 3u wo wit*h* werke*s* of wil
  & dou*n* schal 3e d*r*ive be 3e neu*er* so dere.   120

squires, and listen to my commands.

Ki*n*g ic am, kinde of ki*n*ges i-korre,
  Al þe worlde wide to welde at my wil ;
Nas þer neu*er* no ma*n* of woma*n* i-borre
  O-3ei*n* me wit*h*sto*n*de þat i nold hi*m* spille.   124

I am king of chosen race, and have all the world at my will.

Lordis of lon*d* be*i*t at my ledi*n*ge,
  Al me*n* schal a bow i*n* hal & in bow*r* ;   126

.   .   .   .

Bravely art
thou my
messenger,

the root of
all my rest.

Baldli þou art mi bot,
  Tristili & ful treu ;
Of al mi rast þou art rot,
  I nil chong fer no new.[1]   130

Rex.

Al in wel ic am biwent,
  May ne grisful þing me grou ;
Likyng is wyt me bilent,[2]
  Alyng is it mi behou.   134

Strength
and Health,
my knights,

Strent & hel knytis[3] kete
  Det rift in ded ;[4]
Lak þa*t*[5] for no[6] þing ȝe let
  Smartli to me sped.   138

bring me
bright swords
and shining
helmets.

Bringit wyt þou brit brondis,
  Helmis, brit & schen ;[7]
For ic am lord ofir al londis
  & þa*t* is wel isen.[8]   142

Primus miles, Fortitudo.

Lord, in truþe þou mit trist
  Feþfuli to stond,
þou mit liu as ȝe list,
  For won child[9] is þu fond.   146

I am
Strength,
a none such.

Ic a*m* Strent, stif & strong,
  Neuar is suc non,
In al þis[5] world brod & long,
  I-mad of blod & bon.   150

---

[1] Brandl assigns this stanza to *Regina.*   [2] Skeat.
[3] MS. *kyntes.*   [4] This verse has *one stress* too few.
[5] MS. has *y* for þ.   [6] MS. *ne.*   [7] MS. *schinend.*
[8] MS. *weli scn.*   " [9] MS. *wonschild.*

Hau no dout of no þing[1]
  þat[1] euir may befal;
Ic am Strenyt þi[1] derling
  Flour of knitis al.

Have no fear,

I am Strength, thy favourite.

154

Secundus Miles, Sanitas.

King of lif þat berist þe croun,
  As hit is skil and riȝte;
I am Hele i-com to toun,
  þi kinde curteyse kniȝte.

158

þou art lord of lim & life,
  & king withouten[2] ende;
Stif & strong & sterne in strif,
  In londe qwher þou wende.

I am Health,

162

þou nast no nede to sike sore
  For no þing on lyue;
þou schal lyue euer more:
  Qwho dar with þe striue?

thou hast no need to fear:

thou shalt live evermore.

166

Rex.

Striue? nay, to me qwho is so gode?
  Hit were bot ffolye;
þer is no man þat me dur bode
  Any vileynye.

Who would be so good as to fight with me?

170

Qwher-of schuld i drede
  Qwhen i am King of Life?
Ful evil schuld he spede
  To me þat werch striue.

Of what should I be afraid?

174

I schal lyue ever mo
  & croun ber as kinge;
I ne may neuer wit of wo,
  I lyue at my likinge.

I shall live for ever.

178

Regina.

Sire, þou saist as þe liste,
  þou liuist at þi wille;

---

[1] MS. has *y* for þ.   [2] MS. *with outen.*

Bot so*m*thing þou miste
& þerffor[1] hold þe stille.   182

Think, thou
haddest
beginning :

Thi*n*ke, þou haddist begi*n*ninge
Qwhe*n* þou were i-bore ;

if thou
makest not
good end, thy
soul is lost.

& bot þou mak god endi*n*ge
þi sowle is fforlore.[2]   186

Love God
and Holy
Church.

Loue God & Holy Chirche,
& haue of hi*m* som eye ;
Fo*n*de hi*s* werke*s* for to wirch
& thinke þat þou schal deye.   190

REX.

Thou speak-
est not
cunningly.

Douce da*m*, qwhi seistou so ?
þou spekis no3t as þe sleye.
I schal lyue eue*r* mo
For boþe two þi*n* eye.   194

Wouldst
thou that I
were dead,
that thou
mightest
have another
lord ?

Woldistou þat i were dede
þat þou mi3t haue a new ?
Hore, þe deuil gird of þi hede,
Bot þat worde schal þe rewe !   198

REGINA.

Nay, yet

Dede sire, nay god wote my wil,
þat ne kepte i no3te ;
Hit wolde like me ffull ille
Were hit þareto bro3te.   202

Yet þogh þou be ki*n*ge
Nede schalt haue ende ;

death over-
cometh all
things.

Deth ouercomith[3] al thi*n*ge
Hou-so-eue*r* we wende.   206

REX.

3e, da*m*, þou hast wo*r*dis fale,
Hit comith þe of ki*n*de ;

This is only
a woman's
tale, as ye
shall find.

þi*s* nis bot wome*n* tale
& þat wol þe ffi*n*de.   210

[1] MS. þer *ffor.*   [2] MS. *ffor lore.*   [3] MS. *ouer comith.*

1 ne schal neue*r* deye
  For I am Ki*n*g of Life ;
Deth is vndir myne eye
  & þerffor leue þi st*r*ife.   214

þou dost b*o*t mak my*n* hert sore
  For h*i*t nel no3t helpe ;
I p*r*ey þe spek of hi*m* no more
  Qwh*a*t wolte of hi*m* 3elpe.   218

I shall
never die,
for I am
King of Life.

REGINA.

3ilpe, sire, nay so mot i the ;
  I sigge h*i*t no3t‍ qwherffore,[1]
Bot kin*n*[2] tech*i*t boþe þe & me
  First qwhe*n* we were bore.   222

For dowte of Deth is maist*ri*,
  To wepe & make sorowe ;
Holy writ & p*r*ophecye
  þerof[3] i take to borowe.   226

þerffor,[4] qwhile 3e have mi3te
  & þe worlde at wille,
I rede 3e, se*r*ue God Almi3te
  Boþe loude & stille.   230

þ*i*s world is bot ffantasye
  & fful of trechurye ;
Gode sir*e* for 3oure curteysye
  Take þ*i*s for no ffolye.   234

For God [wot] wel[5] þe soþe,
  I ne sey h*i*t for no fabil ;
Deth wol smyte to þe,
  I*n* ffeith loke þou be stabil.   238

Boast not,

I say it
because
Nature
teaches it
to me.

I advise thee
to serve God
Almighty.

Death will
assuredly
smite thee.

REX.

Qwh*a*t p*r*echistou of Dethis mi3t
  & of his maistrye ?
He ne durst onis w*i*t me fi3t
  For his boþe eye.   242

What preach-
est thou of
Death's
power ?
He durst not
fight me.

---

[1] MS. *qwher ffore*.
[2] MS. *Kin te techit ;* perhaps a case of dittography.
[3] MS. þer *of*.   [4] MS. þer *ffor*.   [5] Holthausen.

Streinth & Hele, qwhat say ȝe
   My kinde korin kniȝtes?

Schal Deth be lord ouer me
   & reue me of miȝtes?   246

I MILES.

Mi lord, so broke I my bronde,

   God yt me fforbede,[1]
þat Deth schold do þe wronge
   Qwhile i am in þi þede.[2]   250

I wol withstonde[3] him with strife
   & make his sidis blede,
& tel him þat þou art King of Life
   & lorde of londe & lede.   254

II MILES.

May I him onis mete
   With þis longe launce,
In ffelde oþer in strete,

   I wol him ȝiue mischaunce.   258

REX.

ȝe, þes be kniȝtes of curteisye
   & doghti men of dede;

Of Deth ne of his maistrie
   Ne have i no drede.   262

Qwher is Mirth my messager,
   Swifte so lefe on lynde;
He is a nobil bachelere
   þat rennis bi þe wynde.   266

Mirth & solas he can make
   & ren so þe ro;
liȝtly lepe oure þe lake
   Qwher-so-euer he go.   270

---

[1] MS. *ffor bede.*   [2] Holthausen.   [3] MS. *with stondc.*

Com & her my talente
Anone & hy þe blyue ;
Qwher any man, as þou has rente,
Dorst with me to striue.   274

Nuncius.

King of Lif & lord of londe,
As þou sittis on þi se,
& florresschist with þi briȝt bronde
To þe i sit on kne.   278

I am Mirth, wel þou wost,   I am Mirth,
  þi mery messagere ;   as thou
þat wostou wel withoute bost   knowest,
  þer nas neuer my pere ;   282

Doȝtely to done a dede   and can
  þat ȝe haue ffor to done ;   bravely do
Hen to Berewik opon[1] Twede   any deed.
  & com oȝein[2] fful sone ;   286

þer is no thing þe i-liche
  In al þis worlde wide ;
Of gold & siluer & robis riche
  & hei hors on to ryde.   290

I haue ben boþe fer & nere   I have been
  In bataile & in strife ;   in battles
Ocke, þer was neuer þy pere,   far and near,
  For þou art King of Life.   and am
                                   without peer.
                                   294

Rex.

Aha[3] ! Solas, now þou seist so,   Aha! thou
  þou miriest me in my mode ;   cheerest me
þou schal boy ar þou hennis go   verily,
  Be auaunsyd bi þe rode.   and shalt be
                                advanced.
                                   298

þou schal haue for þi gode wil   Thou shalt
  To þin auauncemente,   have the
þe castel of Gailispire on þe Hil, castle of
  And þe Erldom of Kente.   Gailispire.
                                   302

---

[1] MS. *o pon.*   [2] MS. *o ȝein.*   [3] MS. *A ha.*

Draw the
cord, Sir
Strength,
I will take
my rest.

Draw þe cord, Sire Streynth,
    Rest I wol now take ;
On erth in brede ne leynth
    Ne was nere ʒet my make.   306

*Et tunc clauso tentorio dicet Regina secrete
nuncio.*[1]

REGINA.[1]

Messenger,
I pray thee

Messager, i pray þe nowe
    For þi curteysye,

go to the
Bishop.

Go to þe bisschop for þi prowe
    & byd him hydir to hye.   310

Bid him
preach to
my lord
the King.

Bid him beware beffore,[2]
    Sey him þat he most preche ;
My lord þe King is ney lore
    Bot he wol be his leche.   314

Say that he

Sey him þat he wol leue noʒt
    þat euer he schal deye ;

is in great
error.

He is in siche errour broʒte
    Of God stont him non eye.   318

NUNCIUS.

Madam,
I tarry not.

Madam,[3] i make no tariyng
    With softe wordis mo ;
For i am Solas, i most singe
    Ouer al qwher i go.   *et cantat.*   322

Sir Bishop,

Sire Bisschop, þou sittist on þi se
    With þi mitir on þi heuede ;

my lady
the Queen
prayeth
thee. . . .

My lady, þe Qwen preyith þe
    Hit schold noʒt be bileuyd.[4]   326
    .   .   .   .   .   .[5]

---

[1] This direction and the word "Regina" occur in the original
before the preceding stanza, but it seems obvious that they must
have been intended to appear here.
[2] MS. *be ware be ffore.*   [3] MS. *Ma dam.*
[4] *bi leuyd.*   [5] Hiatus in MS.

[EPISCOPUS.][1]

þe[2] world is nou so wo-lo-wo,
  In suc bal i-bound[3]
þat[4] dred of God is al ago
  & treut is go to ground.   330   Fear of God and truth are gone from the earth.

Med is mad a demisma*n*,   Meed is a deemsman,
  Streyint betit þe[5] lau ;
Gentyl[6] is mad a cepman
  & truyt is don of dau.   334   and truth has disappeared.

Wyt is nou al trecri,
  Oþis[7] fals & gret ;   Oaths are false,
Play is nou uileni
  & corteysi is let.   338

Lou is nou al lecuri,   love is lechery,
  Cildrin bet onlerit ;
Halliday is glotuni,   and holiday gluttony.
  þis lauis bet irerit.[8]   342

Sot[9] me*n* bet [9] bleynd   True men are blind.
  & lokit al amis ;
He bicomit onkynd
  & þat[4] is reut i-uis.   346

Frend may no man find   Friend, consolation and peace cannot be found.
  Of frouer ne of sib ;
þe[2] ded bet out of mind,
  Gret soru it is to lib.   350

þes[10] ricme*n* bet reuþyles,   The rich are ruthless,
  þe[2] por got to ground,
& fals me*n* bet schamles,[11]   and the false shameless.
  þe sot ic hau i-found.   354

þe[2] ric kyni it[12] is wrong   What the poor do is all wrong in the eyes of the rich
  Al þat þe[13] por dot ;
Far þat[4] is sen day & nit
  Wosa wol sig sot.   358

---

[1] *Mill* : not in MS.   [2] MS. *ʒe.*   [3] MS. *i bound.*
[4] MS. *yat.*   [5] MS. *bet it ʒe.*
[6] MS. *gocyl.* Cf. introd., p. lxv.   [7] MS. *oyis.*
[8] MS. *yis lau is bot irerit.*   [9] MS. *slot, blet.*
[10] MS. *yes.*   [11] MS. *schanles.*
[12] MS. *kynyit it* : dittography, perhaps.   [13] MS. *yat ʒe.*

Men may
think me a
fool for say-
ing this :
but the great,
like fishes,
eat up the
small.

Paraventur me*n* halt me a fol
  To sig þat[1] sot tal ;
þai[1] farit as fiscis[2] in a pol
  þe[3] gret eteit þe[3] smal.   362

Rich men
oppress the
poor,

and think not
of death.

Ric me*n* spart for noþing[1]
  To do þe[3] por wrong[4] ;
þai þingit[1] not on hir ending
  N*e* on Det þat[1] is so strong.   366

They neither
love nor
fear God.

Noþer þai[1] louit God ne dredit
  Noþer[1] hi*m* no his lauis ;
Touart hel fast hi*m* spedit[5]
  A-yeins har ending daus.   370

God give
them grace
to amend.

Bot God of his godnis
  Yif ha*m* gras to amend ;
Into þe[3] delful derkyns
  þe got wytout hend.   374

þer[1] is dred & sorow
  & wo wytoutin wel ;
No ma*n* may oþir[1] borou
  Be þer[1] neuir so fel.   378

þer[1] ne fallit no maynpris,
  Ne super*s*idias ;
þay[6] þe be kyng or iustis
  þe passit not þe[3] pas.   382

Lord, that
died upon
the cross,

Lord, þat[1] for his manhed
  & also for his god,
þat for lou & not for dred
  Deit oppon þe[3] rod,   386

give us grace.

Yif ou gras or lif to led
  þat[1] be ȝour soulis to bot ;
God of Heuin for his godhed
  Leu þat[1] hit so mot.   Amen.   390

Amen.

[1] MS. has *y* instead of þ.   [2] MS. *ficis.*   [3] MS. *ȝe.*
[4] *worng* in MS.   [5] MS. *draut.* Holthausen *spedith.*
[6] MS. *payt.*

TUNC [EPISCOPUS] DICET REGI.

Schir Kyng, þing oppoɴ þin end
    & hou þat¹ þou schalt dey ;
Wat uey þat¹ þou schalt wend
    Bot þou be bisey.   394

Sir King, think upon thine end.

& eke þat¹ þou art lenust man,
    & haddist begyning,
& euirmor hau þout opon
    þi dredful ending.   398

þou schalt þing þanne
    & mac þe² euir þyar
þat¹ Det is not þe² man
    For no þing þe² uil spar.   402

þou schalt do dedis of charite
    & lernen Cristis lor,
& lib in Heuin lit
    To sauy þi¹ soul fre sor.   406

Do deeds of charity, and learn Christ's teaching.

REX.

Qwat ! bissop, byssop babler,
    Schold y of Det hau dred !
þou art bot a chagler
    Go hom þi¹ wey i red.   410

What, bishop babbler !

Go home.

Wat ! coɴ þou þerfor¹ hidir
    Wet Deþ³ me to afer !
Yit þou & he bot⁴ togidir
    Into þe² se igot uer.   414

Comest thou hither to affright us with death ?

Go hom, god yif ȝe sorow,
    þou wreist me in my mod.
War woltou prec tomorou ?
    þou nost uer bi þe² rod !   418

Go home ;

where wilt thou preach to-morrow ?

Troust þou I nold be ded ;
    In mi yyng lif ;
þou lisst screu, bolhed ;
    Euil met þou trive.⁵   422

¹ MS. has *y* instead of þ.   ² MS. *ȝe*.   ³ MS. *deþt*.
⁴ MS. has here *wer*.   ⁵ MS. *triue*.

What should
I do at
Church ?
Wat schold i do at churg ? wat !

Schir bisop wostou eh ![1]

Nay churc nis no wyl coot,[2]

Hit wol abid þer.[3]   426

I leave care
behind,
I wool let car away,

    & go on mi petying.

and go on my
pleasure.
To hontyng & to oþir[4] play

    For al þi[3] long prechyng.   430

I am king,
and have no
need to care.
I am kyng,[5] as þou mit se,

    & hau no ned to char

þe wylen þe.[6] queṅ & meyne

    About me bet yar.   434

EPISCOPUS.

Think, Sir
King,
Thynk, Schir Kyng, one oþir[3] trist

    þat[8] tyng misst son

þot þou leu nou, as ȝe list,

Death will
come soon.
    Det wol cum rit son ;   438

& ȝiue þe dethis wounde

    For þin outrage ;

Wiþin[7] a litil stounde

    þen artou but a page.   442

When thou
art buried
there meet
feet and
earth.
Qwhen þou art grauen on greue

    þer metis fleys & molde ;[8]

þen helpith litil, I wene,

    þi gay croun of golde.   446

Good-day :
Christ in-
struct thee.
Sire Kyng, haue goday,

    Crist i ȝou beteche.[9]

REX.

Farewell,
and learn
better to
preach.
Fare wel, bisschop, þi way

    & lerne bet to preche.   450

                   hic adde

---

[1] MS. *wostouer.*   [2] MS. *cot.*   [3] MS. has *y* instead of þ.
[4] MS. *oir.*   [5] MS. *þyng.*   [6] MS. *ȝe.*   [7] MS. *with in.*
[8] MS. *þat mete ffeyt & molde.* Holthausen : *þi mete is fylt &*
molde.
[9] MS. *be teche.*

Nou, mafay, h*i*t schal be sene,
   I trow, ȝit to daye,
Qwh*er* Deth me durst tene
   & mete i*n* þe waye.   454

Now it shall
be seen
whether
Death dare
meet me.

Qwh*er* artou, my messager*e*,
   Solas bi þi name ?
Lo*k*e þ*at* þou go ffer & ner*e*,
   As þ*o*u wolt haue no blame,   458

Where art
thou,
messenger ?

My banis ffor to crye
   By dayis & bi niȝte ;
& loke þ*at* þou aspye,
   Ȝe bi al þi miȝte,   462

Go thou,
proclaim,

and see
whether

Of Det*h* & of h*i*s maistrye
   Qwh*er* he durst c*om* in siȝte,
Oȝeynis[1] me & my meyne
   W*it*h fforce & armis to ffiȝte.   466

Death dare
come to me.

Loke þ*at* þou go both Est & West
   & c*om* oȝeyne[1] anone[2] ;

Look thou
go East and
West, and
come again
soon.

NU*NCI*US.

Lorde, to wende I am prest,
   Lo now I am gone.   470

I go.

          et *eat* pla[*tea*]

Pes & listenith to my sawe
   Boþe ȝonge & olde ;
As ȝe wol noȝt ben aslawe
   Be ȝe neu*er* so bolde.   474

Peace, listen
both young
and old :

I am a messag*er* i-sente
   Fro*m* þe Ki*n*g of Life ;
þ*at* ȝe schal ffulfil his ente*n*te
   On peyne of lym & lif.   478

I am a
messenger
from the
King of Life.

H*i*s hest*es* to hold & h*i*s lawe
   Yche a man on honde ;
Lest ȝe be he*n*ge & to-draw,[3]
   Or kast i*n* hard bonde.   482

[1] MS. *O ȝeynis, o ȝeyne.*   [2] MS. *an one.*
[3] In MS. prefix is separated.

Ye know that
he is king
and lord of
all lands :
Ȝe wittin wel þat he is king
    & lord of al londis,
Kepere & maister of al thing
    Within se & sondis.   486

I am sent to
know if any
I am sente ffor to enquer
    O-boute ferre & nere,
dare fight
against him.
Ȝif any man dar werre arere [1]
    A-ȝein [1] suche a bachelere.   490

To wroþer hele he was i-bore [1]
    þat wold with him stryue ;
Be him sikir he is i-lore [1]
    As here in þis lyue,   494

Even the
King of
Death.
þegh hit wer King of Deth
    & he so hardy were ;
Bot he ne hath miȝt ne meth
    þe King of Lif to affere [1] ;   498

Be he so hardy or so wode
    In his londe to aryue,[1]
He wol se his herte blode,
    And he with him stryue.   502

· · · · ·

[1] In MS. prefix is separated.

INDEX OF PROPER NAMES.

[In the case of the names of characters from the various plays, the reference is to the first appearance of a particular character.]

Abraham (Habraham), 27/35, 36/1.
Adam, 8/17.
Almayn, 57/17, Germany.
Alysander, 58/21, Alexandria.
Angel, 38/59 ; Angelus, 20/39, 27/26 ; Aungell, 16/100.
Antyoche, 57/17, Antioch.
Aragon (Arigon), 54/11, 56/60, 57/7, 58/50, 63/187, 65/261, and after 87/927.
Aristorius Mercator, 57/1.

Babwell Myll, 74/541.
Bedlem, 1/20, 79/701 ; Bethelem, 1/32, Bethlehem.
Berewik opon Twede, 97/285.
Bosra, 69/363, 368, Basra.
Braban, 57/18, 72/453, Brabant.
Brytayn, 57/18, Britain.

Calabre, 57/19, Calabria, S. Italy.
Caldeys, 58/26, Chaldees.
Caluery, 61/134, 69/369 ; Caluary, 5/31, Calvary.
Calyce, 73/510, Calais.
Cattlyngis, 58/26, Catalauni, inhabitants of 15th century Luxembourg.
Cleophas, 4/6.
Clericus, 59/61.
Coleyn, 57/19, Köln.
Colkote, 74/540.   Vide *Tolkote*.
Colle, 71/445.
Croxston, 56/74.   Cf. Introduction, p. lxiii.

Deabolus, 22/97.
Denmark, 57/20.
Deus, 19/1, 26/1, 37/33.
Doctor, 52/435.
Dolor, 17/111.
Dordrede, 57/20, Dordrecht.
Douyr, 73/510, Dover.

Episcopus, 99/327.
Eraclea, 54/12, 57/6, 59/58, 60/114, and after 87/927, according to the play a city in Aragon.
Erldom of Kente, 97/302.   Cf. Introduction, p. lxviii.
Eva, 10/59.

Farre, 58/22, Faröe (?).
France, 58/22.

Gailispire on the Hil, 97/301.
Galilea, 4/36 ; Galilee, 4/43.
Galys, 58/23, Galicia.
Gene, 57/15, Genoa.
Genewaye, 57/15, Genoa.
God the Father, 13/1.
Gyldre, 58/25, Guelderland.

Hamborowhe, 58/24, Hamburg.
Holond, 58/24, Holland.
Holy Ghost, 17/123.

Isaac (Ysaac), 29/104, 37/28.

Jasun, 61/125.
Jazdun, 61/129.
Jenyse, 57/15.
Jerusalem, 58/25, 79/699.
Jherico, 58/25, Jericho.
Jhesus, 78/638.
Jonathas, 59/69.
Juda, 79/700.

Lachborun, 58/33, Luxemburg.
Lombardy, 58/33.
[Luke], 4/5.

Malchus, 61/137.
Man, 13/25.
Maria ii, 3/3.
Maria iii, 3/1.
Maslphat, 61/133.

GLOSSARY.

O.E. = Old English.   O.F. = Old French.   N.F. = Norman-French.
O.N. = Old Norse.

a, 89/48, she. Cf. *ho.*
achatis, 60/87, agates.
adjutory, 8/7, helper.
afeze, 70/392, drive away, push away. O.E. *fésian.*
agryse, 84/824, am horrified. O.E. *agrisan.*
almundis, 60/99, almonds.
amatystis, 59/81, amethysts.
apeche, 64/222, impeach. O.F. *empecher.*
apert, 7/70, open. O.F. *apert.*
arere, 104/489, rear up, raise up. O.E. *aréran.*
asay, 34/276, 35/316, 37/35, 38/43 ; assaye, 62/146, test, try.
aslawe, 103/473, slain. O.E. *asléan.*
atour, 24/145, at over.
attruenance, 58/48, instruction. Cf. O.F. *estruiance, attruiance* : probably miscopied for 'attrueaunce.'
avoee, 52/428, acknowledge, declare. O.F. *avoer.*
avoyde, 75/570, go away ; awoyd, 71/420, cast away. O.F. *esvuidier.*
awance, 78/657, avenge.

bale, 3/13, 89/32; bal, 90/58; balys, 71/435, calamity, injury, evil. O.E. *bealu.*
banis, 103/459; bans, edicts. O.E. *bann.*
barn, 39/106, child. O.E. *bearn.*
bedene, 5/29 ; bydene, 86/906 ; moreover, also, a common stopgap frequently in use in rhyme-position.
boldyro, 74/534, some part of the body evidently : I do not know of its occurrence elsewhere. It is curious to note that a prominent family of the name of Boldero,

appear to have been connected with Babwell Myll, in Mary's reign, and also probably much earlier.
bot, 100/388, *vide* to bot.
byggly, 61/138, greatly.
calcedonyes, 60/91, chalcedonies.
canker, 74/532, cancer.
cannyngalle, 60/95, canyng of ale, vinegar turned sour.
carye, 90/82, to be anxious. O.E. *cearian.*
cauelacion, 28/71, cavilling. O.F. *cavillacion.*
cepman, 99/333, chapman, merchant. O.E. *ceapman, cypman.*
chagler, 101/409, storyteller, jester, babbler. O.F. *jangleur.*
cham, 90/69, came.
char, 89/53, care. O.E. *cearu.*
charp, 89/53, talk. O.N. *karpa.*
chere, 73/495, face, countenance. N.F. *chere.*
cheue, 61/131, attain an end, succeed. O.F. *chevir.*
chont, 90/68, knew. O.E. *cunnan.*
clink, 25/187, clinch, clench, clink. Cf. Middle Dutch, *clinken.*
clome, 77/630, *i. e.* cleme, smear. O.E. *clǽman.*
clowtis, 69/372, blows, strokes.
colt-euyll, 74/537, a swelling in the genitals, usually referring to horses. MS. reads Toltugℓℓ.
condescent, 58/43, yielding.
congruent, 8/5, accordant, suitable, proper.
connyng, 9/26, 31, knowledge, wisdom.
consayue, 6/59, conceive.
counfer, 33/247, perhaps a miscopying of counter, on account of.

crepawdis, 60/91, precious stones, ? toadstones.

cure, 75/579, take care of. O.F. *curer.*

daliaunce, 26/6, 27/41, pleasure, dalliance.

dau (of), 99/334, killed.

dell, 46/256, 52/408, part. O.E. *dœl.*

deme, 76/602, judge, think. O.E. *dēman.*

demisman, 99/331, judge.

derewourthy, 59/85, derewordy, 52/411, precious. O.E. *dēorwyrðe.*

dight, 34/304; dyght, 70/412, 82/771, prepare, set in order, do. O.E. *dihtan.*

dokettis, 65/236, ducats.

dole, 5/29, grief. O.F. *doel, duel, deul.*

dolloure, 13/19, grief.

doluen, 5/19, buried. O.E. *pp.* of *delfan.*

drenche, 71/421, drown. O.E. *drencan.*

dulcett, 60/98, sweet.

duresse, 80/713, hardship, harm. O.F. *duresce.*

dystrie, 63/200, destroy. O.F. *destruire.*

emerawdis, 59/86, emeralds.

empery, 8/2, empyrean, empire. O.F. *emperie.*

entent, 6/49, takes intent, look after.

eueryschon, 51/401, euerychoon, 71/443, all, every one. O.E. *œfre œlc an.*

fale, 94/207, proper, estimable.

fang, 4/6, seize, catch. Cf. O.N. *fanga.*

fare, 66/289, fayre, 23/140, go; 78/642, behave; 66/291, fare, victuals. Cf. O.E. *faran.*

fee, 20/34, 67/302, cattle. O.E. *feoh.*

fenesters, 21/58, windows. O.F. *fenestre.*

fere, 27/47; company, 29/108, companion. O.E. *gefera.*

fesycyoun, 65/263, physician.

ffel, 88/19, skin. O.E. *fel.*

fond, 6/44; ffonde, 94/189, try. O.E. *fandian.*

fordo, 24/168, destroy. O.E. *fordōn.*

forse, 28/80, no forse, it is no matter.

forthinks, 22/91, regrets. O.E *forþencan.*

fray, 37/24, terror; 69/375, frighten.

frouer, 99/348, comfort, consolation. O.E. *frōfor.*

ʒard, 42/170, rod, staff. O.E. *gerd, gierd.*

gare, 23/112, make, prepare. O.E. *gearwian.*

gate, 75/551, way. O.N. *gata.*

gaynest, 5/9, shortest.

ʒelpe, 95/218; ʒilpe, 95/219, boast. O.E. *gielp.*

ginned, 25/196, devised, contrived. Cf. O.N. *ginna.*

gled, 51/381, fire of burning coal.

glosse, 68/358, flattery, falsehood.

gostlic, 89/51, spiritually. O.E. *gāstlic.*

grenynis, 60/101, grains of Paradise, a very pungent Indian spice.

gret, 5/33, 46/262, weep, O.E. *grētan.*

grou, 92/132, injure, harm. O.F. *grever.*

gryH, 80/708, irritate, be harsh to, act grievously against. O.E. *grillan, griellan.*

hele, 4/39, hiding-place, refuge. O.E. *hel*; 104/491, fate, omen, auspice. O.E. *hœl.*

hen, 29/128, 34/309, hence.

hende, 88/5, 88/9, 91/109, gracious. O.E. *gehende.*

henly, 75/558, vilely. O.E. *héanlic.*

hent, 50/356, seize. O.E. *hentan.*

hest, 38/66, 38/69; hestes, 91/118, 103/479, command. O.E. *hǽs.*

hewe, 7/72, 26/17, hew, colour. O.E. *heow, hew.*

ho, 89/49, 89/51, she.

hoH, 7/72, hollow (*i.e.* with hollow-looking skin and form).

honowraunce, 29/103, honour. O.F. *honorance.*

hoothe, 19/8, probably a miscopying of heethe, heath. O.E. *hǽþ.*

hore, 94/197, whore. O.E. *hóre.*

hote, 91/118, command. O.E. *háte.*

hye, 98/310, hasten. O.E. *higian*; in hy, 1/12, 25/186, 25/188, in haste.

ibore, 104/491, born. O.E. *geboren.*
ifer, 88/1, companions. O.E. *geféra.*
ikorne, 91/114 ; i-korre, 91/121, chosen. O.E. *gecoren.*
ilore, 104/493, lost. O.E. *[ge]loren.*
interely, 80/719 ; interly, 85/881, entirely. Cf. O.F. *entier.*
irerit, 99/342, reared, raised. O.E. *geræred.*
i-wys, 42/163, 56/55 ; i-wysse, 46/247, 258, etc., certainly, indeed. O.E. *gewiss.*
janglest, 73/493, chatterest, pratest. O.F. *jangeler.*
kempes, 91/114, soldiers, champions. O.E. *cempa.*
kepe, 46/252, care ; kept, 29/111, cared, liked. O.E. *cépan.*
kete, 92/135, brave, strong (perhaps a variant of kene).
korin, 96/244, chosen, *vide* ikorne.
kowthe, 56/56, known. O.E. *cúþ.*
kyt, 90/80 ; kith, 90/92, quit. O.F. *qviter.*

lain, 23/137, reproach, scold, blame. O.E. *leán.*
laith, 23/118, loath, unwilling. O.E. *láð.*
largyfluent, 81/746, liberal, bounteous.
lashe, 69/388, lash. Cf. L.G. *laske.*
lede, 96/254, people, nation, race. O.E. *léod.*
leint, 89/34, length. O.E. *lengþ.*
lenust, 101/395, MS. not clear, lenust or lesust, *i. e.* either most transitory, cf. O.E. *léne,* or vainest. Cf. O.E. *leásost.*
lesing, 89/54, falsehood. O.E. *leásung.*
let, 99/338, slowness, hindrance, delay, 35/312, 46/246, hinder, prevent.
leuit, 89/51, loveth.
levyr, 28/80 ; lever, 38/72, rather. O.E. *léofre.*
list, 102/437, please, like. O.E. *lystan.*
lore, 39/85 ; lor, 101/404, precept, teaching. O.E. *lár.*
lore, 98/313, lost. O.E. *[ge]loren.*
lynde, 96/264, lime-tree. O.E. *lind.*

mac, 89/47, mate. O.N. *maki,* O.E. *gemæcca.*
mace, 60/102, mace, a spice consisting of the dried outer covering of the nutmeg. Ital. *mace.* O.F. *macis.*
mafay, 103/451, by my faith. O.F. *ma fey.*
maistri, 95/223 ; maistrye, 95/240, 103/463, dominion, power. O.F. *maistrie.*
male, 60/99, bag, sack. O.F. *male.*
mansuete, 81/751, peaceful, peaceloving. Lat. *mansuetus.*
mased, 6/57 ; masyd, 75/575, bewildered, dazed. O.E. *amasian.*
mastyk, 60/102, mastic.
may, 86/914, maid.
maynpris, 100/379, main prise, bail.
med, 99/331 ; mede, 73/488, reward. O.E. *méd.*
medyll-erth, 37/34, earth. O.E. *middangeard.*
meenye, 22/106 ; meyne, 102/433, 103/465, household. O.F. *maisnee.*
mekyH, 54/13, 56/62 ; mykyH, 79/670, 81/750, mickle, great. O.E. *micel, mycel.*
mene, 89/30, moan, complain. O.E. *mǽnan.*
mene, 56/79, mean, common (*i. e.* irrespective of wealth or poverty).
meth, 104/497, power. O.E. *mǽðe.*
meyne, *vide* meenye.
meynt, 83/798, communicated. O.E. *gemǽned.*
mold, 6/57 ; molde, 102/444, earth. O.E. *molde.*
munit, 89/47, has in mind. O.E. *múnan.*
mynnes me, 1/21, I remember [peculiar to the Northern dialect].
myregrym, 74/535, a headache. Cf. Fr. *migraine.*
mys, 64/213, misdeeds.
mysericord, 83/809, mercy. Lat. *misericordia.*

nay, 22/105 ; naye, 57/13, fail, denial.
necesse, 79/694, necessity.

ocke, 97/293, och ! the Irishman's interjection.

oxennell, 73/506, oxymell, a mixture of vinegar and honey.

petying, 102/428, pushing, instigation. O.F. *boter.*

plasmacion, 8/8, formation.

plawe, 76/586, play, fight. O.E. *plegian.*

plecer, 43/193, pleasure.

plesaunce, 26/8, 28/59, 29/95, 33/259, 34/280; plesance, 58/46; pleasure, enjoyment. O.F. *plaisance.*

pleyn, 59/57, play, *i. e.* mix up with the people. O.E. *plegian.* Cf. "ȝe þat pleieȝ with þe world." 'Ancren Riwle.'

poose, 74/538, catarrh, a cold in the head. O.E. *gepós.*

pref, 34/280; preve, 61/128, proof, test. O.F. *prove, prœve.*

prese, 2/40, in the crowd, "although I do not push myself forward."

prest, 103/469, ready, prompt. O.F. *prest.*

preve. Cf. pref.

prevely, 28/83, secretly. Cf. O.F. adj. *privé.*

prove, 21/74, Holthausen suggests prow, advantage. O.F. *prou.*

provey, 20/31, purvey, provide. O.F. *porveir, porveoir.*

prow, 23/129; prowe, 98/309, profit, advantage. O.F. *prou.*

prynt, 69/387, impression, image. O.F. *(em)preinte.*

pryvyte, 63/196, privacy.

pungarnetis, 60/106, pomegranates.

purviaunce, 26/9, 27/39; purveance, 65/242, provision. A.F. *purveaunce.*

pymente, 68/348, a spiced drink. O.F. *piment.*

pynsonys, 75/577, 77/621, 85/855, pincers.

qvart, 53/462, safe and sound. O.E. *cweart.*

quartan, 74/533, an ague returning every fourth day. Lat. *quartana.*

qwyte, 91/98, requite. O.F. *qviter.*

rape, 76/581, hasten, hurry. O.N. *hrapa.*

raw, 5/24, row, series. O.E. *ráw, réw.*

rawe, 76/588, ? run.

read, 23/121, advice, counsel. O.E. *ráed.*

recuer, 71/442, recovery, recuperation. O.F. *recovrer.*

red, 101/410, 41/143; rede, 95/229, advise, counsel. O.E. *rædan.*

repreue, 69/376, reproof.

reue, 96/246, rob, plunder. O.E. *réafian.*

reut, 99/346, regret, grief, sorrow. O.N. *hrygȝ.*

reys, 60/99, rice.

reysones, 60/100, raisins.

rot, 92/129, joy. O.E. *rót.*

rowe, 20/26, line. Cf. raw. Holthausen suggests 'tow,' as otherwise wood and tow are not mentioned; other suggestions are ' crow ' and ' rewe.'

rowte, 35/320, 77/623, company, rout. O.F. *route.*

royes, 1/15, king Fr. *roi.*

ruff, 22/85, rough-tree (later written roof-tree), a rough, untrimmed mast.

rychesse, 54/18, 58/37, wealth. O.F. *richesse.*

ryff, 22/85, reef, part of a sail, here used possibly for the sail as a whole. M. Dutch and O.N. *rif.*

rynge, 57/19, range, wander, roam. O.F. *renger.*

samyn, 7/69, together. O.N. *saman.*

saurit, 90/71, savoured. O.F. *savourer.*

sawe, 91/116, saying, bidding. O.E. *sagu.*

scamely, 73/506, scammony, a plant of the genus *convolvulus.*

schen, 92/140, *i. e.* schinend or schinand, shining. O.E. *scínand.*

schereys, 37/18, cheers. O.F. *chere.*

screu, 101/421, shrew. O.E. *scréawa.*

se, 97/276, throne, seat. Lat. *sedes.*

seam, 20/26, seam, Holthausen suggests beam. Brotanek translates Schreiner-verband.

sekyrly, 63/182, certainly, surely. Cf. O.H.G. *sichurlicho.*

semblably, 12/1, likewise, similarly. O.F. adj. *semblable.*

sere, 20/48, several, various. O.N.

ser ; sore, sad, is a possible interpretation. O.E. *sár.*

shear, 21/57, cut, shear. O.E. *sceran.*

shope, 27/51, shaped, created. O.E. *scóp.*

sib, 99/348, peace. O.E. *sibb.*

sideyns, 54/9, citizens. Cf. footnote, p. 54.

sig, 99/358, 100/360, say, tell. O.E. *secgan.*

sike, 93/163, sigh. O.E. *sican.*

skaith, 23/119, loss, injury. O.E. *scaða, sceaða.*

skyħ, 26/19, 60/112, 66/283 ; skil, 93/156, fitting, reason. O.N. *skil.*

sle, 32/233, 32/239, 34/288, slay. O.E. *sléan.*

slee, 22/109 ; sleye, 94/192, sly, clever. O.N. *slægr.*

slight, 24/174, skill, cunning, sleight. O.N. *sliegð.*

smaragdis, 60/88, smaragds, emeralds.

sneke, 74/538, a disease, ? worms. [I am unaware of its occurrence elsewhere in Middle-English literature.] Cf. *schneke* (German), a sore between the claws of animals giving out matter in the form of a worm.

sond, 38/68, 41/146, messenger. O.E. *sand, sond.*

soporacion, 8/12, putting to sleep.

sor, 101/406, grief. O.E. *sár.*

sot, 100/360 ; sothe, 77/625, true, truth. O.E. *sóþ.*

spence, 72/451, provision-room. O.F. *dispense.*

speryd, 85/861, closed, shut in. O.E. *gesparrian.*

sprot, 22/86, perhaps a mistake for spout, a round plane ; a meaning derived from the original meaning of a pipe ?

sprout, 22/86, sprout, sprig. M. Dutch, *spruite.*

sprund, 22/86, perhaps a miscopying of spranke, a sprout. M. Dutch, *spranke* ; or cf. M.E. *sprintel.*

spyer, 28/86, spire or spar. Cf. O.N. *spira*, a spar, and Dan. *spire*, a sprout.

stead, 25/202 ; sted, 41/144 ; stede, 30/141, place. O.E. *stede.*

steer, 24/169, ?19/10, strong. O.H.G. *stiuri,* Gothic, **stiurs,* and O.E. *stór.* Apparently 'stere,' a loan-word, has displaced the native word.

stint, 24/164, 7/73, cease, stop. O.E. *styntan.*

stocey, 89/36, *i.e.* stotey, cunning, craft. Lat. *astutia.*

stounde, 102/441 ; stownd, 63/198, 64/234, hour, time, moment. O.E. *stund.*

streyint, 99/332 ; strynt, 89/36, strength. O.E. *strengðu.*

sufferen, 33/273, sovereign. O.F. *soverain.*

suirt, 89/49, sweareth. O.E. *swerieð.*

supersidias, 100/380, *i.e.* supersedeas, a writ suspending the power of an officer or to stay law proceedings.

sure, 63/199, assure.

sustentacion, 13/2, sustenance.

swemfuħ, 80/720, 80/725, sorrowful. Cf. O.E. *swǽman,* to fall into a trance, to grieve.

synymone, 60/103, cinnamon.

ten, 89/48, tene, 103/453, irritate, vex. O.E. *téonian* ; tene, 56/77, 83/799, vexatious injury. O.E. *téona* ; tene, 64/209, accuse. O.E. *téon.*

tent, 20/39, heed, attention.

tercyan, 74/533, tertian, *i.e.* a fever. Lat. *tertiana.*

teseke, 74/538, slow consumption, phthisis. Cf. O.F. *tesiqueux,* Mod. Fr. *phtisique,* and "Et fu si tisique et si sec que à poine pooit il crachier."—'Miracle St. Loys,' cited in Littré.

thee, 25/206, thrive. O.E. *þéon.*

to bot, 100/388, remedy, salvation.

to brast, 55/48, 85/863, burst open. O.E. *to-berstan, to-bearst.*

topazyons, 60/88, topazes.

trayn, 7/67, enticement, stratagem. O.F. *trahin.*

treut, 99/330, truth. O.E. *treowþ.*

treyn, 56/77, afflictions, griefs. O.E. *trega.*

trist, 102/435, trust, consolation. O.N. *traust.* [Brandl translates zusammentreffen, *i.e.* tryst.]

rive, 101/422, thrive. O.N. *þrífa.*
roust, 101/419, believest, thinkest.
O.E. *trúwian, tréowian.*
row, 103/452, believe. Cf. troust.
ruyt, 99/334, truth. Cf. treut.
yte, 23/117, quick. O.N. *tiðr.*
ꝛede, 96/250, country, people. O.E.
þéod.
ꝛrawe, 91/104, throe, pain. O.E.
þréa.
ꝛnlusty, 22/81, idle, slothful. Cf.
O.E. *unlust.*

ꝛeniaunce, 33/251, punishment,
penalty. O.F. *renjance.*
ꝛernage, 68/348, Italian white wine.
O.F. *vernage.*

vanhope, 56/67, despair.
vari, 72/479, curse, condemn. O.E.
wergian.
vayns, 24/152, wains, wagons. O.E.
wægn, wæn.
ve Tib! 1/1, an exclamation. Cf.
'York Chaundeler's Play,' v. 37 *et
seq.* We hudde! We howe!
vedyr, 33/269, wether. O.E. *weðer.*
veet, 23/131, 23/133, know. O.E.
witan.
vel, 100/376, weal. O.E. *wela,
weola.*
velawey, 45/234, alas, an exclamation of sorrow. O.E. *wa la
wa.*
vend, 35/315, 73/495, thought. O.E.
wénde [*wénan*].
vende, 103/469, to go, to turn. O.E.
wendan.
vene, 102/445, think. O.E. *wéne*
[*wénan*].
vere (on), 70/402, in doubt.
vet, 63/188; wete, 62/164; wott,
76/601; wette, 59/67, to know.
O.E. *witan.*
vhünt, 23/114, probably 'quaint' in
the original. Cf. Introd., p. lxvi.

wil of red! 6/54, at a loss. Cf.
York Plays, 424/91, ed. Toulmin-
Smith.
wisse, 5/22, guide, direct. O.E.
wisian, wissian.
wit, 5/15, know. O.E. *witan.*
withnayde, 28/62, denied, disobeyed.
Cf. M.E. *naiten.* O.N. *neita,* to
say no.
wittin, 104/483, know. O.E. *witan.*
wode, 104/499, mad. O.E. *wód.*
wo-lo-wo, 99/327, *vide* welawey.
wond, 57/8; wonde, 59/58, change,
turn away. O.E. *wendan.*
wone, 6/37, one. O.E. *án.*
wonneth, 54/13, 54/19, dwells, in-
habits. O.E. *wunian.*
wood, 80/707. Cf. wode.
woode, 76/596. Cf. wode.
woodnesse, 71/422, madness, frenzy.
O.E. *wódnis.*
work-looms, 22/82, text is evidently
corrupt, probably work-tools.
wot, 6/40, knowest. O.E. *wást*
[*witan*].
wott, 76/601, *vide* wet.
wraist, 5/32, ? wrest, ? wrayest.
wrake, 71/419, ill, misery, vengeance; persecution, 69/379, 90/88,
avenge. O.E. *wracu, wræc, wre-
can*; 35/342, wreck, ruin. Cf. to
wrack and ruin [Prov. Eng.],
O.L.G. *wrak.* O.N. *vrek.*
wreist, 101/416, accuses, molests.
O.E. *wréjan.*
wyghtly, 74/526, 75/560, vigorously,
nimbly.
wyst, 61/142, known. O.E. *gewiten*
[*witan*].
wyt, 42/161, know. O.E. *witan.*

yar, 102/434, ready, prepared. O.E.
gearo.
yede, 64/219, went. O.E. *eóde.*
yilp, 89/37, boast. O.E. *gelpan,
gielpan.*
ylke, 70/415, 71/417, 77/620, same.
O.E. *ilca.*

Richard Clay & Sons, Limited, London and Bungay.